Painted Bride Quarterly
Print Annual 5

Sponsored in part by:

Painted Bride Quarterly
Print Annual 5

Editors	Kathleen Volk Miller
	Marion Wrenn
Poetry Editor	Jason Schneiderman
Senior Editors	Nicole Callihan
	Bryan Dickey
	Daniel Driscoll
	Shafer Hall
	Andrew Keller
	Matt Longabucco
	Paul Siegell
	Elizabeth Thorpe
	Rachel Wenrick
Layout Editor	William Rees
Graphic Design	Drexel University
Associate Editors	Nat Bennett
	Emily Gordon
	Christopher Wall
Contributing Editors	Gregory Pardlo
Editorial Staff	Lindsay Anderberg
	Patrick Blagrave
	Veronica Castrillon
	Miriam Haier
	Todd Jackson
Graphic Design	
Graphic Design Department	April Moralba
Drexel University, Philadelphia	
Legal Counsel	Robert Louis
	Chad Rutkowski
Founding Editors	Louise Simons
	R. Daniel Evans

Student Co-ops

Drexel University, Philadelphia

Lauren Boyle
Jacob Brophy
Catherine Lewandowski
Maia Livengood
Julia Perch
Mark Petrovich
Daniel Savage
Rachel Semigran

Student Interns

Olivia DiPasquale
Kathryn Gardner
Katrina Gaudier
Giby George
Emily Homrok
Michael Filippone
Nicolle Morales Kern
Laura Knoll
Carolynn McCormack
Kurt McCrohan
Sonal Patel
Jordan Schilling
Heather Schwartz
Zack Ssebatindira
Matthew Strickland
Justine Wan

Sponsors
Drexel University
The College of Arts & Sciences at Drexel University
The Department of English & Philosophy at Drexel University
Mid-Atlantic Arts Foundation

Dr. Donna Murasko, Dean, Arts & Sciences, Drexel University
Dr. Abioseh Porter, Department Head, English & Philosophy,
    Drexel University

Painted Bride Quarterly
Drexel University
Department of English and Philosophy
3141 Chestnut Street
Philadelphia, PA 19104
www.pbq.drexel.edu or webdelsol.com/pbq

COVER: "File Boxes, Spring Grove Stale Hospital, Maryland" from *Asylum*
by Christopher Payne

PBQ is a Member of the Council of Literary Magazines and Presses. PBQ is Indexed by the
American Humanities Index and the Index of American Periodical Verse (Metuchen, NJ:
Scarecrow Press)

Painted Bride Quarterly is published online four times a year. Unsolicited submissions
are accepted year-round. Send submissions via US mail to the address above or online.

Please include a hard copy of all submitted work, a short biographical note with phone
number and e-mail, and an SASE. All critical articles should be submitted in MLA style.

PBQ assumes no responsibility for submissions received without adequate return
postage, packing, or proper identification labels. For more information write to the above
address or visit our website.

Subscriptions for libraries and Institutions $20 per year. Subscriptions cannot be
forwarded. Please inform us of address changes by mail.

ISBN 978-0-9728565-4-6.

*Thank you, thank you, thank you and thank you to: President John A. Fry, Dr. Donna
Murasko; Dr. Abioseh Porter; Chris Brennan, Steve Volk, and Danny at the Pen & Pencil
Club, AWP; CLMP; the friendly folk at Bubble House; Allison, Hayley and Chris; Mother
Wrenn, Aunt Betsy, Jonathan Burr and Michael Butler. Thank you, thank you, thank you to
all our readers at our reading series and special events in New York and Philadelphia.*

Printed by Drexel Printing and Mailing Services
Printed in Canada

Distributed by Ingram Periodicals

The fonts used within this publication are Documenta and Univers.

This Print Annual is dedicated to:

Toni Brown
PBQ editor, poet, and friend

Constantine Papadakis
Drexel University President and supporter

Table of Contents

Issue 80

Poetry

Fiction

Prose

Issue 81
The Punishment Issue

Poetry

Fiction

Issue 82

Poetry

Fiction

Prose

Issue 83

The Food Issue

Poetry

Fiction

Prose

Contributors

Rachel Abramowitz

The New Materials (Commuter Train)

ISSUE 80

I was only a module, these things.
If reading a book is the remedy
For walking I've heard your voice on the radio, though.
I believe you for the amount of time it takes
To extract my dinner from its chill coffin
And to remember you across from me, or beside.
Were you the one with the unrecognizable German?
Who copied perfect on your umbrella masterpiece?
I don't believe you dressed faintly in light.
I've been watching your shoes swirl inwardly velvet
Like a reflection and smelling of applewood, carefully.
Once I slept and dreamed my eyes would not open.
Last chance for this beautiful white tent
I've lifted from the lawn, without help,
A harvest of beams shaking off the night condensed.
This is what I'm offering until
It's time to think all about me,
Nine-tenths property and all that.
Remember, we are law together. Despite my splash
And newness, I'll follow you on your errands
And carry your simplicity
For as long as you let me on the ground,
Just crooning by the rink and by.

ISSUE 80

J. Matthew Boyleston

Vision After the Sermon

Gauguin

From the outside looking in,
the ground is a splotched fingerprint in blood
and the curved bar of women bent like Zs
is the windowsill you look through into a room
that bursts with shining things.
You see beyond a land of black and white
to a place where the cost of color
will be a touch to the hollow of your thigh
and the rot of a blessing on your tongue,
at a man and a blue angel with bourbon wings.
Your sight is stuck like love in the throat's nib.

James Engelhardt

ISSUE 80

Regarding the Distance Between Our Suburbs

It was bitter vacation
he will tell you, an ocean
of stinging and poisonous things.
Nightclubs of women wearing only
three starfish, drinking curaçao,
not sharing black cigarettes with him.

Home is not vacation,
the bitter man will say,
at home, children come to the capitol
for the football championship.
They are soft and incomplete
but imagine their incomplete deaths
by suicide to be hard-edged, glittering
and so beautiful you will wear
their pictures around your neck.
They cannot follow your directions.

The neighbor's girl has a telescope
she uses to see into the earth.
The bitter man, walking through crickets,
stops to talk with her.
She holds her knees to her chest
and tells him about the grinding
she sees under the skin of the earth,
the weeping of boulders,
the grit and metal of hot confusion.

ISSUE 80

Eryn Green

This Slowly Stampeding

Teakettle on the stovetop, no more
boxes we thought. The white roof's sudden razing,
the storm a hundred miles off—not bad news,
bad luck. Without notice, windows
won't budge. Tiny far-fetched flickerings
pass like paper from a windy deck—I've learned to
hold a shadow in a box. By the evaporating shore,
past the river, we strain through horsehair
to see which shapes are people
and which are reeds.

ISSUE 80

Brian Patrick Heston

An Echo

How you once nursed your Guinness
listening to the Phillies on the scarred
mahogany radio you bought before

the war: speakeasy days before gram,
asbestos days on ships rickety as planets
before the old house of Christmases

and Easters. In my dream you stroll
ungodly hours, a broken lamp buzzing
as a boy forms from above.

You watch his twisted descent
through stratosphere, through cloud
canyons, until he lands in a thud

on the sidewalk, bony arms
and legs splayed, wings charred to ash,
breath lodged in his lungs. You struggle

to your knees, Guinness in one hand,
hammer in the other. After putting your ear
to his chest, you breathe through his blue lips;

only the wheeze of your own air
comes back. That's when you search
shadow windows for another pair of hands

not as jittery, but every curtain
is closed. So you lean again, keep at it until
your lungs are finally spent. Then a sound

does come, at first faint on the breeze.
You tap your hearing aid to be sure
then hear it clear, the broken guttural song.

ISSUE 80

Kathryn Hunt

The Visitation

Last night a black fox
came to the door, its eyes turning to ice
when the light caught them.
It considered me through the glass,
loped away while I ran room to room
to go on seeing.

At the hour for zazen
I ate chocolate instead.
A bird pecked away at a tree
like my mother drumming her nails
on the table. A pile driver
clanked in the distance, a sound
not as beautiful as a temple bell
but still, in its own way, essential.

In my grandmother's diaries,
she records her day as "raspberries,"
"a jardinière filled with gold."
The just-kissed color of the berries,
isn't that holy?
And the irritating little bird,
is that God talking? And what of longing?
Is it really a refusal?

Last night after the fox
disappeared in the grasses,
I stood in the incandescent light
of the kitchen and ate the sacrament
of vegetable soup. *Don't call me,*
my mother said. It was the last time
I talked to her. *I'm going out,*
I probably won't hear you.

ISSUE 80

Siel Ju

Cleaner

Something about the noise makes me want to raze the place, build
up a new world with steel lego blocks. Clean lego men who don't
sweat. All polished efficiency. A quiet chrome aligned and arranged
to fit. Manual labor like pushing paper, bricks in pristine rows, power
tools with firearm silencers. Birds hop in and out of a shadow's
precisely demarcated outline. The symphony of muted machines.
Soundless joy.

ISSUE 80

Siel Ju

Longer

The clear truth of the moment is that it'll pass. Any sort of desire
or impetus or agency or ability of emotional closeness you feel
right now – that'll pass. What's left'll be the vague sense that you
wanted something that may or may no longer be worth the effort.
If it helps picture the happy reverse too. As in, if we work quickly,
that too will produce illimitable desire, perhaps. I'd like to think that
the individual is unique, but act a certain slutty way, and they'll all
react back in the exact manner you imagined. Let it go and just write
shorter poems, though you'll find it easier to do so if you've already
published. Otherwise you'll simply come across as lazy, will you not.

Keetje Kuipers

ISSUE 80

Speaking as the Male Poet

I would like to write the fistfight poem, which I have never had
the pleasure of (I hit him once but he wouldn't hit me back)

or I might visit a prostitute (girl, woman, professional or not)
and then confess to you my shame (oh, to be the doer of the deed!)—

the death of a pet, a reference to Greek tragedy, a snowy drive
    in the dark,
a hospital room I wouldn't have to describe because just knowing

I am perhaps very bad and very broken and certainly very, very,
very smart would be enough. you might then want me to cook you

scrambled eggs in my boy-kitchen or simply ignore you from
behind the black rims of my not-really-necessary reading glasses

and I could say things to make you swoon, things like Codeine,
Oldsmobile, shortstop—words that were ordinary but now, coming

from my pen, my born in the suburbs of Boston pen, my son of trains
leaving every hour pen, my jeans tangled around my pale white
    calves pen

might have a new meaning that would make you think twice, as in,
why didn't I think of that? and they would be clever and sad

all at once, and wouldn't you want me, would want to wonder at me,
how I came to be transformed, and maybe who my mother
    is (lost child,

peter pan) and how she feels about the lies I'm telling you.

Christina LaPrease

A Mirror, Dissolving

Someone sneezes & I remember learning
to say *symptom*, how we grew into the hush:

caught coughs in a mask, pocketed morphine
in rabbit furs & practiced numbers

by the show of our bones. Once, we gathered
pillows for a reason of rain & bedded down

in a tub, chasing dragons. A junk calm blazed
between us, until our rooms, unkept by pilot lights,

took in the river. Haunted by the watermark,
we let our cushions go & the fathoms folded

us apart. These days, I trade accents & faces
every few years. Fall in love, meet a father,

save small fists of coasts in pill bottles & stop
dreaming *good morning sunshine*. I rise & am still

one hour too many. I move on a cut of sleep
& somewhere, a clock pushes its sharp circles of noise.

ISSUE 80

ISSUE 80

Teresa Leo

The Heart Has the Capacity to Break and Reset a Million Times

But it's the million and first, say,
that begins in a cab to Woodside, Queens

with a hockey player, who's also a musician
and a city planner, who might be a one-night stand,

but he's the best kisser you've come across
in years, with a face that's all elegy and nostalgia,

edges but smooth, the Mekong Delta in June,
the mouth, clementines flown in from another country,

what only stays on the shelves briefly before
it disappears for a year, and before you know it,

everything in you is moving in his direction,
your head gravitates to his chest, his fingers,

anywhere you can hear a stress or a pulse,
until the 4/4 beat becomes 6/8ths,

a compound time signature,
because he's every place you've ever

climbed or crawled that knocked the wind out,
like the Grand Canyon or the Cu Chi tunnels,

a vapor that expands to fill even the largest
of rooms, and you can't breathe, in this cab,

going to his apartment, you're 18 again
in some kid's parents' basement listening to Dylan

for the first time, stoned, or maybe not stoned,
it's that lead singer voice whispering in your ear

across 42nd Street and through the Midtown Tunnel,
and now you're 16 riding in the back of a Senior's car,

making out but not the way you did at 16;
he could be taking you anywhere, but he's taking you

back to a time before you ever fell in love,
before any transmutations of the heart,

resetting its counter, and he makes up
for every football player who ever left any girl

sitting at a table at the Junior prom to dance
with the head cheerleader, because tonight,

you are 14 and you've carried his hockey stick
through the streets of New York, the way at 14

you carried the quarterback's cleats to the bus,
and even though in the morning he'll take you

to the platform to get the train back to the city,
even though you'll both become 40 again

by the time the train rolls into the station,
even though he'll say *this but no further*

just as you turn to board, tonight, in this cab,
you are 13, your bodies unbearably strung,

lips unendurably ready, and when he leans in,
everything else in the world is forced to evacuate,

when he leans in, you are both young and beautiful
without even a trace of sadness.

ISSUE 80

Teresa Leo

Online Dating

A year of surfing the profiles, where the men
look for women the way women shop for shoes—

ordering their size in a variety of styles:
slingback, hook & loop, stiletto, the most

impractical ones with points at the toes
not built for a human foot, but the excitement

of how they look in pictures, images
that can be scaled up to examine the make,

the workmanship, the alternative views that show
all the angles, how they look with a dress,

with jeans, then the thrill of the box
arriving at the door, the couture packaging,

until, finally, inside the fancy wrapping,
disappointment, just an ordinary pair of shoes

that pinch, the claustrophobia of them,
with an edge awareness that presses in,

each step a bullet to the brain, and though
there's a brief thought of taking them out

on the town for a fancy dinner, or at least
to a bar for a game of pool, they rarely get past

the front door, their value already diminished,
the cost too high, the shape not elegant enough,

no room in the closet, and they are reboxed
and sent back with a little less care

than the way they came in. Within minutes
of their return, they are easily forgotten,

and it's back online to find something else,
something that's less Sunday in the park

and more Bangkok at night, something
that promises to stand out in a crowd,

some version of it, and in this way,
there will be many new arrivals,

introduced to compete each new season,
last year's styles removed or clicked past,

no arch or heel high enough, and for each
new arrival, for each dazzling possibility,

an equal but opposite, brilliantly fit,
stunningly sensible departure.

Ada Limón

ISSUE 80

Return to Rush and Flutter

You're the persistent fish swimming
the same surviving river, un-skinned
and unhinged by a year of bad weather.
Lost ones in the bones, your water
damage, your rage of flood and fire
and still, all along Warm Springs Road
the naked ladies have the nerve
to flower pink and full. A choir
of constant blackbirds and bees and
you cannot miss them more. Go bury
your head in the tough and wasted
weeds so you can hear the beating
deepen, the blazing suddenness of
a wound overcome by wonder.

Jeff G. Lytle

ISSUE 80

Maybe We're Quakers

Cataclysm. The juice of the
ever after. A hard look from
the Saint. But hey, even

mediocre deaths are deaths,
breathless and blue. Happen
on a busted egg amid

the garbage and gum of
the sidewalk, its puny cargo
ejected, naked and bony,
into dead December. Or a

divot in the foot of blizzard
gathering on the playground, then
the wing marks left like arrows
as a pigeon lifted itself and dragged

forward for an hour before it
quit, then the wind that shuffles
its feathers and the snow that
overcomes it. Maybe it breathes

there awhile or maybe its heart
gave out already in mid-flight.
Just birds, and the death of birds.

Not so much as a box of
hair in a hurricane. Flint and tinder and

breath. Snuffed. A reliquary
of old nonsense. Light,

sharp as gin, catches on the
iced stalagmites of snow banks
rotten with oil and black dirt.

An abandoned city infected
with rust. The dark stairs home.

Light etching through cracks
in the drawn blinds. Light always
withdrawing, failing us.

ISSUE 80

Marilyn McCabe

In Vino Veritas

I.

Sacred as a blessing, profane
as a drunk; we always
break the glass:

Just as the pulp slips
from the skin so the ferment
bares something in us. Opens
us, a cave

mouth. Angels
stream in as the whistle
of wind through mallards'
coasting wings; or demons

issue out in gaping
voiceless howl, depending
on the hour we drink: how
late the night, how dark.

Those sugars, the tannins,
the diacetyl acid and fruit; or
is it the process, slow
precipitation
that gathers truth like rain:

Is that why wine takes
away my words, settles
them gently like mud?
Truth is gloomy like that,
and best said in
nothing. Or

I have not drunk
enough.

ISSUE 80

II.

This mercy falls
far short of holy,
though it's all
we, earth-
bound, can hope for:
dirt and vine,
sun and time
ferments something
odd and wilder than
that from which it was born.
We are all
squeezed from our
ruddy skins,
revealed
in our slow
translucence.

Kerrin McCadden

Say Sing

This is my one life. Say you know.
Say this means many things, say snowy owl,
say three feet of snow, say kestrel. My one
life is here at the table, next to me. Say you know,
say fine night for soup, glad to have you,
how was your drive. Say there is only one ridgeline
worth knowing, one swale between three hills.

Wonder why the mountains are named
Lord's Hill, Devil's Hill and Burnt Mountain
Say we should go there sometimes, when we are
lonely like this, stand in the center, gear shouldered
and wonder where to camp. Say bear claws and
hawk circles, say grass chewed low. Say here,
One Life, settle in with us. Here is the fire.
Say here is a warm stone. Say sing.

ISSUE 80

ISSUE 80

Ashley McWaters

Lesson

The body of work takes off her clothes,
intending to shock. She is a skeleton;
her shadow a warrior. I ask her
what is her *nom de plume,* she replies
she eats no chicken. I ask her to show
what she wants, she draws a knife
from under her foot and begins dancing
a waltz with the blade held high.
She motions for me to put down my work
and come. We are in the belly of a whale
or we are spat out on dry ground. We
are dancing. We are moving our fingers
and holding still. The blade glints
and standing sighs. She is still teaching
tricks with the knife. She is tricking me
to teach with the knife. She is knifing
the trick so there is teaching: hook, needle's
open eye. I stay, quiet the blade. *Come
closer ever closer come. Let me tie
your hands together. Tangle your fingers.
Knot your wrists.* I stay still, quiet
the clicking needles, swallow
the spitting edge. I wait.

Yvonne C. Murphy

Nests

ISSUE 80

Queens, NY

I can't get settled, the floor scattered with boxes,
each day filled with unpacking, placing and building.
Pigeons shuffle on the fire escape or sleep with heads tucked
into iridescent necks, pacing on the windowsills, gray
bodies anchored by pinkish feet. *Zut, zut* – nests plastered
with shit, feathers and dirt, flu and viruses levitate on wings.

All day the demolition of single family houses, wrecking
balls make way for condos outside my third story window.
The boarding up of yards before each building's collapse,
piece after piece comes down: old refrigerators, bathtubs
idling at the curb. Each room an empty case exposed
through the cracks in graffittied plywood – pink bedrooms,
skeletons of plumbing, brick facades torn away, tar-papered,
once stately before the long boring into the ground.

The pigeons mock me, this family of five, their burbles,
white eyelids fastened to blot out the day, always coming back
to rebuild in layers of twigs and crap, imbrications of filth
flaked through windowscreens. Pest species, opportunists
surveiling from the sides of their heads. I ruined their nest
with the end of a broom, watched it crumble,
disassemble on the grass below.

ISSUE 80

Charles O'Hay

Junk

All night the city had spent
turning itself to licorice: red
black, the streets and buildings
getting loose, trying on masks.

At the bar, Nola's on stage
stripped down to show how gypsy
hair can fall across a body
not yet gone to hell from junk.

A guy with a wedding ring
tells me she's the kind of woman
on whom he could spend hours
kneeling at her altar,

But when she takes the seat
next to mine we talk instead
about cameras and crucifixions
the death of Elvis, Jim Morrison.

I wonder about clean sheets
and she wonders about clean
needles, each thought moving us
further from that narrow strip of land,

Where the jukebox sings Clarence
Carter Clarence Carter Clarence
Carter and the light comes down
from the honeyed lamps in spoonfuls.

ISSUE 80

Charles O'Hay

The Life

Slouched on a park bench,
the daily storm kicking cans
in your head

You watch the faces
move in slow parade
among the tulips and bronze:

Shoppers, retirees, students
workers spilling from glass towers
for a hot dog and a moment's sun.

The faces are wet cigars, creamed
corn, barbed wire, broken clocks;
the faces are wars nobody wins.

You wait for one fiery syllable
from the sky, or some rich woman
to fuck some sense into you.

But neither arrives, only shadows,
sparrows, burses wheeling the old
toward death.

Tonight you will press some bills
into a man's hand. You won't know
his name. You won't need to.

He will have what you came for.

ISSUE 80

Josh Rathkamp

For the First Time in Years

She reached in
to the second drawer down,

the one beneath her socks,
the one that held everything:

Nyquil, allergy pills,
a bag of spare toothbrushes,

and in her hand she offered a green one to me,
lead me down the hallway,

showed me
the toothpaste behind the bathroom mirror,

the shelf
above the toilet,

the place to leave it
in case I needed it again.

ISSUE 80

Tomaž Šalamun

Letters

I

Love, spinning
like geometry, where are you?
Should I really believe in
myself, as—you say—you do,
you, the tree with tenants,
soil with hoops, earth with
rain? I am not that perfect,
also animals, copulating, are not.
The dragon with the dragon, the sheep with the sheep,
the light with shadow. And after all, what did my
esoteric method, my lust for translation
take away from you? Didn't I bring
everything back? You refused me,
because you are a shallow and impatient
reader, because I said I was God and you
believed me. You thought it was cruelty
when it was fire, water, air. Is it better for you
now, up against other shoulders?
Other, much more exhausted
forms than I was?

II

Fuck you! Don't you get it,
you were already gone? And with that
you crumbled like some loathsome
plastic toy. How
terribly boring, this eternal
theme of yours! This vain little system
of painting and usurping living
people! Any woman would go crazy.
You drank my air like the greediest little
toad. Find yourself some Veronica or
Magdalena, if now, too late,

you realize that your conspiracies with
the apostles are unnatural. Nature, you see!
Of course I believed you, and who wouldn't,
before they saw. But slowly you will
realize, or maybe already, that what you were
playing at was also kitsch for history, not just for
a woman. Yes it's better for me now that I am
leaning against other shoulders.
I'm fine. And that thing about »exhaustion«,
I feel sorry for you! Enough with that ridiculous pale
face of yours, with that »suffering«, for which
you are not the least bit talented. These black holes
that you draw for yourself are hardly
love or responsibility towards children, but the same
sort of painted background as »your
Maruška« that never was. And print
this, as your have everything else:
You are out of the game.

III

I am sitting on a chair.
Like some dead priest whose blood
they've sucked.
They blossom, they blossom,
the almond trees.
We are all going home.
The cloud is air.
From up close you can see
That you can't caress it.
Steamboats wait to be
unloaded in the harbour.
Yesterday it rained.
Today the sun glitters.
They blossom, they blossom,
the almond trees.

Translated from the Slovenian by Joshua Beckman and Ana Jelnikar

Tomaž Šalamun

ISSUE 80

Stork, Lift Your Weight!

Oh blindness with red cherry hands behind
a wire that bars escape from the tunnel!
Blindness is a bowl.
I am blind, I am blind!
Blindness is terrible rusted wheelbarrows
with skin, smoldering marble.
Blindness is a handkerchief.
Everybody is counting eyes!
Blindness is Christ's wounds with a grid of netting.
Saws and files being sketched by carnivorous
animals.
Blindness is rocks banging against each other,
chafed by chains.
The insects break their sex.
Scales tumble over cliffs and twist their
mouths.
There is no pier!
No getting away from oneself!
Blindness is the thunder of little frogs, a thousand in a pile,
smooth.
Wrap a little bun inside a kimono, bucket!
They have come for you!
They have come for you!
They have pins on their faces and soft slimy buttons.
They open like tentacles in red water.
Rabbits gather on the teeth of harrows.
A staff of calm people smiling behind the
nibbled hands.
Cattle low from the drought but we don't hear it.
Sheds stream down hills like
black green lightbulbs.
The spirit of the universe is compressed.
Savages in packs tear their earrings from their fields.
Blindness is a bloated pear.
Sails slaughter like razor blades to cover with snow.
Burns drip from the bones.
Lava kills itself before a bulk of boiling air.

ISSUE 80

The altar peels only scales.
Papers do not change the direction
of the slaughter by the Red Hand Brothers.
I can hear the saber crying.
Bandits sniff around like Cherokees.
A salmon is struck dumb.
Blindness is a Slav, black destiny of a Slav.
There are no clear lakes.
Nor larch trees that would push off the banks as in a fairy tale.
It sucked the air from the bees
and now there's no more work.
At home there are peacocks.
Blindness is a string thunder.
A house that acts the part of a janissary.
Paper hats trampled themselves beneath lentils.
Bach mines, mines of slings, gray slings!
Wind is yellow, with a yellow head.
Under Komarca the forehead and concrete clashed,
pavement and concrete, a scarf and concrete.
Convicts drink the gulps of their parents.
Everywhere there are posters.
SUGAR FOR THE BEAVER!
THE BEAVER IS OUR BROTHER!
DRAGON FLIES FALL INTO SKILLETS.
THE BEAVER SAVES THEM!
THE BEAVER HAS LITTLE CLAWS ON RAILS AND IN OUR
JOY!
White scabby roads.
Dewey diamonds leaves.
Bosch, Bosch, not the painter but the porcelain
head in the doghouse on Tito Street, there you can
also order a washing machine,
a Miehle,
horses with their organs out,
junkers on steps.
Blindness is beer froth on a tablecloth.
Out of the catalogue grow terrible potatoes.
The cigarettes are full of rouge.
Through the door blows ornamentation.
Machiavelli, you who have a thick sense of touch, why do you
spin?
Crickets on whales are coated with sage.
Fathers scrape oaks and give them to their mothers.

A file hangs from the light.
Blindness is a corant that bangs his face
against an icy stream before the chance of spring.
Herds carry medals in bundles.
Yellow guys with trucks supply dew.
Oh blindness with red cherry hands behind
the wire that bars escape from
oneself!

Translated from the Slovenian by Joshua Beckman and Ana Jelnikar

ISSUE 80

Mathias Svalina

Animal Chase

(for 5 or more players)

Two bases are marked off, at either end of America. Each child takes
the name of an Animal. One child is It. He stands in the center of
America & writes newspaper columns about the decline of America.
He starts a radio show & becomes tremendously influential. He
begins to see himself as no longer It but the voice of the people.
When he goes to sleep at night his mother tucks him in & whispers
"Sweet dreams, voice of the people." When his father drops him off
at school he calls out "Have a great day, voice of the people."

The Animals lurk in the darkness of the forest & the shadows of the
demolished factories. When stray children pass the shadows they
pounce on them. Licking the blood from their claws & beaks they
whisper to themselves "I am Animal. I am Animal."

When the first game ends all children trade names & a new child
becomes It.

Mathias Svalina

Frog in the Sea

(for 6 or more players)

One child is the Frog. He sits cross-legged in a circle about 3 feet in diameter. The other children tease him by calling:

> Frog in the Sea
> Can't catch me

They step in & out of the circle, teasing & poking the Frog. They poke him with sticks & they poke him with chimney tools. They show the Frog pictures of beautiful actors & actresses. They read to the Frog from histories of atrocities. They leave hand-written notes on the Frog that say things like "Ribbit" & "Frog." At night each child thanks his lord that he is not the Frog.

This is an especially good game for teaching the shy pupils to become a bit more daring.

ISSUE 80

Mathias Svalina

The Spy

(for 12 or more players)

Four beanbags or rubber balls are used in this game. Beanbags can be made from shells or wooden blocks. Beanbags should be heavy. So heavy that the child can barely hold them. So heavy that if the child wanted to steal one & take it home he would tire while walking home & fall asleep in the forest. So heavy that when he falls asleep the other children gather around him & create a wall of rubber balls so thick that when he wakes up he can never escape. So many rubber balls that tiny rubber balls can be found inside a child's mouth.

Chalk marks are made on the ground at desired lengths. A chosen child throws the beanbag into the box. The boy in the circle of big rubber balls keeps the tiny rubber balls in his mouth. The remaining children walk through the woods searching for their lost classmates.

ISSUE 80

Mathias Svalina

The Stomach Ache

(for 1 to 6 players)

One child is the Stomach. The other children are the Aches. A rectangle is drawn in the dirt & the Stomach is blindfolded, ear-plugged & made to lie inside the rectangle. The Aches run in an oval around the rectangle & scream. As they scream the Aches bump into one another, trying to knock the other Aches into the Stomach. When a bumped child lands on the Stomach he is out.

The Stomach must remain stoic within the rectangle. He must chant to himself "I'm not listening. I'm not listening." If there is only one child playing he is safe from the Ache. The more children playing the more Ache the stomach endures. The game ends when the Stomach takes his blindfold off.

ISSUE 80

Mathias Svalina

The Walrus Dance

(for 3 or more players)

One child is the Walrus. One child is the Trainer. The other children sit in the sun fanning their programs to cool their sun-flushed faces. A circle is drawn in chalk on the asphalt & the Walrus lies facedown inside a circle.

The Trainer commands the Walrus to turn over, to waddle, & other such dance moves. The Walrus obeys the commands, but sneaks slowly toward the Trainer. When the Walrus is very close to the Trainer he pushes the trainer outside the circle into the icy water, wherein the Trainer either drowns or freezes. The Trainer should act either death with much screaming.

The other children sit in the sun, complaining about the price of popcorn & the long lines at the soda fountain. They look at each other's red faces & say "You're getting such wonderful color," & "Your skin will soon be so brown that I will barely be able to see you," & "Will you go to the churches with me?"

ISSUE 80

Rob Talbert

The Last Scene in Casablanca

Everything's already for sale
so I shoplifted color from the world,
brought you and I closer to static
on dead channels. Now I confuse
flowers with garbage. Now I can
say your eyes are the same as airplanes.

I still desire flight in this world, waiting
greedily for my turn, my path through
the city. We'll fly over the art gallery
and sigh, land in central park and try
to guess whether it's autumn. Some
will be angry. They'll say it's all over.

What demands ever sprang from metal?
That it never stay warm? Never only kiss you
in a crash? Strangely enough here we are,
held up and breathing, also in love but I
never did ask to be sure.

I've made up my mind to believe in gray,
to take from this trip the miracle that the
actions you take are what backgrounds
are made of. The city knew this years
ago and tried to tell me with sirens and barking
dogs but how could I realize? If the sky still exists

without blue then you can be a better lover by
taking me up into it. Far away from all things
expected and made of traffic.

Rachel Chalmers

Light Industrial

1. A streak of blood

"Darling, it's me, Pats," says the telephone. John wipes the crunchy bits out of the corners of his eyes and tries to wake up.

"Talked Nige into it. You're on. Can you start today? Before he changes his mind. When can you be here?"

It's seven am.

"Come as soon as you can. Heather's in this morning, and Laurie said he'd drop by this afternoon."

Laurie's name has a pause before and after it, for emphasis.

John can't decide what to wear. All his new clothes are for driving a truck. His student clothes are old. He settles on a thin green t-shirt and khakis. His hair is too long. A ducktail curls up at the back.

He swears at his Ford Falcon when she hesitates before starting. He swears at the traffic all the way down William Street and up the Cahill Expressway. Driving over the Harbour Bridge, he swears at the stockbrokers and real estate agents sailing their yachts on the water far below.

At a quarter to nine, John drives into the Gore Hill campus of the Australian Broadcasting Commission. It is not imposing. There are red brick warehouses to his right and to his left, temporary buildings up on cement blocks. Heat rises in waves from the asphalt parking lot. The cicadas are deafening. The red and white broadcast antenna looms high over his head. He hasn't had any breakfast. He is hungry, and his head aches for coffee.

"Working for Patricia Bray," he says to the guard in the booth. "Starting today."

ISSUE 80

ISSUE 80

"Make sure she gets you a permanent parking sticker," says the guard. "Right at the T, up the hill and should be some parking on your right. Good luck."

John turns the Falcon and drives up the hill. Pat's daughter Melody is walking down it. She's wearing a tight fawn velour t-shirt and a short brown suede skirt. She carries a bulging manila folder. She sees him and makes a big surprise-and-welcome face. John stops the car and opens the window.

Melody wears thick fawn and brown makeup to conceal her bad skin. The head has come off one of the pimples, and a streak of blood has soaked into the makeup.

"Darling!" she says. "What are you doing here?"

"Starting work," he says.

"Nige said yes? Nige said yes!" says Melody. "Yay for you!"

"Running late," says John.

"Oh I won't keep you," says Melody. "Doing some photocopying." She brandishes the folder. "College applications!"

"Good luck," says John.

"Oh, you, too," says Melody, and winks. John puts the car in gear and drives on up the hill. He finds the last space in the parking lot, next to a convertible Mercedes. There is no shade. The car's vinyl interior will bake in the heat.

A woman stands at the door smoking a cigarette. Her forehead is the exact height of John's mouth, and he already wants to kiss it. Her hair is clipped to peach-fuzz. She's wearing combat pants and a black sleeveless T. Her eyes are green. One eyebrow is pierced. She squints at him through the blue smoke and offers him a cigarette.

"John?" she asks.

"Heather?"

They shake hands. His are sweaty, hers are small and strong.

"She's in the toilet," says Heather.

"Sorry I'm late," says John. He admires the way her round breasts stretch the thin black cotton.

"Late? It's not even nine. I fuckin' hate getting up this early. All she's done is talk about Nige and how brilliant he is, Laurie and how brilliant he is, you and how brilliant you are. I've been bored shitless, no offense."

"None taken," says John. "I drive a truck, me."

"Oh, she eats that shit up," says Heather. "You're her noble savage, you are. Did you really come first in your Honours year?"

"Second," says John.

"Typical. She always has to lay it on with a trowel. Congrats, by the way. George Orwell, right? And now you drive a truck. Down and out in Penrith and Longueville. How ro-fucking-mantic. I mean, good on you and all, but she's... Oh, never mind."

"She's given me my break," says John.

Heather looks up at him, squinting against the sunlight. He casts her as the star of his own amateur porn flick, all apricot highlights and violet shadows. She flicks her cigarette butt into the gutter.

"You don't need Pat," she says.

"There's always work for a truck driver," says John.

Heather grins.

"Right. Fallback plan. Me, I got this offer to do a kung fu film in Hong Kong."

As she leads him inside, she demonstrates her best kung fu moves. "Haii-YA!"

She is remarkably supple.

2. Brutal, brutal

There is a computer printout tacked to the door. "Under The Skin," it reads. Inside is a conference room with a long table and plastic chairs. A glass-walled office opens off to one side. Pat is behind the glass, talking on the phone. She's wearing a crushed orange linen suit over a pink silk shirt. Her greying hair is layered and lacquered and permed.

"Well, he's coming now," she says. She looks up, sees them, waves a bejewelled hand. "In fact he's here." She listens. "Of course not. Of course not. I would never do that."

John and Heather sit at the conference table. The plastic chairs are amazingly uncomfortable. John fears for the circulation in the back of his thighs.

"Yes it will. It always is, isn't it? In the end," says Pat.

Heather yawns and stretches and lays her head on her arms.

"You do that. You'll feel much better. Call me later. Dinner. Yes. Lovely."

The carpet is a sick shade of olive. The wood-veneer is peeling off the conference table. An electric fan rattles impotently. Sweat drips down John's side under his shirt.

"Love you, darling. Love you. Kisses. Bye."

Pat puts the phone down and comes out of the office.

"John! Darling! You made it! At last! You two met, then?"

"International freemasonry of smokers," says Heather.

"Oo, fun," says Pat. "Next time I wanna come with."

She draws up a chair and sits herself down.

"That was Nige. Brilliant, brilliant. He'll like you, John. He was the toast of London as a young man. Came out here from the Beeb. The BBC. Auntie Beeb, they call it. Misses England dreadfully, of course. Their loss. British TV, brutal, brutal industry. Chews people up, spits them out."

Heather rests her nose on her crossed arms and looks imploringly at John.

"Anyway," says Pat. "I'm glad we're all here. We can start. But before we do," - her bright tone modulates, becomes more formal - "I wanted to talk a little bit about what this project means to me, personally. Are we cool with that?" Back to bright. "Are we, you know, down with that?" Her pink lipstick has leaked a little into the wrinkles around her mouth.

Heather and John nod obediently.

"So John, I don't know if you know this, but my father -"

"Ray Bray," says Heather in a deep, newsreader's voice.

"Yes, thanks, Major Ray Bray, was - among other things, he was a World War Two pilot..."

"Air Ace Ray Bray," says Heather.

"...but after that – he was in politics, and at one time he was minister of police."

"Under Askin," says Heather.

"Yes, thanks, Heather, but he never has anything to do with the dreadful corruption or anything like that. Anyway, at the time, I worked for the equivalent of ATSIC, John, that's the Aboriginal and Torres Strait Islander Commission or Native Affairs as it is back then, and I wanted, we all did, to do something, for these poor, poor people. Because they are so, you know. But there was so little we could do. And now I feel a great sense of, you know, of obligation.

"So. Now, of course. Television," says Pat. "Television drama. I feel, strongly, that if we can portray the reality of these peoples' lives, then we can be a force for change. A force," she paused for emphasis, "for good."

She looks around with a smile. John nods gravely. Heather grins.

"So, John," says Pat, "I know you've never been in a story meeting before, but we're still trying to knock the, the outlines into shape. You know. The bones of the thing. So we can get to, to the meat of

ISSUE 80

it. Do you have your outline? You don't have your outline? Heather, what have you been doing, if I may ask?"

"Smoking," says Heather.

"Ha! Of course. Look, do you kids want some coffee? I need coffee, and donuts too I think. Is Melody back yet? Melody! MELODY!"

Melody sticks her head around the door and is sent to buy donuts and coffee. The coffee is vile, but his headache lifts like fog. He is so clumsy in his hunger that he drops a donut in his lap.

"Don't do that," Heather scolds. "You'll traumatize your genitals."

"Potty-mouth," says John approvingly.

3. Not this place

"I notice," says Heather, "that she didn't bother boasting to you about her sister. Agnes."

"Agnes Bray? Wait. No," says John.

"President Agnes Bray," says Heather in her newsreaders' voice, "of Australians for a Constitutional Monarchy." They are walking down the hill to a sandwich shop near St Leonards station. The cement footpath winds past muffler repair shops and warehouses where photographic supplies are sold in bulk. The sun glares down. The sweat is like prickles embedded in John's skin. The air smells of eucalyptus oil and of ozone from the electric trains.

"Storm tonight," says Heather.

"The ACM won't like this series much," says John.

"Oh no," says Heather. "It's the slippery slope, innit. Aboriginal rights equals a republic, equals anarchy, equals a thousand year reign of darkness and terror. The end."

"So Pat's working off her guilt?" asked John.

"Straight guilt, liberal guilt, white guilt, guilt at being such an obscene and stupid cow," says Heather. "God I hope my kung fu film gets funded. I feel sick. She never washes the coffee cups properly, she just rinses them out with cold water. I bet I'm coming down with something."

"If you do," says John gallantly, "I'll bring you chicken soup."

She grinned up at him. "I like you," she says. "Keep the aspidistra flying."

John badly wants to see her expression when she comes. He imagines himself rearing over her naked body as she writhes.

"John! John!" calls a voice. It is Melody running down the hill to catch up with them "I wanna sandwich too!"

She takes his arm and looks up at him confidingly. She's washed her face and re-done her makeup, but she stopped at her jaw and there are greasy smudges under her ears. She smells faintly sour.

"How did the college applications go?" he asks.

Melody shrugs. " They just want you to jump through all these dumb hoops."

"College?" asks Heather. "So you finished school in the end?"

"Nah, this is for junior college, I wanna get my international baccalaureate," says Melody. " The High School Certificate's not recognized anywhere else in the world."

"Did not know that," says John.

" There's a lot you don't know," says Melody naughtily.

" This is the place," says Heather. The food sits in stainless steel trays behind glass. There are sweets as well, Freckles priced at one cent each, jelly babies and sugar teeth at two. Heather orders a salad roll. John has roast beef. Melody opts for peanut butter and jam.

"A PBJ," she says. "Only in America, the J is for jelly."

"Shouldn't we get something for Pat?" asked John.

"Oh, Mum doesn't eat during the day," says Melody. "Only donuts and things." She gazes fondly at John: "Sweet of you to think of her."

"There's a liquor store around the corner," says Heather.

"Miaow," says Melody.

"How's your auntie Agnes?" asks Heather.

"My family is so embarrassing," says Melody to John. "And people wonder why I want to study overseas?" They collected their sandwiches and started back up the hill.

"Mum's the best, though, she knows all the coolest people," says Melody. "Is it true Laurie Freeman's coming in this afternoon?"

"S'posed to be," says John.

"Ooh, I want to meet him! I wonder what he's like?"

"He's lovely," says Heather. Melody stares at her.

"How would you know?" she demands.

"Met him on a film we did last year. He got me this job," says Heather. To John, she ads: "He's exactly, exactly how you'd imagine. Tall, sexy, funny, charismatic as all get-out. Basketball genius. White people secretly wish all Aborigines were like him, then there wouldn't be any problem."

"Ouch," says John.

"He's so good at it," says Heather. "First time I go to his place, he's living in this dump of a rental in Glebe and he says, 'How do you like my home?' And I'm all, 'Uhh, actually, Laurie, it kind of sucks.' So he points at this huge painting on the wall, of the Kimberley, where he's from, and he says, 'Not this place. My home.'"

John doesn't know what to say. He wants to get Heather alone again. But on his other side, Melody is trudging up the hill, nursing her PBJ and sulking.

ISSUE 80

4.Gateway drug

Pat has received a distressing phone call. She hears the kids coming back and straightens her shoulders. She has done her best to be an exemplary mother, but her efforts have been in vain. Nevertheless she has to endure with courage the ordeal that lies ahead.

Heather, John and Melody come bounding into the conference room, their gestures large and free, filled with the heedless energy of youth. She intends John for Melody, that's why she gave him the job, but those plans will have to go on the back burner now that Noel has plunged her life into chaos. Her heart contracts as she looks at John, such a decent, studious young man. More a son to her than Noel, who doesn't appreciate any of the sacrifices she has made for him. She remembers in unpleasant detail the pain of Noel's birth.

She emerges regally from her office.

"Mum, Mum, can I stay when Laurie comes? Please say yes, please!" says Melody. "Heather's already met him, why can't I?"

"Melody, please sit down, I have some bad news," says Pat with noble calm.

"Do you want us to leave?" asks Heather.

"No, we're all... family, in this," says Pat.

"What is it?" asks Melody, not particularly alarmed.

"I've just been on the phone with Terence McAllister," says Pat, "the principal of Noel's school."

"Oh God, what has he done now?" asked Melody.

"He was acting inappropriately in class. His bag was searched, and the school found... Melody, I'm sorry to have to tell you this..."

"Jesus, just say it."

"They found ...marijuana."

Heather snorts.

ISSUE 80

"What?" snaps Pat.

"I am sorry," says Heather, at once, contritely, "I truly didn't mean to be rude, but the way you built it up I thought it would be something worse."

"Worse," says Pat levelly. "Worse. My son is on drugs. I have taken steps. I have booked him into a detox facility."

"You've done what?" says Heather.

"Marijuana is a gateway drug. Noel has so much potential! He's a brilliant, brilliant boy. I can't permit him to waste himself in this way. This has to be nipped in the bud."

This time John has to bite his tongue. Heather laughs out loud.

"Listen young lady," says Pat sternly. "The only reason I took you into my confidence like this is that I expected you to act in a mature manner and treat this issue with the seriousness it deserves. If you can't show me that kind of respect, then I don't know about our working relationship. I just don't know."

It is an awkward moment. John holds his breath.

"Well?" asks Pat.

"I'm sorry," says Heather quietly.

"I beg your pardon?" asked Pat.

"I said I'm sorry," says Heather.

John hasn't been so embarrassed since he left school. He risks a look at Heather, whose face betrays no expression at all.

For a while no one says anything. The fan rattles in its cage.

"All right," says Pat. "Apology accepted. You've blotted your copybook, though."

"I," says Heather, "I might just duck out for a smoke.

"Don't be too long," says Pat.

John goes after Heather. She is sitting on the front step with her fists clenched.

"I hate her," she says. "Christ, how I fucking hate her." She is shaking with anger. "She'll fuck up that poor kid of hers the way she's already fucked up Melody. Detox. Christ."

"Screw her," says John. "Let's go. Let's get on the plane to Hong Kong."

For a second he sees it all: their apartment in a high-rise, 747s passing the window on their way in to land, the pair of them eating noodles out of cardboard containers and drinking Tsing-tao, squabbling over the fate of their Triad antihero and his kick-boxing librarian girlfriend, and if Heather starts to win the argument he will throw her into bed and hold her down by her ankles.

Heather exhales and starts to laugh.

"Wouldn't it be great?" she says, and digs up a cigarette. "John Woo, Bruce Lee, Jackie Chan?"

"What are we waiting for?" asks John.

"For the universe to stop with the mighty sucking for just one half of one second," says Heather.

John sits down beside her, crestfallen.

"You might as well hear it from me," says Heather. "Pat'll just turn it into a movie-of-the-week. I've got a sister at the Spastic Center. She's great, but there's only me, so I can't go anywhere."

"Oh," says John. "Sorry."

"Me too," says Heather. She squeezes his hand and kisses his cheek. Her skin is velvety and smells of smoke. "We can't change things, any of us, really. That's what's so awful."

5. *Last thing I need*

"In a way it's a blessing," says Pat. "I was just saying to Melody.

Aboriginal people have such terrible battles with substance abuse, and now, in a small way, I share their pain."

Heather presses her pencil into her notebook until it broke. John's hard-on aches. The phone rings.

".Will you excuse me?" says Pat, and ducks into the office. "'Under The Skin', Patricia Bray speaking," she says. "Oh, Laurie, Laurie darling, hello, hello, how are you?"

The fan rattles. Heather sharpens her pencil.

"Oh, oh dear, I am so sorry to hear that."

A bead of sweat crawls down John's back. Heather licks the end of her pencil.

"No, of course, you do what you have to do. I know exactly how you feel. Exactly. Believe me, I do."

Melody yawns. She has a yellow cavity in one back tooth.

"Yes, yes, whenever. Bye darling. You take care now. Bye."

Pat puts the receiver down and comes out of the office.

"Laurie's not coming. Family emergency, he says," she told them. "He'll try to make it tomorrow."

"Oh well," says Melody. "Can I have some money? Bunch of us going down to the pub."

Pat took her purse from her handbag and counted out fifty dollars. "Don't get wasted. Last thing I need is both of you in detox."

Melody pockets the money and leaves.

Pat gazes into the middle distance. "Typical Laurie," she adds. "He on blackfella time."

At four-thirty Heather says: "Gotta run."

ISSUE 80

"Give my love to your sister," says Pat warmly. John watches the way Heather's bum moves as she walks out the door. When she is out of earshot Pat begins: "Really, she's a saint. Her sister..."

"She told me," says John.

"Ah," says Pat. "Well, We've all suffered our measure of personal tragedy. I think that's why we're drawn to this project. Nigel, for instance, lost his only daughter, to cancer. With that, and not being able to get work in England any more, he's a wreck of a man, really, a shadow — Oh, that'll be him now."

The door bursts open. Behind it is a tall, bearded man in a beautiful linen shirt and black pants. He brandishes a bottle of chardonnay and a corkscrew.

"Fucking weather, eh?" he growls. "You must be John. Pat. PAT. Where do you keep the fucking wineglasses?"

"Desk, darling," says Pat. She kisses him. "John, this is Nigel, of course. Our executive producer. Our EP."

"Very pleased to meet you, sir," says John, suddenly sick with nerves. He doesn't want to go back to driving a truck.

"Sir? SIR? D'you hear that, Pat? Fucking brown-nose!" Nigel calls from Pat's office.

"Told you you'd like him," says Pat. Her eyes glitter.

"Love him. Love it. Fucking sir," says Nigel. He comes out with two glasses. "All I could find. You better get a mug," he says to John.

"I'll pass," says John. "I'm driving."

"The fuck you will," says Nigel.

"I'll get it," says Pat, and heads for the kitchen.

"How's she treating you?" demands Nigel. He opens the corkscrew and twists it with relish into the cork.

"She's, she's great."

"Liar. Did she shitcan that punk chick yet? No? Good. Bitch can write. Nice arse, too. Pat's a fucking retard. Have you heard her with Laurie? 'I'm gubba,' she says, 'you can call me gubba, I don't mind. Gubba, gubba, gubba.' Cunt. She thinks it means governor."

He pauses to wrench out the cork.

"What does it mean?" asks John.

"Eh?" Nigel overfills the glasses and thrusts one at John. "Drink that. She can have the fucking mug. Sir."

"Thank you. What does gubba mean?"

"Garbage," says Nigel. "That's what they call us. Fucking garbage. Bottoms up." He drains his glass.

John tastes his. It's amazing wine, all oak and sunshine, the best he's had. Pat comes back with a coffee mug.

"Started without me?"

"Took your fucking time," says Nigel.

"Oh," says Pat gaily. "I on blackfella time!"

They roar. They remind John of the pigs at the end of *Animal Farm*. You could almost mistake them for people. She loves her son, he reminds himself. Nigel misses London.

He looks at the sunlight playing in his glass. Something inside him eases, that had been wound tightly for a long time. What the hell, he says to himself. What the hell. I can do this.

He drinks.

Wendy Fox

The Fire Time

ISSUE 80

In the fire time we lived for days without sunlight or air.

You and I grew up in the eastern Washington desert, the dry side of the Cascades, where we spoke of rain the way we spoke of the dead: with reverence, with longing, without hope of return. We lived in the country, and I mean all of us. Everyone we knew in the world.

Even as small children we picked rocks, piling up the pebbles and larger hunks of shale and granite into little pyramids around the perimeter of the gardens, where there would be a thicket of marigolds—bright-yellow-and-orange ruffles planted because the stink kept the insects down.

But if we weren't doing our chores or at the neighbors, we spent time out on the low, brown hillsides, trudging among the trees turned brittle and along the dirt cow paths. Up in the land behind our respective homes, there were spindly timbers and scrub and dried lichens on the exposed rock. So, we would find a walking stick and get to it.

The year of the fire, it had not rained for months. Maybe it was a decade with no rain; no one knew. I remember the sizzle of everything, the way my hair had gotten dried and broken at the end, and I was all static electricity and dust. My parents' well was failing. Our yard was long gone, and the lilac bush slumped against the side of the house, blooms dropped and drying around the base. The strawberry beds and the raspberries were paper. We had a plot of wilty potatoes, a cherry tree, and brittle greens, though nearby our southern neighbor's heat-loving wheat fields glowed as gold as a pharaoh's polished tomb. The fields were on a plateau, where the land was mostly flat and open, but there were a few pines poking out through the yellow stalks or fallow dirt; shade and topsoil were precious, and the farmer had not wanted to cut the trees or destroy the root systems that held the ground in place when the wind blew, even if it meant extra turns on the combine.

ISSUE 80

In the fire time and before, we all spent a great deal of time concerned with food. My family cleaned meat and honey in an outbuilding off our house. Part of which we would trade for the northern neighbor's cheese.

There was an extractor for the honey—a big, galvanized barrel with screens inside that the combs could hook into. It was manually operated, and I could turn it if someone would get it started for me. The honey splattered out of the matrix of wax and was collected from a spigot at the bottom, amber draining into the glass gallon jars we also used for milk jugs.

In season my father would hang beef or pork or venison from the winch that was mounted in the rafters. Before he took up bow-hunting, he made his own bullets, melting down wheel weights to smelt lead into shot for the muzzleloader or carefully filling shells with gunpowder and saltpeter. The winch had a big hook attached to a chain, and it wasn't initially there for a butcher—he had installed it so he could pull an engine. If there was nothing up, my brother and I and sometimes you would yank the pulley chain until the hook was a good height and swing back and forth on it. But when there was an animal there, I was set up with a bench and a low table and two big, stainless steel bowls. One bowl held scraps and one held ground meat, and it was my job to run these scraps through the electric grinder, which was painted tractor-green. Every once in a while, the grinder would clog, and then I was to run a piece of hard fat through it, and I enjoyed the sound it made as it churned through—almost like popcorn popping.

But besides that part, I did not like these chores, the sticky smells, the glassy eyes of a deer (my father, for years, would toss the buck horns on top of the woodshed, and there they stayed, pointed bone, until, fearful of fire, he moved the wood away from the house and tore down the shed). Or the beef hide, rotting down on the burn pile: I saw early on that even a fast death was pretty slow, but we turn cold easily, and the blood of different beasts looks the same where it pools around the exit wound, sinks into the ground, and disappears.

The night the fire started, I didn't know where you were. I hadn't seen you that day, because I'd been absorbed in a stack of old, over-thumbed magazines my mother had brought home from her work's lobby. It was hot. If I stayed perfectly still, I was almost comfortable, but the minute I moved, the heat would swirl around me like when I ran bathwater with too much red and not enough blue.

I remember how clearly I wanted night to come and along with it the promise of at least a minute of cool, but instead, the sky opened, electric.

My mother let me stay up past midnight, so we could watch the hillside blaze. Even from miles off I heard the sound of the trees exploding, a hundred years of pine gone. I don't know how I felt besides in awe of the ignition or if I had a sense of the way flame moved.

A day or two later, after little success as our fathers scratched at the dirt with their axes, trying to loosen enough earth to suffocate the flames, the families on our rural mountainside tried to control-burn their own land and barns before the lightning fire got there—an attempt to leave no fuel so they could at least save the houses. The roads closed. The gardens were singed. Our mothers cooked whatever they could find to feed their lovers and husbands, grown and half-grown sons, including a pig they took down with little more than a kitchen knife. Any one of them would have known how to handle a small rifle, but even circled by fire, they killed her the clean way—bled her into a trough before the gutting.

Perhaps my mother did this. She was good with a knife or even a hatchet. In my lifetime I couldn't count the number of chickens I'd seen her behead—picking them up by their legs, flinging them onto a round of wood, and lopping them off at the neck. They really will run for a bit but it's only a second or two.

They decided then to evacuate the children and send them to live for a few days in the nondenominational church in town. In the heat a helicopter landed among the wheat, and you were there with me in the back of a silver van with heart-shaped windows. Where was my brother, your sister? I don't know. But I sat next to you in our getaway vehicle, your sunflower hair and eggplant eyes, and I prayed nothing would separate us, ever. More helicopters came— we were children who played war and who would chop the heads off snakes with a shovel or a sharp rock, but we had never seen anything like these choppers, as we so expertly called them— dropping enough buckets of red fire retardant to make a little portal along the roads, and that's when we went speeding through in the silver van on the way to the church, and we watched another huge machine touch down among the charred alfalfa and the ruined wheat.

ISSUE 80

At the church we both heard two of the town men discussing the fire. We heard them talking about what kind of people lived there, on our mountain, how it was just a bunch of hill people anyway, how we deserved to burn. I remember your face. I think we hadn't known this then, that we were that different. As an odd job, my father even drove the school bus that wasn't really a bus, but a converted four-wheel drive panel van painted yellow with DISTRICT 404 stamped on the side. We had barely started our years of education then, though we knew that some people had inside toilets and all their food came from the store and they didn't wear hand-me-downs like we did. We just didn't know it mattered.

My parents kept their home, their barn, their outbuildings. Their upper tract burned, but, ultimately, we were out little. Even our well came back and came back clean. I had a pony—not a fancy ribbon-in-his-hair pony, but a work pony with lower GI distress, who farted constantly when he walked, and he got a stick in his eye, but one of my father's friends extracted it.

You, though, you lost nearly everything. All that was left, by the rock outcropping where your parents had built the home you all shared, was a blackened concrete foundation slab where your house had been. The chicken coop stood, though even the chickens were ash.

Years later we hiked back there on the trails we had traveled as children, with our grown shoes too wide for the paths, and from there we opened the coop door, which came unstuck with a sound like cartilage separating from bone. Inside there was nothing much: the molting of long-dead birds and a smell from a time when we sat in a church where we were not members and cried so hard we choked. Remember how I cleaned one of the Sunday school rooms, even putting all the chairs up on the tables so I could crawl along the floor and pick the scraps out of the carpet, and then you and another boy came behind me and knocked it all down, upturned the bins of broken crayons and tubes of glue I had sorted, and shredded the picture books? I think you already knew then, with a certainty I still cannot match, how the fire would change us.

Before the ground had even cooled, your family and most of the others left the mountain. You moved to a house in town, and thus began our parting. I stayed on our hillside, learned to gather the morel mushrooms and the stands of fireweed that grow in the years following the torching of a forest. My family harvested the scorched pine and tamarack and used what was left of it in the woodstoves through the deep winters. We took only the trees that were dead, and every year, during the summer and fall when we'd go cutting, we'd be dusted in charcoal again, the burnt bark crumbling in our hands.

I still fear electrical storms and a spark in a dry place. I still remember the way the sky darkened and the smoke bloodshot our eyes. I still remember the ethylene sting of crackling-dry air, and I remember how, the day you visited and we cracked the seal on the chicken coop door, with the evergreen needles and sage around us that had started to grow back in violent-green, how I hoped, like I hoped for rain that summer and how I hope for you now, to come home.

Father Image

ISSUE 80

Timmy and his younger brother Chip waited at the door of the Brooklyn Gardens shuttle bus. The bus leaned to one side, hissed and threw open its doors. "Thanks, mister!" they yelled to the driver as they jumped to the sidewalk. Chip loosened the necktie noose that had been strangling him through the Mass. "Why do you gotta get dressed up for the dead people?" he asked Timmy.

"'Cause it's outta respect. Anyways don't you think it was nice to get dressed up for Chris?"

"Yeah, I guess so. But I don't think he woulda done it for us."

"Don't talk like that."

Chip grabbed the back of Timmy's belt and let his arm swing back and forth as they walked home. They had their orders - come straight home and change out of their good clothes. When they reached their stoop, they stopped and looked up at the third floor. The window was closed. Timmy looked down at Chip, and they nodded their heads and smiled. They ran passed their stoop, around the corner and stopped in front of the color tiled window of the corner pub. Timmy, shading his eyes, pressed his face to the colored glass. Chip stood on a standpipe and did the same. "Do y'see'im? Is he in there?" asked Chip

"I think so. C'mon."

Chip clung tightly to his brother's pocket as they went through the huge wooden double doors. The pub was filled with familiar faces from the neighborhood. Occasionally, a face would turn, smile and raise a glass. They could see Tony the bartender scurrying about scooping up change and passing out glasses. At the far end seated on the last stool in the corner, was Uncle John.

"Tony, look who came to visit," sang Uncle John, "my two roving nephews, back from the spreadin' of the Good Word, no doubt."

Timmy and Chip could tell that Uncle John had spent most of the afternoon in the pub, because, because, whenever Uncle John spent most of the day there, his lips would stick out under his nose. Fish Face, Chip called it. The boys ran over to him, and Chip ran into his Uncle's arms. That's when Timmy saw that picture again. It was the only picture of Him that frightened Timmy. The Head was tilted back, and the Eyes looked Heavenward. Sad. Pitiful. Blood dripped from the Crown of Thorns, and the Mouth gaped open. Abba. It wasn't like any of the pictures in his religion books at school. Even the statue in the church vestibule wasn't as frightening. Once Timmy even touched the wax Nail in the wax Feet on a dare, and that wasn't scary. He did not want that picture to touch him. Chip didn't mind; he ran right into it. Why would anyone want that picture, Timmy thought, and to have to see it when you get up in the morning, or whenever you had an itch. Uncle John must have liked it to have it tattooed to his arm. Uncle John held out his arms and caught Chip, and planted him on a stool. When he was younger, Timmy used to think that the Blood would rub off on his clothes.

"Tony, two sodas for the boys," said Uncle John.

"Here y'go." said Tony placing two colas on the bar.

"So what's the good news, boys? You keepin' your noses clean?"

"Yep, they're sparklin'," said Chip before he gulped down his cola.

"So what's with the fine tie and trousers?" asked Uncle John.

"We had to go to the - you know - funeral," answered Timmy, fidgeting on his stool.

"You remember, John," said Tony. He reached over and drew Uncle John over an inch. "Smitty's kid," he whispered. Uncle John sat straight and reached for his drink. Timmy could see the Eyes, and the muscles clenched when the glass was grabbed.

"Terrible thing," said Uncle John, "So young. But for a twist of fate, it could have been either of you. Terrible thing." Chip wiped his mouth and belched. "Here, here," said Uncle John.

"We better be gettin' home, Uncle John," said Timmy. "Thanks, for the sodas."

ISSUE 80

"By all means. The last thing I need is for your mother to start accusin' me of corruptin' you."

Timmy grabbed Chip around the waist and helped him off the stool. "Now, you be good," said Uncle John as the two brothers rushed through the doors out of the dark taproom onto the street. The boys squinted at the bright sunshine. They walked slowly, and Timmy peeked around the corner. "Is she waitin'?" asked Chip. The street was deserted and all the windows were shut. Timmy pulled his brother, and they ran to their stoop, as the click and screech of a screen was being raised.

"Timothy! Philip! Where the dev'l have you been?" screeched their mother hanging halfway out of the window. "Get in and change." They rushed up the stoop, and Timmy saw his mother continue to look up and down the block.

Each successive flight of stairs brought the boys higher into the heat; the third floor was always the hottest with the approach of dinnertime, and the kitchen heat billowed through the door and washed over them. Their mother was at the stove, working. The table was already set, but he was not there. Chip ran into their room and tumbled out of his good clothes forgetting, or not caring, to hang them up. Timmy followed his brother and picked up each piece as it was discarded. After he changed, Chip sat on his bed leafing through a stack of comic books he dragged out from under his bed. Timmy changed, and then opened the window letting a breeze into the room. He stepped out onto the fire escape and sat down. The breeze was stronger, and he forgot the heat in the kitchen. He looked out over the yards and felt the metal bands rub into his backside, so he shifted to get comfortable. The dry paint flaked away from the bars and he absentmindedly picked the flakes away and watched them flutter down through the bands, past the floors, until he lost sight of them as they landed someplace in the yard. Clotheslines, some heavy with damp laundry and others with dry sheets, swayed back and forth from each apartment. Looking over the yards and down the block it looked like party streamers haphazardly strung at different heights.

Chip climbed through the window with a comic book in his mouth. He slowly sat down next to his brother and opened the book. "He's back," mumbled Chip. He turned the page and Timmy looked over his shoulder at the superhero. Chip moved his lips as

ISSUE 80

he read the dialogue. "Are they gonna..." Something crashed in the kitchen. They were both on their feet, hearts thumping in their chests, before the comic book hit the floor. Timmy grabbed the rung of the ladder leading to the roof and climbed up with Chip following.

The screams and yells from their apartment mixed with the street sounds. Rumbling diesel engines - *This has got to end* - squeaking pulleys - *Every night...* - rustling trees - *I can't take this.* Soon the church bells drowned out everything.

The sun was low and cast a red haze over the horizon of Brooklyn Gardens giving the city skyline a rusty shade. Each tower and skyscraper reflected the waning sunlight in differing patterns. "That's pretty,' said Chip. They sat in the center of the roof far from the edges next to an old duct that was boarded over. "Could y'tell me the names for the buildings again?"

"We do this all the time. When will you remember for yourself?" Timmy snapped.

Chip nodded and pulled his knees up resting his chin. "I wish I brought some comics." The church bells stopped, and they heard a door slam below. "Do you think Chris died because he did somethin' bad?" asked Chip.

"No. God's not s'posed to do that."

"Maybe he thought somethin' that was a sin?"

"No. That's not s'posed to happen either."

Chip rocked back and forth, away from and into Timmy. Mr. Malk, the grocery man who lived in the apartment house across the yard, stepped through the door onto his roof. The boys waved, and Mr. Malk stopped short, saluted and walked over to his pigeon coop. Loose feathers flew around the opened door as Mr. Malk slapped the side shooing everyone out. He picked up his long stick with the white rag on the tip and made wide circles with the stick. The pigeons flew together in a wide circle that stretched from his house to theirs following the pattern of the rag stick. The flutter of the white and gray pigeons could be heard with each pass. The boys watched them fly high in an arc and pass directly in front of them every time Mr. Malk drew his rag stick in a tight circle; then they

ISSUE 80

heard more cooing and fluttering, but not from Mr. Malk's pigeons. Mr. Mann from the building next door had let his pigeons free. His pigeons were all white and flew in quicker circles when Mr. Mann waved his own rag stick.

"They gonna do it?" asked Chip.

"They like it too much."

"Who you thinks gonna win?"

"Nobody really wins. They kinda trade. Watch."

The diameter of each circle of flight increased. The men waved their rag sticks until their pigeons flew in overlapping routes. They flew together ten times mixing with each other until each man stopped his circle making and tapped his respective coop top. Gradually, all the pigeons hobbled into the shade, fresh water and feed of the pigeon coop. Mr. Mann stuck his head inside his pigeon coop, and the boys watched him grin as he grabbed a pigeon in each hand and waved them at Mr. Malk. He put the captured pigeons back into his cage.

"Timothy! Philip! Get down here! Dinner!" screamed their mother.

* * *

Timothy, Chip and their mother sat down to eat. The meal was delicious, and the table was silent save for the scraping of knife and fork, and Chip's chewing. Once the plates were cleaned, they went back to their room. Timmy went directly to the window and onto the roof. He sat on the edge and watched the skyline slowly light the night. He could hear the bazaar in the churchyard begin to open. Chip walked up behind his brother and softly tapped his shoulder. Timmy stood up moving away from the edge and looked at Chip holding his hand out with a rubber ball. Timmy grimaced and shook his head. "I don't feel like it." He walked near the duct and leaned against it. Chip walked next to his brother and knelt down beside him. "You gonna leave one day and leave me," he said,

"I can tell. You don't wanna play with me anymore like you used to. No more cat burglar. You don't even hit me with your pillow no more."

"It's not you. You didn't do anything," answered Timmy.

"I guess."

Timmy grabbed Chip with one arm and hugged him. "You know you're my best pal."

"You're just sayin' it," said Chip struggling, "You're gonna leave me all alone."

"I can't leave."

"Would you take me with you?" said Chip slowly.

"Sure."

Chip smiled.

"C'mon, let's go to the bazaar. I got some money."

They climbed down the ladder and ran through the apartment to the street below. The sounds of buzzers, ringing bells and popping balloons from the churchyard drifted up the street to meet them, enticing them, drawing them quickly through the chain link fence. The tents had green and white stripes with narrowing awnings over open counters. Patrons slapped coins down and the old women spun the huge numbered wheels. Some booths had two wheels spinning in opposite directions waiting to see if the number fell under the tiny red strip guaranteeing the third shelf prize. The wheels buzzed in every corner of the yard. After inspecting each booth for the best booty, Chip decided: "C'mon, this one."

Timmy picked Chip up and let him put the coin wherever he pleased, occasionally changing his mind and switching at the last possible moment when the old women's hand left the wheel.

Seven coins. Seven spins. No prize.

Chip looked up at Timmy, cocked his head to one side, and gave a half-hearted smile. "It's okay." His eyes were glassy and filled. Chip wiped them with his arm before anything more happened. Timmy rummaged through his pockets, frantic and hopeful.

"We can go home," said Chip hooking two fingers through one of Timmy's belt loops.

"Hey! "yelled the older brother retrieving a coin from the folded recesses of a back pocket.

"You do it!"

"No, you do it!"

They ran over to the nearest booth, and Chip blindly slapped it down from Timmy's shoulders. The wheel spun and buzzed and clicked. The second wheel spun. The red patches blurred until the whole wheel turned red. They both waited for the wheel to show the number and the color. The wheels slowed and the tab clicked off each nail. Forty-Two. Thirty-Five. Three. Twenty-Five. The tab stopped between two nails over Forty. Chip looked down at the counter. Their coin was nestled over the hole in the four of Forty.

"What will it be children?" Anything on the first shelf," said the old woman scooping up the change.

"It's on the red," said Chip.

Timmy looked at the wheels. The narrow red stripe hung over the tab pointing to Forty. "It sure looks like it," he said.

"Sorry boys, you're mistaken. It looks to me like you're off by one nail," she said putting the change in her apron pocket.

Timmy moved closer to the edge of the booth near the wheel. "What do y'think Chip?"

"It looks like we're bein' gypped. But it's okay. I'll take that." He pointed to the first shelf.

The old woman handed Chip a plastic box the size of a folded newspaper. Chip took the lid off and looked inside. "Perfect." He climbed off Timmy and grabbed the belt loop.

"What did you get that for?" asked Timmy.

"I'll tell you later."

"I got no more money."

ISSUE 80

"Can't we just walk around a bit and see everything before we go home?"

"Sure."

The lights on the booths blinked, and the music piped through the paths of people huddled around a stage. They could smell popcorn, chocolate and beer. Huge stuffed animals were tossed over counters to the waiting arms of teenage boys who immediately passed them over to the girls at their sides. Timmy and Chip walked near the card and dice games in the auditorium and were shooed away by the men at the doors. They rested on the back steps of the school and startled a kissing couple in the shadow of the steps. Soon the lights blinked on and off, and three priests came out from the rectory and walked around the yard ringing bells. The bazaar was going to be closed for the night.

"We'd better be going," said Timmy.

"I know, but I don't wanna go home."

"C'mon."

They walked home slowly. Chip kept one hold on the belt loop and the other around the plastic box. They crept up the stairs waiting for sounds, any sounds. The kitchen light was on, and the apartment was quiet. Walking through the living room on the way to their room, they heard the deep voice, from the shadow on the couch-the heart-stopping, breath-holding, hold-up-your-arms-close-your-eyes-voice- "Get to bed."

Timmy closed the door. He walked to the window opened it and gazed at the clear night, the stars and moon. Chip put the plastic box on his bed and rummaged for something under his bed.

"What are you looking for?" Timmy whispered.

"For this." Chip pulled out a handful of comic books and placed them in the plastic box and put the cover on top. "So if you leave and you take me with you, I can carry this."

"Yeah, sure."

Chip scrambled on top of Timmy's bed, resting next to his brother.

"You betta get changed for bed."

"I'm gonna sleep just like this, with my sneakers on," Chip answered back. "Just in case, so I won't have t'put them on. Promise to tell me which buildings are which." Chip climbed onto his own bed clutching his comics' box.

"Sure. G'night." Timmy and Chip closed their eyes and waited for the time when they both could leave.

ISSUE 80

ISSUE 80

Andrew Palmer

Homage

A series of conversations about breaking stuff.

"I really don't want to talk about this."

"Fine. Okay," said Kate. This was just last night. Long silence for a phone conversation, maybe ten seconds, maybe even fifteen or twenty. Not twenty. But long. Maybe fifteen.

"But," he said, "we're gonna talk about it anyway, aren't we," and he started talking about how they'd had this conversation like twelve times already and while he didn't think another one would be necessary after they kissed and made up after the last one like a month ago right after he finished gluing the shower curtain ring back together, it seems it is, more for her than for him but he's not trying to be contentious.

"Well you are."

"What?"

"Being contentious, without even trying, you're a . . . a real pro."

"At being contentious? At breaking stuff?"

"Okay, Alex, Alex, you can stop now, I get it. Okay? I get it. We've had this conversation before and we don't need to have it again, so let's not."

"It just seemed like you'd forgotten all the salient points from our last conversation, so I was—"

"I remember your points, okay, and fine, 'salient,' whatever, I don't need to hear them again. You can stay at my apartment, but no more than two nights though, okay?—you leave the morning after the concert."

"That's all I'm asking for."

ISSUE 80

"Okay," she said, ". . . okay."

"What."

"Okay, I'm just gonna come out and say this, just to add one more element to the breaking things conversation, but we're not going to argue about it, okay?"

"I stopped thinking about it two minutes ago."

"Okay, I just wanted to say this, just so it's out there. You think my argument doesn't have any logic behind it, but I think the reason you've broken so much of my stuff and none of your own—which, by the way, I doubt is true—is that you're more careful about things when you're in your own apartment than when you're in other people's apartments or houses or . . . workplaces."

"Okay, I agreed not to argue, so I'm just gonna say that's bullshit and hang up the phone. And thank you for allowing me to stay with you for two nights."

"You're welcome."

"Okay."

"Good night Alex."

"Good night Kathryn, see you soon."

As soon as he hung up the phone, or right after he shook his jowls—or his cheeks, he's too young to have jowls, probably never will: he relaxed his cheeks and shook his head back and forth—and tussled his hair to get his mind off the conversation and onto other things, something he often does after talking with Kate, anyway so right after that he started thinking about this whole breaking stuff argument, how'd it ever reach this level of recurrence, to the point that it sometimes seems like it's really threatening to ruin his friendship or whatever it is now with her? He really should have thanked her for allowing him to stay with her for two nights—or should've said "three nights" to get a laugh from her—now berates himself for pretending he did. Berates, reprimands, scolds, whatever. Reproaches. So say what you really said: "Okay, I agreed not to argue, so I'm just gonna say that's bullshit and hang up the phone"— something like that, anyway—and then, he's almost sure, it was just last night, "Good night Alex," "Good night Kathryn"—"Kathryn" because he'd recently started calling her Kathryn on the phone instead of Kate because he knew it made her laugh or pretend to or at least smile. But there was no "thank you for allowing." Also there was some overlap between his "so I was" and her "I remember," but he didn't know how to convey that on the page or didn't care at the time—but he got the gist of the conversation so on to an earlier one, about nine months ago.

More of a monologue than a conversation, or a diatribe, his: "Fuck you!" more vehemently than he'd said it in the past few years, as far as he can or could (he thinks) remember. "Fuck you for even insinuating that I come over here to break your shit on purpose!" then, "I don't want to be here right now," then, "Shit, shit, shit!" then, "I come over here to cook you dinner, probably the best dinner you're going to"—or "gonna"—"eat the entire month and you're seriously scolding me for possibly breaking a tiny plastic piece of your fire detector?" then, "Coincidence, Kate. Three things in two months, that's a coincidence, and you treat it like it's some kind of character flaw. Like I can't help breaking your priceless *things*, two chairs and a fire detector, Jesus," then, "Next time I come you'll accuse me of breaking something before I take my fucking shoes off, no, no next time!" He couldn't and can't remember being or acting this angry and loud to someone other than himself since... he doesn't know when. He was in her kitchen, small and narrow with a small round table at the end, next to a window. Sat down at the table. "Do what you want with the salmon, I'm eating Cheerios, I bought them anyway. May I have some milk?" She'd walked into the living room, probably sat down on the couch. Probably crying or about to. "May I have some of your milk, please, Kate?" No answer. "Kate! Fuck this, I'm going home," and he did.

Got over it, as always, both apologized, he for yelling and cursing and she for implying that he broke her stuff on purpose. He didn't break anything for the next two months, then she moved to St. Paul, came back to Madison for a friend's wedding and stayed with him, he didn't break anything, neither did she—before she came, on the phone, jokily: "You can stay here, but one rule, Kate: No breaking stuff"—and they got along great, agreed things hadn't been this nice between them since the summer after they broke up for good, more than two years ago. Bliss, when they were together, as friends, the two years since the breakup, not bliss, but real happiness, which was rare for him during that period, and then, this was what, a month

ISSUE 80

and a half ago, he went to St. Paul to visit some friends, including Kate, stayed with her, broke a shower curtain ring—was reaching for his towel and trying to steady himself in the tub by holding onto the shower curtain. She wasn't home at the time. He put the broken ring, a boutique plastic one, on her coffee table, left for an art museum. Came back and she was there and as soon as she opened the door for him: "Can you explain this?"

"I don't believe this is happening."

"You did it again!"

"I—Kate I can't believe you're doing this."

"Alex, you break stuff! You stay in my apartment and you break my stuff!" She's wide-eyed. Incredulous. Says, "Three chairs, a fire detector—not to mention that fire you set in my oven—and now"— some overlap here, he started probably somewhere around her "set"—"I'm going for a walk," and he did. To the hardware store three blocks away. Two and a half, maybe even two depending on how you count. Dialogue obviously imperfect, same with the salmon and Cheerios monologue nine months ago, but that should go without saying and will from now on. He thought as he walked about how he'd yelled at her about seven and a half months ago (though at the time he probably didn't think about exactly how long ago it was) and how calm he'd stayed this time in comparison. Something close to self-congratulation, not even seething now, just calm, happy—not happy, necessarily, but calm and satisfied—on his way to the hardware store, where he'd buy some superglue to repair the shower curtain ring, Kate wouldn't be so upset when he got back, he'd fix the ring, they'd have a levelheaded conversation, he'd make a joke about how this probably has to happen every few months in order for their dysfunctional relationship to continue to function (though he really thought there was no way she'd have the gall to bring it up in the future after this really quite mature gesture of friendship, unless as a joke, like making "breaking stuff" into a euphemism for something, as he and his roommates had made "checking stuff" into a euphemism for masturbation sophomore year in college, which he guesses is why the word sophomoric means what it does—not "why it means" that but semantic evidence, something) and they'd go back to being friends, which is more or less what happened. No way she'd have the balls to bring it up again.

But then, last night, gall, balls, so after he hung up the phone and did the relaxed cheek shake and thought about the conversation and earlier ones for awhile—maybe five minutes—he decided he'd write an email. One to end this ridiculous back-and-forth—though really it's always Kate who brings it up (but she'd counter with But it's always you who breaks stuff). He has all of his emails automatically saved when he sends them so this is verbatim unless he trips up as he transcribes it, but he'll type carefully: "Date: Sun, 18 Apr 2006 23:30:37 -0800 (PST) / From: "Alex Keeler" <alexkeeler@ifp.com> / Subject: breaking stuff / To: "Kate Bergen" <bergen_partylikeits 18_99@hotmail.com> / Need to get this off my chest. Re: breaking stuff: there's simply no reasonable case to be made against me. We can both agree that I don't come to your apartment with the intention of breaking something. You suggested that I'm less careful because I'm not in my own apartment. This is false. Evidence: a month in Will's parents' apartment, in which nothing was broken, two and a half months plus another week at Monique and Benoit's apartment—nothing broken, several days in Alex G's parents' apartment—nothing broken, several days in Rex's two NYC apartments—nothing, and Annie and Aaron's Brooklyn apt.— nothing again, several nights in Sara's Minneapolis apt.—nothing, and a week in Sara's SF apt.—nothing broken, and four nights in Krista's apt.—nothing, and a few days in Alex Sandoz' apt.—nothing, nothing, Kathryn. Those are cases within the past three years, two of them with other Alexes, and they don't include the dozens of non-overnight non-Alex visits to such apartments as Steph's, Nicole's, Bryan and Kat's, Will's, Rex and Scott's, Manny's, Mike J's, V's, V's boyfriend's, my cousin Beth's, my cousin Matt's, and Sue Z Q's. / Your only remaining argument, one you've at least hinted at, would be that I'm more careless only at YOUR apartment(s), or that I somehow subconsciously don't care about your stuff. Well, that would be simply wrong: insofar as I think about stuff, I don't care any more or less about yours than I do my own, or anyone else's. I respect your property, and I even allow that your stuff is somewhat nicer than much of my stuff and many of my other friends' stuff, a sentiment I think I've expressed to you in approving terms. / There have four incidents (correct me if I'm wrong): 1) January or February '05, Madison, broken chair; 2) April or May, Madison, burnt chair; 3) May or June, Madison, fire detector; 4) February '06, St. Paul, shower curtain ring. All of these items I've either paid for, offered to pay for, or fixed. For all of them I have been yelled at. Before these incidents, we knew and hung out with each other—and even for a period declared our mutual love—for about three years: during

those three years, would you characterize me as someone prone
to breaking stuff, mine or others'? / Coincidence, Kathryn. Weird
coincidence. / We're never to speak of this again. / Kathryn, / Alex."
Sees now he left out a "been," third paragraph, first sentence, and
doublechecks to make sure the error's in the email and not just the
transcription—it is—but doesn't think that had much effect on the
rhetorical impact of the email. Something like that would bother
him if he saw it in an email he got, but not Kate, he's pretty sure.
Very sure. He forgot to mention that he'd not only started calling
her Kathryn more often but that they'd both started using Kathryn
as both a salutation and a goodbye—like Aloha or Shalom—and the
joke was fresh enough and goofy enough that he was sure it'd make
her laugh or at least smile and the email would be taken in the right
spirit, which was serious but not too and over the top but in a funny
way. He was right, Kate sent an email earlier today saying basically
Okay, you're right, no more talk about breaking stuff funny boy,
and that should have ended it—he means all thoughts on both sides
about breaking stuff—but then he started thinking and writing about
the whole thing, and—why didn't he remember this before? (hits
himself on the side of the head with his palm)—there's that essay
about breaking stuff he wrote a few years ago. Four and a half. (He
should mention he burnt the chair with a hot frying pan—salmon,
for her, another fine meal ruined by her yelling at him, or, to be fair,
by him being a little careless and then her yelling at him. No need
to mention the inside jokes with some of the names in the email,
not important.) He fishes up the essay from his files, thinks it might
give him some ideas about things to add to what otherwise is just
a pretty mundane account of a series of fairly minor arguments
between exes, with a bit of contextualizing for the reader's sake. It's
called "On Throwing Things." It's long, so best to summarize and
quote. It starts out by saying he just got a phone call from someone
who told him he's going to have to work more than he'd planned
in the next week. He (in the essay) hangs up the phone, feels angry,
feels like throwing something, doesn't, pours himself a glass of wine,
feels like throwing it across the room, doesn't, then ruminates on
throwing things. Essay He's thrown things in the past—a bat at a
friend, a chessboard at his brother, pens, pencils, notebooks. Essay
He thinks again about throwing the glass of wine across the room,
"the wine spilling onto [his] floor and then kitchen table tablecloth,
the glass rotating like a satellite in *2001: A Space Odyssey*, then
crashing against the wall, spitting centrifugal shards." Essay He
thinks about a story by a writer named Stephen Dixon in which the
narrator (why not just say Dixon, since that's who it certainly seems

to be? to paraphrase his four-and-a-half-year younger self) imagines punching through a window out of anger for not winning a literary award. EH "thinks about the supreme prudence of a person who converts his destructive impulses into fodder for creative endeavor—how [he] would like to be such a person! [He] took a sip of wine and set it down on an end table. There would be no throwing tonight." But then EH thinks about how in some of the throwing-things cases there was a long period of deliberation and hesitation between the initial anger and the act of throwing, and how in these cases it still felt orgasmic—he uses that word—to throw whatever he threw. The essay ends—best to just quote the end: "You may think that these kinds of tedious-deliberation-spawned throwing incidents might not afford the same gush of satisfaction as more spontaneous hurls. Not so: anger and frustration can take a long time to dissipate. It is almost never too late to throw something. Which means it is not too late for me to throw my glass of wine. [He]"—but why not drop the third- for first-person substitutions?—"I am sitting on my loveseat. There is a quarter-full glass of cheap Shiraz-Cabernet sitting on an end table to my left. My heart is beating very fast! I pick up the glass of wine. I throw it against the wall"—with a paragraph break between "something" and "Which."

So—any insight or instruction here, vis-à-vis breaking Kate's stuff? His essay deals with breaking stuff intentionally, while his recurring argument with Kate—which seems like it won't recur after last night's email and her response today, though there's no telling with her and him—was about breaking stuff unintentionally (though Kate might say half-intentionally or subconsciously intentionally). But he's broken stuff intentionally in the past. Thrown stuff. Besides the bat, chessboard, pens, pencils and notebooks, he's thrown books, guitar picks, T-shirts, tennis rackets, crumpled up pieces of paper, an empty marjoram container—though most of that stuff didn't break, except maybe a couple pencils and a book—*The Ghost Writer*, by Philip Roth—which tore and which he now regrets throwing. And he's never actually thrown anything at someone, he just thought saying so would make for a more interesting essay. "So," Kate might say, "just more evidence that your suppressed anger manifests itself in breaking my stuff." "Okay, Anna Freud," he'd say— "Anna" because Kate's a woman. And he still gives no credence to her argument, even if it only applies to his breaking her stuff and no one else's, since his relationship with her is fraught and often filled with unspoken or displaced annoyance, not to say anger, not to say malice, and much more so than his relationship with any of the people he mentioned in his email (Sara maybe excepted), so she may have brought up the breaking stuff stuff for any number of reasons, but then maybe he really does break stuff because he's suppressing anger or something similar or even, still, admit it, lust—a point she could have made in her email response today but didn't. Which means she'll probably bring it up like a month from now (she'll be wrong), as this argument, like so many others, not the least of which was the one about whether or not they should stay together when they were a couple—they broke up three times, four by her count, before the last one two and a half years ago—seems to be predictable. Periodic. Nothing he can do about it. (Temptation to do something literarily or linguistically interesting with "breaking stuff" and "breaking up" and maybe even "broken hearts." Any possibility of that ruined by including this thought here.)

This is becoming more rant-like than he wanted it to be. He actually really likes Kate—and this was supposed to be a story about breaking stuff, all of the stuff he's broken over the years and especially the last few months (and here he could have said "and also all of the women he's broken up with" or "and also all of the times he and Kate broke up" if he hadn't closed the door or gate on that narrative path with the above parenthetical). Bring it back to that. He breaks stuff, it's true, and not just Kate's. But more stuff than average? In the past month he's broken a Bunsen burner and a wine glass (both at the same party, science-themed, and he was drunk and dancing, which is no excuse—but he certainly harbored no anger or bitterness against the host (that was for you, Kate)), and ......
that's it. Except for maybe some toothpicks and matches, etc., which shouldn't count, he's pretty sure that's it. Conclusion: no evidence of either breaking-stuff aggression or sheer clumsiness—and, though this isn't the point, Kate has no case against him. And he's actually still in love with her. And he wrote the "Throwing Things" essay a year ago, he just said it was four and a half years to distance himself from a piece he now dislikes. And he never threw *The Ghost Writer*, though there were times while he was reading it that he wanted to. And the reason he said "a writer named Stephen Dixon" was to hide or obfuscate the fact that he's not only familiar with Dixon's work but holds it in high regard or just "likes it," and not only to hide that but also that he thought this whole story was and still is way too stylistically similar to a Dixon story he just read, and used and is still using too many of the same tricks Dixon uses in that story and a lot of his other fiction (and "tricks" is the word Dixon would use, has used in his stories)—long paragraphs, self-corrective sentences,

ISSUE 80

dropping pronouns and articles from beginnings of sentences, other kinds of sentence fragments, self-directives, real or apparent evidence of searching for the right word, dramatically collapsing time, slipping into the conditional, leaving in or planting apparent errors and later correcting them, acknowledging the work as fiction—up to and including this trick of pushing himself or pretending to push himself to a higher level of honesty or transparency. And he changed all the names in the email to conceal their real identities. And Kate's name isn't Kate. And his name isn't Alex. And Alex is me. And me isn't he, and she isn't she, and we aren't we. And most but not all of the conversations with the character I call Kate really happened, though the dialogue only approximates reality, though I admitted that before. And, though I didn't mention it in my essay, it took me about 45 minutes after I threw the glass to clean up the shards from the floor and wipe off the wine from the wall. And if Kate were to read this she'd call it more evidence for my vanity. And she'd be right. And that's part of why I love her. And I believe in love. And this is getting too confessional—not confessional exactly but muddled—not muddled exactly but directionless. Muddled. In other words worthless. I chuck my laptop out the window. Not really, but now. Not really, I need it to email Kate about the possibility of staying three nights instead of two. And to suggest other things. And it's never worth it to break stuff on purpose.

Joseph Rogers

Go Children Slow

There are a few different routes from here; it all depends who's in the car with you. Say it's her—she's probably beside you on the front seat of a '78 Impala with all your friends' initials carved into the maroon foam on the roof. Her initials are right next to yours. They were the first ones. It was her idea to scratch them in with a dead pencil, and soon everyone wanted their jagged letters up there; something to be remembered by when everyone went their way after graduation. But everyone didn't go their way after graduation. Everyone's still right here. At least SB and DF are taking classes at Quinsig—more than you can say for yourself. When you come by their apartment each night, you know exactly what you're in for: a handful of dudes pulling bong hits and staring at SportsCenter.

If she's in the car, no doubt you're late getting her home. Head down Grove St. to the Walgreens, hook a right on Forest, and follow Forest to the elementary school. There's that exterminator's in the old three-decker with the PEST OF THE MONTH billboard bolted to the roof—you want the left just before. That's Paddock Ave. Lots of kids in the neighborhood so go children slow. Climb the hill and bang a left. It's three blocks up on your right.

But maybe one quick stop first: that bakery next to the packie is still open. When you pull over to the curb, she'll say to the windshield or the dashboard or wherever it is she's looking that's nowhere near your eyes, "I said I didn't want one." Go in anyway and buy her that Sesame Street cookie she likes. The blue one. Grover. As you come up on the Walgreens you'll remember one of the many times you said, "Maybe we should stop." And she said, "Yeah, we really should start using them." And you said, "Seriously, we really should" as you drove right on past.

Look at her when you pull up to the light at the exterminator's. She'll be all the way over there with her head against the window. Look at the hair she dyes black once a month; the touches of acne on her cheeks; the tiny hole in her nose where she's taken out her silver stud and stuck it through her bootlace because her mother still somehow doesn't know. Stare at all the front seat separating you and think, There's so much maroon between us. It will seem tragic and poetic, but you won't be sure. She likes tragic and poetic, writes everything down in those notebooks she keeps in her backpack, the pages so filled with words that none of it looks like English. She says she's just going to keep on writing.

You'll wonder if you should say it, what you were thinking about the maroon, but opening your big fat mouth is what started this silent treatment in the first place. You said a stupid thing, which isn't rare in itself, but you said a stupid thing at the wrong time. Remember? Your trapped voices bouncing louder and louder off the closed car windows until there was only one place you knew to look for a way out: math. What was it you said? "Two plus one can equal zero sometimes, you know." Brilliant.

Sitting there in her silence you might start thinking about PD, standing under fluorescent bulbs in his Price Chopper uniform, scanning and bagging and scanning and bagging. How he told you the words "paper or plastic?" begin to merge after a while. "Papeplast?" he says, "plast?" he says, "pluh?" as shoppers file through. Then he slides his timecard, stuffs a bag of Funyuns in his jacket, a tube of cookie dough in his pant leg, and heads across the street to SB and DF's.

If it's December it might have just stopped snowing. Only an occasional car on the road, crunching forward, headlights glaring off all that white. The billboard bolted to the roof of the exterminator's three stories up won't show the Bald Faced Hornet or the Subterranean Termite, it won't say PEST OF THE MONTH. Every year it's the same joke: a smiling, fat-faced Santa Claus watching over everything. Above him: GUEST OF THE MONTH.

The hill will be icy, shift into low. You've got eight cylinders but no front wheel drive so don't push it too hard or your tires will just spin and spin and then where will you be? You hate the smell of car heat but her feet are always cold so put the hot air on full blast. The defroster will still be shot so crack your window and keep wiping fog off the inside of the windshield. Notice those power lines above you, how they plug into home after home, how they link everything together. How it's all so makeshift. Those wooden poles and swooping wires, it'll seem to you technology from another age. This whole neighborhood, this whole town, lately everything's been looking grainy and washed out, as if your eyes filmed it decades ago.

ISSUE 80

Maybe you're a visitor from the future. You're homesick for someplace you can't quite remember; it feels like someone's vacuuming out your stomach. There's only one thing you'll be sure you remember about the future: the sky there is maroon.

Snap out of it—your ass is in a fishtail. Go easy. Imagine tires digging into packed snow. Don't force it.

Forget it. You can't make it. Let yourself slide back-asswards down the hill. She won't even turn to look at what you're sliding into; she'll stare straight ahead, holding onto the cookie in its waxy bag. When you stop sliding and get the car steadied, you'll find yourself in the middle of the intersection. The snow-covered street will be deserted, traffic lights bouncing off white. Green. Yellow. Red.

Maybe being the only car out there will have you remembering the empty school last summer—you and MW sweating your asses off in that greenhouse of a classroom for six weeks. English never was your best, but summer school? How can you ace Calculus and flunk English? "Because you can't prove any of these answers," you'd say to yourself and raise your hand to go to the bathroom. You loved the feeling of wandering those deserted halls, your sneaker squeaks echoing off lockers. Like a nuclear bomb had hit and somehow you were the only one who survived.

You won't be sure about making it up that hill, the hill that winds up to a house where she'll have to stay for another year and a half before there's even the possibility of graduation. Her mother'll be waiting up, no doubt about it; maybe she'll have popped some of those pills she keeps in the junk drawer and she'll be scrubbing the kitchen walls with a sponge. Dad's ass'll likely be down in the room he made for himself in the basement, ZZ Top on cassette and a can of Hamm's. Remember one day he started going into the vegetable drawer in the fridge and offering you those cans? Liked to take you downstairs and tell you what a nice piece of ass his wife used to be. You and dad played it like regular pals for a while, didn't you, but you don't go in that house much anymore. Not since the afternoon dad's talk shifted from wife to daughter. To how it seemed like only yesterday she was in diapers, and what a little lady she was growing into, and how tasty her fat ass looked in those skirts. Remember how your hand started shaking when he said that? It was your insides trying to bust out and leave the rest of you sitting in that basement. And words, they were nowhere to be found. Until finally you thought of her notebooks.

Somehow that got you standing, and you told him the only thing you knew for sure in that moment. "She's just going to keep on writing," you said, and you walked back upstairs.

In front of you, Midland Elementary, a concrete playground and classrooms you sat in just six years ago. And that parking lot where so much has happened since: your first sip of beer, first hit off a joint, first time inside a girl. This girl. Imagine, all that preparation, that practicing yourself until you were empty, in your bedroom, in the shower, in the garage, and still you had no idea what you were in for, how real skin would feel, how warm her around you could be. And here you'll be parked in the middle of an intersection and she'll be a hundred miles away over there against the window. At least she'll have that cookie in her hand. You can watch her lick the frosting off like she does, her tongue getting bluer and bluer.

Don't even think about turning on the radio; this silence is yours to endure. It'll give you plenty of time to think about how MW wound up failing summer school. How he never did graduate. But how still, there you are right alongside him five nights at Yellow, loading freight into trucks. Trucks your pops drove the country in before that forklift went through his thigh. Now he doesn't leave the house much and coming home's always the same scene: your mom in the kitchen, smoking with the windows closed, her feet in her favorite pink slippers, the plush faded and brittle with dust. When you come in, she hugs her head into your chest and says, " There he is, my knight in shining armor." There's something in the frying pan, always something in the frying pan, something from the cabinets always overflowing. She just keeps feeding him. You think maybe this is her plan. Maybe this is what she thinks about while she sits at the kitchen table staring off at nothing, her cigarette turning to ash. Maybe she's trying to kill him. Your pops. If you need him he'll be reclined in the La-Z-Boy, snoring, with the remote on his big belly and his hand on the wooden lever like maybe he was just about to get up.

Put it into gear and head for the elementary school. Go ahead and pull around back, you know the spot. " What are you doing," she'll say. Her lips will be blue. " You think this is funny?" The car will slip and slide in the unplowed parking lot, but keep going until you're beneath the basketball hoop. Speak. Say, "Look, I didn't mean it." Say, " You caught me by surprise is all." Say, " We can figure this out." Move your hand to her and rest it on her stomach. Notice: nothing:

feels different. She'll let you stay there a few long seconds before she says, "Spare me" and puts your hand on the seat between you.

The cookie will be in her lap, Grover's hands missing from the ends of his skinny arms, his face smeared and smudged. It'll start you thinking about JG and KC. Not their pasty skin and sunken eyes, not those gruesome bruises. Not even about the two of them waiting in bushes to knock over old ladies at ATMs. What you'll be thinking about is how last time you went down to Walpole for visiting hours, someone had beaten KC so bad he'd had his jaw wired shut. With bubbly spittle glazing his chin he was trying to tell you what went down, but no matter how much he squinted and contorted his face all he could do was make sounds like wet moans.

Taking her there to that spot beneath the basketball hoop is how you'll be trying to say things you don't have words for. Words will be there somewhere for you to use, but everything you'll search will turn up language you won't understand. Numbers on the dash, letters on the heater, all those initials above you. You'll look and look trying for a hint of how to form language to give her, but it will all have become nothing more than lines, curved and straight, in patterns you won't remember, hieroglyphics you won't be able to decipher. Turn the car off. Over the low roof of the school behind you, across the street, in the rearview, you'll see Santa smiling at you from atop the exterminator's.

She won't look at you; she'll keep picking and picking at Grover, his legs and arms turning to crumbs in her lap. Reach for the cookie. You'll get a finger on it but she'll yank back. "Fuck off," she'll say. Then all at once she'll bite off a chunk. Grover's head. She'll chew with her mouth open and put the cookie right in your face. "Here," she'll say. She'll almost be yelling. "Go ahead." When you don't move, she'll let out a breathy sigh and pull away. She'll tilt her head back and stare up at the roof. You'll look at her eyes for everything you want to say, but by then her eyes will be closed.

And you'll know so much in that moment, too much. You'll see it: driving her to that place in Main South with the old guy out front shouting Psalms; sitting in a pea-green waiting room pretending to read *Sports Illustrated*; pulling over at the curb in front of her house, a hug but no kiss, and watching until she gets inside. Knowing that's the last time she'll be in your car; knowing you'll leave this place soon, and that this whole thing is what it took to get you gone.

Forget all that, some future you think you see. For now, she's your girl, and she's so far away over there.

Take the cookie from her. Set it on the seat between you and place your hand on her knee. She'll brush you off once, and again with a little less, but keep on. Move your hand beneath her skirt. She'll say, "Cut it out" but won't make a move to stop you. Feel the warmth of her more and more up her thigh. Move your fingers over soft cotton and feel the bristly hairs beneath. She'll say, "We can't" as she reaches down and pulls her underwear aside. She'll say, "This is what got us here in the first place" as she moves her legs apart. You'll be trying to tell her: that night of all the nights we parked here in this very spot, I do not regret.

It's now she'll let you lean in and kiss those blue lips. Your mouth on hers, this will be how you're hoping words that are somewhere inside you spill into her, and when she feels them land in her belly she'll know you're trying to say: remember us that night how we laid back across the front seat and sweated our naked bodies together under an itchy blanket, and how we looked up at our initials of all the initials etched into the foam roof, and how those letters that added up to us, they were constellations in a maroon sky.

Francine Witte

Trust

Sarah had given up on trust. Then she met Harley. He was so oozy with charm, she stopped being careful. He would tell her how pretty she looked in her print dress even though she was wearing a pantsuit. And just as she was about to correct him, he would give her his dazzle smile, and that was that.

Soon, he persuaded her to open a joint bank account. Of course, most of the money was hers. Her dead husband, Wendell, had left her quite well off. As time went by, and Sarah asked where all the money was going, Harley would wink and tell her they could live on love.

One day, the dentist called and told Sarah her check had bounced and would she please give her teeth back. "With all the time I've spent on them, they're really more mine than yours," the dentist said. She hung up and started to look for Harley, who was nowhere to be found.

Months later, he calls and Sarah answers the phone, toothless. "I'm sorry," Harley says, and she can almost hear his teeth sparkling in the morning sun. She doesn't want to forgive, doesn't want to trust again, but the words *come home* rise up her throat, past her tongue and fly out into the moneyless air.

And who knows what other words are liable to come out of her mouth with her teeth no longer there to stop them?

Nathalie Anderson

Review of Teresa Leo's *The Halo Rule*

ISSUE 80

Teresa Leo's *The Halo Rule* centers on a paradigmatic situation familiar in our culture: the woman who ventures to open herself to love, to a man, to commitment, and the man who holds back, holds out, withholds. The archetype embodying this paradigm features Narcissus — so fixated in self-regard, in self-absorption, that the woman whom he ignores and takes for granted wastes into nothing, into Echo — herself so obsessed that her every syllable traces his latest utterance. Teresa Leo updates this relationship in a satiric sequence at the heart of her book — her Narcissus, identified as N, attends meetings of Narcissists Anonymous, cruising for affirmation from potential Echoes even there, always on the lookout for "an elegance // he'd chip away at and have, and not have, and have / until it was a broken thing, a bird unwinged" — and this queasy dynamic spills from the Narcissus sequence to impel Leo's entire volume. The man in these poems "will push / your head back to the bed so you can't see him // not seeing you"; will answer a declaration of love by replying that he's "not // all the way there yet"; will, in "Engagement Sonnet," "take back the ring"; will, after four years, still "say my name wrong, / say it outright without hesitation"; will favor in his women "all that looks good / and doesn't speak." And the woman in these poems knows the score, "listens carefully, arches her back, / murderous and sentimental, like a staircase"; berates herself for breaking his rules by letting her feelings show: "*Idiot.* What I said 7 or 8 times in the bathroom after." It's no wonder that his voice on the phone "call[ing] to remind me" of their ended affair in "Anniversary" makes "the three years blow open again": "there is no witness protection for the lost."

In tracing this paradigm through *The Halo Rule*, I'm reminded of Olga Broumas's more straightforward 1977 poem "Cinderella," which famously considers the token woman "alone / in a house of men / who secretly / call themselves princes." A self-appointed prince requires a paramour who is worthy of his eminence, but whom, because he's the *sine qua non*, he'll never see as his equal, never take as his queen — another familiar paradigm, perhaps particularly in the literary world, where we've too frequently seen uneasily established male writers condescend to take as lovers young poets whose work they meticulously, punctiliously, will not praise. Leo's poems acknowledge the powerful attraction of a man who uses words as lures, whether the first crush who "could say *stay* and *always* in two languages, // a corrupt tongue and a body I believed," or the mature poet who "said my hair was a creature / unto itself, a dark and dangerous thing / that could set the world on fire"— and notice how his words here invite the woman to assume he's complimenting her potent "dark and dangerous" mind while simultaneously allowing him to deny any implications beyond her mere appearance. "Acknowledgments" gives us the aftermath of such relationships, as the speaker finds in fact no acknowledgment of herself in her lover's book or, by implication, life — "Not a word, a mention, a nomenclature or coda. / No wedding rings, cock rings..." — but feels the diminishment intended in his inscription to her: "W/ Love," that casual "W/" spotlighting the insincerity of the "Love," "the innocuous ways / men sign off." "Poets in Particular" makes the man's refusal of commitment explicit — "No apostrophes here," no possessives – "as he rises and falls to the rhythm of / the *can't*, the *don't*, the *yes but*, the *not*," a sequence nicely providing titles for the four increasingly equivocal poems that follow.

Broumas's "Cinderella" concludes by rejecting the prince's castle for "my sisters' hut." Teresa Leo doesn't make that move, and — although I assent to the feminist analysis in the earlier poem — I'm also glad that she doesn't go there. Leo's poems grant the neurotic paradigm its full potency, enmeshing the reader in desire, disgust, appalled recognition. If this Narcissus is more conscious and thus more purposively cruel than his classical precursor, the Echo figure inscribed here is also more aware and thus more open to transformation. Indeed, even as *The Halo Rule* tracks sardonically its paradigms of condescension and acquiescence, manipulation and self-abasement, it reminds us that becoming conscious of such patterns is itself a political process. Even while enmeshed in obsession, Leo's protagonist recognizes the insidiously seductive "bereft / theft rhyme of desire and seizure / under our skin"; she's already asking, "How, if at all, / does agency fit in." By the book's conclusion, Leo has conjured up evocations of early sexual experiences that gesture towards the origins of "the pull-back caveat // of *I like you but*"; still more significantly, she's recalled a grandmother whose "arranged marriage" and "forfeited world" intensify and complicate the meaning of self-abnegation and sacrifice; and in "Love at the End of the 20th Century," she's opened her volume to a striking alternative paradigm: "you, // conscientious objector, accident, rapture," with whom "I may be dangerous but I am not armed."

This paradigm shift constitutes the significant and satisfying crux of *The Halo Rule,* but how it's conveyed: ah, there's the pleasure. The book's teasing phrases, its fracturing juxtapositions, its slippery syntactic turns, its potent repetitions remind me often of poets like John Ashbery, but less invested in the surreal effect or the non-sequitur for its own sake, more pointed, more purposive, more excoriating. Here, *"harm"* — the word, the premise —"fulfills / all of its properties of grammar and rage," and that idea – that emotion inheres in our very syntax — reverberates throughout the volume, in "the staccato of conjunctions that kept each noun at bay," in "a little subjugation, verbs / he'd take a shine to," in "the felonious turned formalist." I especially like the quick runs of words that crop up variously throughout the volume — "dilapidate, diminish, diffusion, ruin" or "bypass, sidestep, around-the-bend, through" or "stun gun, flame thrower, / harpoon, maimer" or "the ricochet, // the arsenal, the ambushed heart." And isn't that Echo's quintessential tactic — through repetition and rumination to amplify the implications of Narcissus's well-defended evasions of emotional responsibility?

ISSUE 80

No Discourse to Her Beauty: A Tragic Proem in Thirty-Two Acts

I.   (It began with a disagreement. We dithered over Fortinbras, Claudius, who of them made the better Prince: Reference Machiavelli, read strategy, but Hamlet's line? ... snuffed out.)

II.   *With this regard their currents turn awry,*
And lose the name of action. – Soft you now!
The fair Ophelia! Nymph, in thy orisons
Be all my sins remember'd.

III.   We talked late into the night, what if, Ophelia HAD conceived, what if, there had been a child. It was never enough (for me) that Prince Hamlet had nearly wasted the ghost's gray hours, or had whipped so many corpses into their holes. He had perhaps fathered an heir. "Could this have been?" "Which scene?" "Would there have been time?" The doubled sharpness of lines in the margins – "You are keen, my lord, you are keen," and "It would cost you a groaning to take off my edge." What groaning could she lay claim to, his playing with her, at her expense, no matter how preoccupied his mind with revenge and fury? No--I stay close to my greater mistress, the child-made-mother by his majestic play, and his toying embraces. Ophelia--my Ophelia.

IV.   *Get thee to a nunnery: why wouldst thou be a*
breeder of sinners?

V.   (We manufactured this plotline — beautiful — the gravedigger raised the young girl, cropped her hair, [what with so many Norwegians occupying Denmark in the years *after* Laertes and our sweet prince came together at

Elsinore].) Long after her mother drowned herself, having not taken her fullness to a nunnery where she could have concealed in habit the child she had in secret. Ophelia did not go, not quickly enough, and as her temple waxed, what quickening she might have found in all the herbs meant not for poesy, but abortifacients, every one, each one gone wrong and her pale face drowned, never knowing the thing lived past one sad dusk. Mad? Of course she was, no waffling here; to be or not to be pregnant is no question for pondering. Only that she was, and if her dress was unkempt, it was fortuitous concealment, if her face puffy and dazed, no wonder. Fatherless, fatherless, either way, *all of us.*

VI.   The midwife would have known the way to the cemetery, and undertaken many a night burial in those days, when too many women birthed in darkness or in secret, their orphaned fairy-children bound for the crossroads, or these little lumps of flesh barely formed, who would never have had a chance anyway; well she knew the stone path to the grave-maker's house, the "First Clown" of the bard's Mouse-Trap, to catch us all unawares, and absolute, as each character might be any one of us. Which one of us?

VII.   To be or not to be. The bundle the woman would have given the clown might have been bloodied, might have been washed, but either way it would have been sheer chance that this thing die or live, too early born to blistering mad and unknowing mother and father, each in their separate spheres. "A rat, a rat!" of a grandfather freshly entombed, no chance that her mother live after what she had done, but only picking flowers now for a grave she was speeding toward herself, under the willow boughs. No one's seed had made her child form in no one's womb, and still, Beckett many centuries off and later, claiming: "They give birth astride a grave, the light gleams an instant, then it's night once more. On!"

VIII.   The Maker of Houses built the little den of stone found on the edges of newly erected tombs and had there a wife perhaps, more likely not. A man cannot live with death for very long before he makes conversation with it. He might have lain his little unwillingly claimed bundle on the hearth, merely waiting out the process that would signal a return to his work, but it didn't come. When she cried, he brought warm buttermilk up along the rag-thumb and suckled her, surprised by her strength. And when she passed the filthy meconium he buried that instead (like the milt of a foal's tongue), careful into the earth, as some passage fare for her to live, for by now he had become fond of her, made peace with her strong will.

IX.   The Midwife speaks: " That corpse-child lives while her mother makes exchange of her soul. You've been made a gift, one I cannot take back. It was me who made the mix who brought her forth and I won't have such a reminder in my house of all the days I've made women of children by making death happen in their wombs. You keep your token, architect. Make my house fine when I leave soon enough. But know that the grave you dig on the morrow is the mother of your whelp."

X.   In *youth when I did love, did love...* he sang, all the while too aware of what silence could not remain. One day he'd have to tell her, too far away to imagine. He dug and drank deep of the stoup his helper brought, and in a pause, let dribble some into the earth. The dead woman would have that, in exchange for the new box in the corner of his home where a secret slept.

XI.   *Hold off the earth awhile.* The digger had seen many go into the graves without such a scene as this, brother battling lover, but watching and working were not the same thing, just as these men who bore some relation to the woman were not the same thing – but surely, the gravedigger wondered – the mad Hamlet, father? So struck upon this corpse and conversant with her that he could announce before the royal court "I loved Ophelia?" She had a name. Nothing that he could have done then but watch, lone eye of a sorry spectacle. Still, he privately worried – the babe's soiling cloths would need tending to, her feeding time close. Who cared whether these royals understood the value of life? They scrapped in plots over this affection or that love when such proof lived in the graver's mansion. Hurry now, the babe will be hungry. Hurry now, cast your flowers down.

ISSUE 80

XII.   *The readiness is all.* Of all places, just before the duel,
the opportunity for our Dane to slip his signet ring into
Horatio's palm. ("Since no man has aught of what he
leaves, what is't to leave betimes?") Horatio, who would
have understood enough to hear the fatal going of his dear
friend. He would know that were Hamlet to survive, this
ring's return would be an afterthought, though a man's
heart was in it. Hyperion to a satyr aside, royalty would
understand the press of this image against the wax, the
shapelessness of plots and plots . . .

XIII. News of the deaths spread, and the digger was busier
that week than ever. He planted into the earth all parents
and uncles and granddames to the child he knew, and
considered them each well gone. Now no one could claim
her, and her stay was bought in blood. She would remain,
grow stronger, little Danish abiku. Still there was the
trouble of eyes and Norwegians and soldiers, longer in
Denmark than just a passing through. Progress made to
Poland could be delayed – there was an unpeopled throne.

XIV.   (Here it is, the trouble: "She is Hamlet, Queen of
Denmark," I say, unwilling to lose the name. "Hamlet
II" and then, "Hamlet III" then back to "Hamlet II: The
Rest is Not Silence . . ." We imagine voiceovers and movie
contracts, copyrights and action figures. Soon we have
become absurd.)

XV.   "Help me Horatio, you're my only hope. You served my
father well in the Polack Wars." (O dear o dear o dear.)
Star Wars and *Battlestar Galactica* collide and we consider
Starbuck a model for our young Hamlet, a short-haired girl
raised to fence, to boyishly study the bawdy language of
soldiers under the care of a wearied graves-man, a girl who
will eventually seek out Horatio in her twenty-fifth year.
What better way to make good on a father's request?

XVI.   *Things standing thus unknown, shall live behind me!*
If thou didst ever hold me in thy heart
Absent thee from felicity awhile,
And in this harsh world draw thy breath in pain,
To tell my story.

ISSUE 80

XVII.   ("It must be done right, that's the main," among our battalion of concerns. A novel. A screenplay. "You keep seeing this as a movie?" Go ahead. "Let's do short pieces." NO, NO, NO. Fine. I'll write it.)

XVIII.   *Sweets for the sweet.* But look here, this is what I keep seeing. Horatio's attendance to the sites of memories in years previous, his obligation to Fortinbras fulfilled, his planned journey back to school, to Wittenberg. He walks his farewell among the cemetery scene where he sees a child play free within the stones. "You boy, come here." (Or something like this, some drawing near of friend and friend concealed.) "What grave is this?" "Why no grave at all, Lord, but a bed." "A bed?" "For man and woman to lie upon when all their lies are past." And some deep remembrance still further to Horatio who feels low in his bones a familiarity he cannot fathom, till the aging gravedigger surprises him in greeting. "The child is yours?" And a suspicious glance. "Who wonders?" ("Go child, take this packet to the maid at the meadow's edge.") Horatio's worry: "I will be gone a long time and cannot tend these beds – I knew them well."

XIX.   *Even while men's minds are wild; lest more mischance*
            On plots and errors, happen.

XX.   (Here we break ways, my love to his home, several hours away. I to my work and son, alone these ten nights. Who will write it? And did we ever decide how it is that Horatio becomes aware of the child? How it is that she gains the signet ring?) There are other matters--of Fortinbras, of an occupation, for it was his own father's land taken in duel between Prince Hamlet's father and Old Fortinbras that so distributed the lands of Elsinore. We cannot leave this plot unmanaged: there is an occupying army and a bastard child to the throne. Oh Shakespeare would be pleased, or not, though there is nothing like resolution, dénouement when badly sought. Some end to this tragedy, perhaps enough that the fathers and sons have their work behind them. But of the daughters? I want to understand the unraveling of Ophelia's fate to drown indirect from Hamlet's imperious fury, to suffer so much for her father's death. It would be her daughter's inheritance, this unavenged accident-

ISSUE 80

murder of a grandfather by hand of the father. What awesome parentage! Only the house of Atreus could outstrip this soured and repetitive wheel.

XXI.   *Too much of water hast thou, poor Ophelia,*
         And therefore I forbid my tears

XXII.   "She was a mother to that'n, and there be the father fifty paces yon in royal house, the finest. His was the greater train. This'n was mad in heart, not mind, and found her edge by the willow bank. This child is of 'em, and still strangely, the very light of me. But my lord, you know her future better, take her on. I am a poor man."

XXIII.   But Horatio could not have thought too long on her circumstances. What madness had he already seen? Too many years past, and what might have been the truer intuition he might have blamed on wishing; he could not believe a man who might have reason to lie. Is it money, old man? Do the pockets of the dead carry little freight in these late days of peace in Denmark? I cannot have a child where I am going, I do not have the time. But his words caught in his throat before he could say them, perhaps because he sensed something greater at stake, or recalled a jollier frame, of a joking clown at work on a grave that was, for a few minutes the last spectrum of a good friend's wit and gaiety. This man had been the same, now he is sure, who parried words with a prince and managed some cuts, but now, stony dullness to his play, which was not play, and all gravity.

XXIV.   "If it be her wish to know, send her to Wittenberg to seek Horatio. I will see her grown and given the message of her origin. But take this. Do not sell it, nor allow any to see it until she is master of her silences. You would be killed for having i – this you know. This purse is on account – her passage to seek me. I will see it done that a stipend is set for you in my absence. You have served Elsinore these years enough, dug enough graves. Some pardon from death's company, to tend a better home?"

XXV.   And so it could be that fifteen or more years pass. Many years.

XXVI.   Years and years.

XXVII.   HURRY UP PLEASE IT IS TIME

XXVIII. But you stopped calling and there were no letters. We let this sit in some file or another, waiting. I packed up my things and moved. Then I moved again. You never came. I wondered why. Memory and desire. I began to write you every day.

XXIX.   Days.

XXX.   (I guess this is what happens when professionals fall in love: the critiques overwhelm the art. We begin to edit one another out of our too busy schedules.) So I'll have to write your sections for you, though I can do no justice to the "sledding Polacks" of your imagination; you've always fancied yourself a Hamlet, but I too have seen myself in mode of a Dane, and just to be fair, Ophelia needs some second life beyond the watery silence, one that makes sense, some exchange.

XXXI.   Was it enough? The night you and I imagined a second part, it was to find a way out of our own impossible love. (Harp lager with lime.) Queen Hamlet was our child as much as she was Ophelia's, or Hamlet's. Who plays what part and why do neither excite? This freakish third is our Hegelian synthesis. The "could be" and "could have been." This is why we'll never finish our novel, why there will be no new play. Potential, potential, potential--this is what I whisper in my empty bed while you are hours away. We might as well be one mad in Denmark and the other stowed in England. A cold, unfinished exile.

XXXII.   We'll never get to the rest--the great battle between the rightful Queen Hamlet (who learnt fencing from Norwegian soldiers, recall) and Fortinbras, after his attempt to marry his way to the Danish throne. The love of Horatio for the young queen, her willingness to know him, a return of love befitting her father's daughter for his dearest friend. May and September: Here is Freud before Freud, anticipating what we know about human hearts and tragedy. We all want to make up for mistakes that were not

ISSUE 80

ours by loving our mothers and fathers. Just as I believed that you and I could be for one another what no one else was ever – mother, father – the midwifery of foolish dreams. Were I Eliot, and you, Pound, or you, Eliot, and I Pound, we could make no land but only waste of this mess. Without the homoerotic parity--what? – this we can never know. I'm only Ophelia, *Ophelia forever,* and my gender makes it so, despite my wild imaginings.

And whether there is a spring to speak of, for Horatio, for the victorious queen, neither of us can say. This is our game, and no one wins. We've all poisoned the tips of our pens, each for one another. And there will always be the same result — a pile of corpses, a pile of pages, and a terrible, fluttering wind.

Jene Beardsley

Sniper

The shots come from somewhere overhead--
Small-caliber raindrops
That pick off one by one the yellow leaves
Crowding the black maple.

ISSUE 81

James Cihlar

Metaphysical Bailout

"Your father had an accident there: he was put in a pie by Mrs. McGregor."
–*The Tale of Peter Cottontail*, Beatrix Potter

My endeavor is an assemblage of tissue, bone, and nerve
whose code is to lift me up. The engine of music, an enterprise of cells,
a corporation of one. Even though she's seen it a million times, the projectionist
lets the well-worn movie run itself out. With so many plotlines,
a variable of success is where she could choose to stop it

but doesn't. Wasting away, his winnowed frame left paw prints all over the house
in the Pied Piper's apocalyptic jig toward death. Even then,
he waited until the last minute before opening that door.
Who wouldn't milk the most out of what he's got,
gambling on fate's prerogative to reverse itself?

Scott said, *I choose not to portray my father.*
Sometimes we don't have a choice. We have to go until the going is gone.
Once the gears start turning, all sorts of mystical things happen,
a web of causality. Somewhere is the part that doesn't move.
We are storing it for the future. Bless the active quiet around it,

the value of space surrounding. I will pump ions in the air
with my pink fibrous bellows, a campaign declaiming stasis
but banking on a fall. A child is too young to manage his body,
biting down on pennies, scratching a pox. How the physical can change in an instant
due to bad decisions, a head stuck out of a car window on a bridge,

a severed finger in a bowl of chili, Nerds and Pepsi. I've made it past
those fears of life-altering fragmentation: unwittingly committing a crime
and going to jail, honestly answering a question that betrays my parents.
Shouldn't it go both ways and the world slip so that what was red is black
and what they all know they now admit?

How I wish to be lovely. Once the frame of reference changes
our signature qualities will emerge from the postdiluvial silt
to shine hallelujah. When the world rights itself, bears will turn into bulls,
mammoths into racehorses, heavy dinosaurs into fine-boned birds.
We'll be seen for who we are, and the past won't matter any more.

James Cihlar

Mr. Purvis

"You might die writing a five hundred page novel" –Alice Munro

What we must know at seventy-eight. The thrill a veteran with
    leukemia gets
when comparing his slutty masseuse Roxanne

to Alexander the Great's wife Roxanne. Earnest Bottoms,
a country scholar's nickname for Ernie Botts, her neuter cousin.

Death is on the horizon. We can see what takes us. There's more.
Please use your own personals, my roommate wrote. Whatever

we did then, we do forever. In youth we have premonition.
In age, memory. Notions, whatnots, sundries,

on the Tenth Street Rexall Drugs billboard. I get it now.
No one is out to help us. No masters and apprentices.

Just confidence games. Henery Hawk
frying Foghorn Leghorn's foot in a pan. My dad

loved that southern blowhard, and Wile E. Coyote and the Roadrunner.
I like the TV designer in heels pounding a picture hook into the wall,

the soap actress stabbing a salad with a fork repeatedly.
We learn even the simple present tense must end, but there are clues

the world goes on: its bad habits of rerunning seasons
and eroding solids, its penchant for coups d'etat.

The dying man's sexual charge out of playing Chinese checkers,
and my cat turning his head on his paralyzed body

to lick ice cream. "Sometimes we cannot satisfy each other."
Let's admit it. And not blame ourselves for where the body goes.

Jona Colson

Mother, Rest

I, too, felt anxious, and snared—
so when I left the house
I didn't wave goodbye,
didn't look you in the eye.
I knew I would not come back
to that room, that sound of stars
crashing against the window mesh,
that color of loss sword-flashing silver
in the dark hall. I couldn't take you

with me. I couldn't take all
those bruised scraps. Just try to rest, Mother,
rest against the fence. I'll hold you
here from outside.

ISSUE 81

Blythe Davenport

Relief

What do you do when your sculpture
stares back at you? Poke its eyes,
if it has eyes? Stone pupils can't feel pain.

When your statue gazes
with a judgment that says
I'll protect you from you
have you done it right or wrong?

The bas relief mastiff on the Fidelity building
hides his nose behind a paw
in frowning disappointment: rough.

Do you reach for your chisel
or change your ways?

ISSUE 81

Sean Patrick Hill

The Flaying of Marsyas

This unavoidable pilgrimage is my self-portrait:
Wandering through poppies in the Provençal fields,
I heard spades sink in gravelly ground, an old woman digging
Turf. In the furrows, a flute fallen among sunflowers.
I played peasant songs for plates of boiled potatoes
To commoners and wanderers in the shadows of a cypress.

Night painted no moonlight on the road, only a cypress
With a star—how beautiful yellow is for an honest portrait
Of a child, one raised on the taste of potatoes
And the long furrows of green corn in the fields,
Eyes opened to the almond groves, like sunflowers
Hung from the walls of Troy. I am digging

For images of peasants in coarse blue linen digging,
Sewing, weaving on black looms, clearing cypress,
Building turf huts and farmhouses, sowing sunflowers
And irises in asylum gardens. But this portrait,
Instead, is of two women bent over a dark field
In a dumb fury of work groping for potatoes.

Athena's flute made the world a still life, a bowl of potatoes.
My music brought the attention of Apollo; the god ceased digging
For gold. I met him with his kithara in a blossoming field
And challenged him to a contest beneath the lone cypress
And lost. I was tied to that very tree, a portrait
Of pain, a dog lapping red paint, and Apollo a garland of sunflowers.

My limbs were stiff like four cut sunflowers.
I saw the color of hard labor required to pull potatoes
And go down and down for the good turf. This portrait
Wears bandages, shows butcher's blades digging
Into flesh bound upside down to this cypress,
Alone in harvest time, the pallid gold of fields.

I see haystacks, the high yellow note of fields
Swathed, illuminated like a row of sunflowers,
Then eclipsed in the shadow of a cypress.
He flays the flesh from my chest; in the cold smell of potatoes
Molding, skin curls like flourishing irises. He is digging
Behind my eyes, to what I see in this portrait;

Almond blossoms, I say. The poverty of potatoes. A vase of
sunflowers.
Rows of poplars, peasants digging into Roman graves. Aloft over
wheat fields,
Crows in blue fire. The portrait, an empty chair. Swirling like dark
flame, the cypress.

ISSUE 81

Ada Limón

The Story of the Pencil

He takes the pencil out of his shirt pocket and gives it to her. It turns
into a dragonfly and then into her only reason to live. She is poor and
carries the dragonfly-pencil in her apron and writes him notes all day
on paper towels. In the night, when everyone else is sleeping, her
notes fly to him and cover his window with bigger messages about
safety and human kindness. He is perfectly blond and shaped like a
horse, like a horse-man, but also he is very gloomy. So he makes a
wish he's not supposed to make and she comes to him wearing only
her dragonfly wings. They kiss and play chess. And ring bells that
make songs and tell stories. Then, it seems over and happy, but it's
not. He grows bored and turns her into a pencil. She is a pencil and
no longer a girl, but she can still write notes with herself when it is
quiet. The next day, he goes to school and gives the pencil-dragonfly-
girl to a newer, even poorer girl. This time, the pencil grows wings
like a pallid bat and cannot be controlled. But this new girl is smart,
and she pretends not to notice. She pretends that the pencil is only a
pencil, says, Thank You and walks away.

Laura McCullough

Button

His hands felt like paws or flippers, big and inarticulate, as if the
spaces between shoulder socket and elbow joint and between the
finger bones had all fused in the August sun, a kind of annealing, so
what had once been uncured now had been except that mobility and
utility had been replaced with one function, appendages for show,

and this is what he sees now when he looks in the mirror, a created
thing, a ceramic puppet whose arms stand like glass stems, whose
hands burst flower-like from the tips.

If he waits long enough, perhaps he will be visited by bees, but for
now, it is only ghosts, the children he hears splashing behind him as
he retrieves his tilting guitar.

If you meet Buddha on the street, kill him, he recalls some saying once.
He thinks a fly has landed on his chest and brushes it away, but it
is nothing but a fleck of thread sticking out of a button head come
suddenly loose.

ISSUE 81

Laura McCullough

The Ways Water is Used

Her youngest daughter's thick curly hair
should not be washed every night;
she knows this,
but her daughter begs her to do it,
loves the ritual, the smell of the shampoo and cream rinse.
It is becoming a chore, the mother thinks,
the child getting big enough to do this herself.
Her own hair is a large knot of curls
kept at bay on the top of her brown forehead
by a plastic comb, the light streaks she has painted there
spiraling away like sweet pea in the garden
she keeps with her girls.
Every night, she folds the tea towel across her child's forehead
to keep the sprayed water from her eyes and face.
Don't drown me, Mama, the girl always teases
and they laugh, but tonight she hears the word from the news,
the one about the way water is used
to simulate drowning.
Her daughter's neck in her hand feels startlingly strong,
the eyes that look up at her disconcertingly wise,
and below them, the tub water shimmers
with foam infected with light,
reflecting it in pink and purple.
The daughter suddenly splashes the mother
who lets the child go
and threatens to send her to her room for the night.
The girl goes under briefly and emerges sputtering,
wipes her face of suds,
and says, *If you try to send me to my room, I will fight you.*
The mother taught all three of her daughters to swim
by throwing them in the deep end.
It is how she learned herself.
What can she say to the child,
but *Come here; let me rinse you again.*

ISSUE 81

Dante Micheaux

Mary at the Torture

Everyone was out that day, for a show.
Sure, it was sad for people who knew him
but she was his mother, slinking about
the rabble in that dark halug, veiling
her face with a headscarf—as if no one noticed her.

Some say it served her right,
letting her son run about the countryside
the way she did. Poor Joseph,
for all efforts at teaching the boy
a skill, never succeeded,
hadn't a chance against Mary's coddling.

But how could she just stand there, watching?
Each time the scourge met flesh she didn't even flinch.
No cry, no lamentation—most unlike a child of God.
Any other mother would have had to be contained,
would have put herself between lash and child,
would have succumbed to conniption—at the least,
rent her clothing. Not one tear.

She was always strange, though—quiet,
dark days about her since she was a girl.

It wasn't easy: the scandal before the wedding;
him getting into trouble with the law.
Perhaps, she was relieved.

Susanna Rich

Now That We're Done I Need to Retrieve Something

...no, not the
birthday whatever,
bagged holiday,
or drugstore *forgive-me*
thing;

nor the lend/misplace/forget or
hand-me-over migrations;
nor the fix/yard sale/consign
on my behalf
I'm missing

some feathered part of me
that swims starlight
waves sage brush, chants
summer dreams...just let

me breathe what you nevermind: your freezer's
atmosphere, your attic fan's
exhaust, the air between
your window and the storms...

ISSUE 81

Robin Beth Schaer

Contrition

A keening culprit, I came unzipped,
unwed. My penance, to be province, to lie
across a millstone bed, ground to powder,

to be wife again. And you, my conspirator,
my paramour, you strapped your longing

to a sail, sent from town, sent to be lost.
But trilobites cluster beneath your feet
on mountaintop that was once ocean floor

and our crime is a revelation that awaits
the murmur of sonar to be found. Beloved,

off the Chalumna River, a coelacanth was pulled
into a fishing boat. Returned from Cretaceous,
returned ugly and spined, but insisting on itself.

ISSUE 81

Britton Shurley

A Plot Against the Robots
(after Wallace Stevens)

First Girl

When I hear their metal boots
clacking through the garden,
trampling down the daffodils,
I will dance by this patch of violets;
I will call down hours of rain.
Their rusty knees should halt them.

Second Girl

I will set the herbs ablaze—
the lemon thyme, the chocolate mint,
the blooming pineapple sage.
I will hand them fistfuls of lavender;
they will not know what to say.

Third Girl

I will play them a tune
on my broken harmonica;
I will write them the words for a song.
If only one would start to hum
like the sweet, green legs of crickets,
even you & even I
would begin to come undone.

Hillery Stone

Losing Another

Again they're taking a tooth,
this time a molar at the very back.
It's dead, they say. *Rotting
the gum right through.*
It's all so definite: a sweep
of the occlusal surfaces; a hulking
metal plate jammed in.
This is the way with things gone bad.
The root is where the justice
is. What is rotten will go on
leaking it's own poison
and then you can't turn back. Still,
I meet my lover on the corner of 104th
and the cold hums under my jacket
like a pulp chamber. My jaw aches;
I can't find the words to remove
him. I want to say, *It's too much
loss*—But I know the hollow space
that comes after, the hole
your tongue can't help but return and return to.
You can fill it with a plastic doppelganger,
a welded paradigm, but it's never the same.

Lauren Watel

Now I Wonder

(Eurydice still in Hell)

Now I wonder if he looked back
on purpose to get rid of me

and commit to living with grief,
a less demanding companion.

As he mourns me in solitude,
the songs that cascade from the lyre

make gods, humans, and animals
intoxicated with sorrow.

He wrenches water from granite
and wrings rain out of cloudless skies.

I'm collecting the beads that seep
through the soil and rise in the heat,

although each day I'm here it grows
more arid. If I heard singing,

I wouldn't be tempted to look.
The future has forgotten me.

Eric D. Anderson

Strawberry

Hector came out of the gas station and saw that his date had driven off. Perhaps that's it, he thought, perhaps it's the Milky Way in my hand. Perhaps that's the dealbreaker. Who eats these anyway, besides children? He stood on the curb and ran through the catalog of possibilities that could explain this development—a carjacking, a mother suddenly pregnant, a friend in danger, an urgent sweepstakes redemption, inexplicable vaporization, a loss of memory and sudden spike of initiative, a fit of embarrassment, a dysfunctional transmission stuck in drive—but knew simply that he had been abandoned—Occam's Razor and all that—abandoned for the sake of a good story. The boy was proceeding farther away every second, windows rolled down, reggaeton up on the stereo, black hair flying, chuckling on his cell phone with his amigos while routing Hector's calls straight to his voice mail and its cleverly worded greeting.

Part of Hector felt relief. Now he wouldn't have to worry about the unfavorable way things would turn out—abandonment at a gas station was minor in the spectrum of potential humiliations, after all. He had experienced much worse. With a certain amount of detachment it was actually kind of funny—the way his car had broken down, the fact that the boy had to drive out to rescue him, the immediate disappointment on the boy's face when he saw he was more beautiful than Hector. And now this.

The earlier lightheadedness was gone—replaced by adrenaline, or something. Hector slid the candy bar into his pocket and started through the gas pump area, head down. A white panel van was parked there with a green nozzle in its tank, fueling automatically. A bald Latino man with a handlebar moustache and a tattoo on his neck was in the front seat going through some papers. It was difficult to see past the overhead fluorescent tubes reflected in the windshield, but there was something familiar about this man. The right front tire was low on air and the tailpipe had a black crust to it. If Hector had been at work he would have run a check on the license plate.

The man spotted him, cranked the engine, and began to pull away with the fuel hose still attached. The hose stretched but the nozzle

ISSUE 81

held firm in the van and a low, loud report come from underground. Everything was still connected, barely—the pump, the hose, the nozzle, the tank—but a widening circle of gasoline advanced from the base of the pump. A bell was going off—someone had engaged the emergency shutoff switch—but no one was coming out of the station. There was just this man, this neck-tattooed man standing outside now, surveying the damage and lighting a cigarette, arms folded. " The fuck you looking at?" he said.

Hector turned out of the station and headed north in search of a bus stop. Night was coming on, he was eighteen miles from home, and he had just three dollars in his pocket now—yet another long and embarrassing story. He pulled on the strip of facial hair that ran from beneath his lower lip to the tip of his chin—an extended soul patch—and wondered if it did in fact make him look more manly.

The sidewalk rumbled and he felt a blast of heat on his neck. His shadow appeared in front of him, shortening up as the fireball rose thirty feet into the air. Another explosion rocked the station; acrid black smoke billowed as the building settled into some serious burning. Behind him a van was falling out of the sky.

#

The counselor said that Hector had joined the military for all the wrong reasons. Mainly to stuff his awakening sexuality back into some hidden place. This according to the counselor. Hector did not argue. The sessions were more about the counselor unpacking Hector's "haunting military experience" than they were about Hector. The truth was Hector had thrived in the army. He found great comfort in submitting himself to the pyramid of command and its endless bylaws of conduct. There was nobody from the barrio to remind him what a fairy he was, nobody to perpetuate the tradition of ridicule. He could reinvent himself however he wanted. The army was just as homophobic as the neighborhood, but Hector learned that he did in fact have a masculine side. He learned that he was a gifted marksman and that he could kill if he had to.

Though fifteen years out of the army, its regimented order still governed his life—in his security guard job, his tidy one-bedroom apartment, his sleeping habits, and his stilted and old-fashioned politeness toward elders. Hector never experienced actual combat— he had been kicked out right before Desert Storm—but he knew the randomness of it would have broken him in half. Similarly, he was still unwilling after all these years to dive into the thriving gay scene downtown, into those forbidden meat markets swirling with techno music, alcohol, and anonymous liaisons in dark corners.

ISSUE 81

#

He knew that coming down here was foolish, but he had done so—and probably would again—for of the possibility of love. Now Hector was stuck in what he had left behind: the barbed wire, the taquerias and roach coaches, the pirated DVDs spread out on the sidewalk, the check-cashing places, the men standing in circles drinking from paper sacks, the unreadable graffiti on buildings and the broken glass below, the awful ranchero music blasting from business after business, the cluster of day laborers around every hardware store, the counterintuitive marriage of poverty and obesity, ghetto birds and ghetto knocks, drug deals in the parks, wrecked furniture on sidewalks awaiting Bulky-Item Pickup, multiple families in one-bedroom apartments, automobile maintenance in the street, three dots tattooed to the fleshy part of your hand between the base of your thumb and forefinger, *mi vida loca.*

Hector felt the urge to vomit. He was six years old again, getting his face ground into the dirt and his pocket money stolen by the Carlos Gang. It was in southern Mexico, in Oaxaca, right before he and his parents came to the States to live with a distant cousin. Pinche maricon, they said, over and over, kicking him. They drew bright red lipstick all over his face. *Chupalo. Chupalo, mariposa.*

#

"Where can I catch a bus?"

Hector approached four men loitering outside of a corner store. Three wore painter's hats and overalls speckled with white spots; the other sported a stained wife-beater and had bits of grass around the edges of his running shoes. They were drinking Coronas from a ripped-open half case at their feet. Some kind of literary mural rose up behind them—books by Marquez, Paz, Neruda, Esquivel, Allende and others floated in a starry blue ether, open to their title pages, connected by the scrawl of gray graffiti. Hector had read none of these authors though he certainly had heard of them.

"¿Adonde vas?"

"Into the city."

The biggest of them had a sculpted beard comprised of quarter-inch wide strips of hair that intersected at two nodal points on his chin. He eyed Hector's dress shoes and pressed tan pants. *"¿Por qué no estas llamando un taxi, amigo?"*

"Because I don't have any money."

The big guy was the leader but the sullen, silent gardener was the most dangerous. He was swaying back and forth while staring low and outside at a point off of Hector's hip. There were four of them and one of Hector and no less-than-lethal munitions to implement a proper restraint and control strategy—no electromuscular disruptive tools, no chemical agents like tear gas or pepper spray, no blunt-trauma weapons like beanbag shotguns or stun grenades that would shoot hard rubber balls in a thirty-foot circular pattern, no diversionary devices, no flash-bang grenades.

If he had to, he'd dispatch the gardener first—slip his punch, grab the wrist, spin, snap the arm over his shoulder, and then shove the guy to the pavement. The big guy would be easier; he'd barrel in too fast, hunched over and simian. Hector would rotate judo-style—using the man's energy against him—and hurl the man into the street, out in front of the maroon Lincoln speeding through the yellowing light fifty yards up. After that the other two would flee. If not, he could break off a beer bottle or resort to a throat chop or an eye gouge followed by joint locks and pressure point work.

"Go three blocks this way." The big guy waved in the direction Hector was traveling. "Go to Hobart. Right on Hobart. Go two blocks and you can catch a bus there."

"You happen to know what bus number it is?"

"Hey, ¿por qué no hablas en español?" The gardener lobbed his beer bottle over the chain-link fence and into the vacant lot beyond. *"¿No eres mexicano? ¿Eh?"*

"Thank you very much, you guys," Hector said. He continued past them down the busted-up sidewalk. One of the men shouted after

him and when Hector turned back to look, still walking, he noticed
the neck-tattooed man from the gas station emerging from the
corner store and joining the group. The man stroked his moustache
and pointed.

A low whupping sound in the distant background became a roar as
a helicopter elevated over some buildings and bore down on them.
Palm trees pitched and convulsed in the downwash of air; garbage
blew neatly into the gutter. Three were rifle shots further down the
block and then something throatier and more dangerous that shook
the ground under Hector's feet. The bright follow-spot settled on
them from above. Hector watched the group of men scatter in all
directions, but the guy with the tattoo on his neck was slow to flee.
There were two or three brief popping sounds—nearly buried under
the white noise of the helicopter—and then the neck-tattooed man
was reeling against a beat-up white Toyota parked at the curb. Blood
squirted from his stomach, then from his mouth as he yelled.

Hector turned and walked away. Palm fronds crashed down around him.

#

This was the difference: Low explosives burned quickly whereas
high explosives detonated. Low explosives usually utilized black
powder, fire, and confinement to achieve an explosion. High
explosives contained a volatile chemical composition that could go
off many ways: via impact, fire, or sometimes even water. The nature
of the composition and state of ingredients determined reaction
rate, noise, flash, and the appearance of flame. Often they were used
in tandem, with a low explosive acting as a propelling charge that
launched the device and then ignited the high-explosive agent.

Blasting caps were another example of the high and the low
coming together.

#

Hobart was filled with smoke. Ordnance flew past Hector's head,
striking one of the vandalized, broken-down phone booths behind
him. He picked his way through the abandoned couches and
mattresses blocking the sidewalk. The rumbling of explosions was
constant. Faces lined the street, staring into it.

ISSUE 81

He grabbed his stomach and propped up against a palm tree. His blood sugar was perilously low—he would faint if he wasn't careful. How many people have urinated up against this tree? he thought. His pants were caught on something—the springy part of a gutted mattress poked through his pocket. A deflated soccer ball lay off to the side and a grown man in a blue-and-red striped jersey gave it a kick as he ambled by. Hector watched the yellow writing on his back as he receded. "Ronaldinho" it said over a blocky number ten. *Futbol*, he thought. *Futbol*. He realized the mattress holding him was actually a makeshift soccer goal.

Hector frowned. There was nothing picturesque about it, not even the shave ice man with his shopping cart, big old-fashioned block of ice, and dozen dubious bottles of flavor. These people were poor and they were Mexican and this is where he was from: the tamale vendors pushing their carts and jangling their bells, the young women navigating strollers through broken glass, the teal-and-pink ninety-nine-cent store across the street, the disrespectful thump of *tecno-cumbia* (or whatever was blasting out of the apartment behind him), public urination, packs of unwatched kids running amok and breaking things, the spread of garbage and lack of civic pride that led to it, the total disregard for nutrition, the bars on apartment windows, the propped-open front gates and side doors undermining all notions of security, the machismo of Latino men and their brazen sexual overtures, votive candles and the not-so-effective yoke of Catholic guilt here in the *barrio*, the girls with dark outlines around their lips and too much eye makeup, the population density, the warbly car alarms, the culture of loiter, the grip of poverty , the idiot senselessness of vandalism.

He removed the Milky Way from his pocket and tore the wrapper. The chocolate outside was pale brown—nearly white—from melting and hardening repeatedly. The surface was fractured into a dozen tiny triangles. He shoved the entire candy bar into his mouth, chewed three or four times, and swallowed hard. It slid down a little and lodged itself midway in his esophagus. Hector inhaled but nothing happened. He tried to swallow again, but the candy bar was parked in his windpipe.

A red articulated bus pulled up to the covered waiting area on the other side of the intersection. People clambered aboard while traffic piled up behind and veered into the next lane. He had almost made it. Only forty yards to go. He could see angry drivers laying on their

ISSUE 81

horns but all was quiet. All of the fireworks had stopped as well. When he turned around, though, he saw the air was filled with smoke and blasts of fire and color, just as before. A regular Fourth of July without the soundtrack. Something was going on with Hector's ears. It was like someone had pressed the mute button.

He still couldn't breathe but he wasn't panicked. Two girls were drawing a picture on the sidewalk a half-block away, and though things were exploding inaudibly overhead, the squeak of the chalk against the pavement resonated. Insects rustled through the dried-out square of grass next to them. Hector felt faint. His legs were weak and spindly; his brain screamed. An Accord drove by and Hector locked on to its out-of-tune engine. Farther away a cat was crying, sounding everything in the world like a little boy. Hector knew he was going to die but still he didn't want to be the center of attention. He failed about and tried to hawk up the thing lodged in his throat, but the springs of the mattress goal had him through the pocket and held him fast.

What now? he thought. Is this all there is?

Something pulled at Hector. One of the springs ripped through his pants and through the flesh of his leg and then he was free. Someone was grabbing him from behind; Hector's feet flew into the air until they pointed across the street at the people watching from the third-story balcony. *Hola*, he thought. *¿Como estas?* Then he was falling forward. His feet slapped down to the earth and the neck-tattooed man jerked hard on his abdomen once more. This time the half-chewed candy bar ejected from his throat and arced into the street.

Hector took huge gasping breaths. His head felt champagne fizzy. His face prickled. He could hear again.

"You're blue! Your face is blue!" the man said. "Are you okay? What happened?"

"Blue," Hector repeated. Like the sea. Blue like the sea. He held his stomach and sides. Tomorrow there would be dark bruises where the man had grabbed him. It was the closest thing to an embrace he'd had in a long time.

"Are you sure you're okay?" someone asked.

"He's fine," the neck-tattooed man said. "Just had something in his throat, that's all." He grabbed Hector by the shoulder and pulled him over to a nearby driveway. A group of kids huddled around a giant purple-and-gold rocket awaiting launch.

The man pulled a silver Zippo out of his baggy jeans and held it out. "Here, you do it," he said.

Hector reached for the lighter but his reflexes weren't recovered and he nearly bobbled it. He held it in his hands, marveling. The lighter was smooth and warm and heavy in a good way. Down below, the fuse trailed off the rocket long and curly like a rat's tail.

"Go ahead."

Hector kneeled in the carbon-blackened driveway and lit the Zippo. The fuse caught fire and crackled its way toward the rocket.

"¡Cuidado!" someone yelled.

"¡Cuidado, cuidado, cuidado!" the children shouted gleefully.

Hector stumbled backward.

The fuse ignited the powder in the cylindrical purple-and-gold casing. There was a strange, longish pause—not unlike the few seconds that pass between the moment you cut yourself and the moment when the pain actually arrives—and then the rocket climbed into the sky. It did not describe a safe, vertical ascent—it veered erratically and shot down the street in the direction Hector had come from. Everyone turned to watch, quiet and serious.

The volatile chemical mixture near the nosecone of the rocket would be robbed of its oxygen when it finally detonated. This is how it works. In effect, the beautiful explosions were intensified by this suffocation—by chemicals getting brutally choked out—just as Hector was moments ago. But he wasn't thinking about that. He was trying to track the now-lateral flight of the rocket into the distance. He lost sight of it—as did everyone else—and just when he was starting to give up and feel responsible— preposterous, he knew, but he couldn't help himself—just when the pause had grown long enough to make people suspect the rocket was a dud, it detonated up against the night sky, big and red and round, like a great, glittering strawberry.

ISSUE 81

There was a collective "Ooooo" and for a moment all the apartment buildings lit up pink. The crowd clapped and hollered and gathered around Hector, congratulating him. He started to object but thought better of it and just grinned. Everyone was patting him on the back now, patting him as if he were somehow responsible for this beautiful explosion. Which, in a way, he was.

Julie Conover

The Voucher

"It's Marge from accounting," says the voice on the phone.

"Oh, hi Marge." I try to remember who Marge is. Is she the pudgy woman, about thirty-five, with the thin lips and grey-flecked sausage curls who stares at me in the elevator? Or the skinny redhead with pasty skin who always wears a Flyers jacket?

"Say, Marge, I'm a little rushed. Can I get back to you?" I'm expecting another call. I realize, too late, that I should have let my secretary pick up.

"Actually, this has to do with the voucher you submitted last Friday. It's the end of the month, so I have to process it today." She's the pudgy one, I realize. The one who looks like she went to some high school named after a Cardinal or an Archbishop. The redhead is Franny.

"OK, what's the problem?"

"The voucher, it can't be processed like you submitted it."

"It's just a parking voucher, Marge."

"Yes, well, that's the thing. You submitted two parking vouchers at the same garage for the same day. We can't process that." She says this like she's a state cop stopping a speeding motorist on the turnpike, shining a flashlight down on me, the guilty driver behind the steering wheel. A voice tells me to just go along, just go along. But I can't.

"I don't see why not. I drove my car to work and parked it, then I drove to a noon lunch with a prospective customer, and when I returned to work I parked in the same garage. So both parking expenses were legit."

"Well, now, the way you explain it makes sense. But the expense voucher rules say that we can only reimburse for one parking

ISSUE 81

expense at the same garage per day." I remember now that Marge applied for a job in my department last year. I didn't even interview her. I hear she's pretty smart, but she's the type who puts her coat on at 4:45 and races for the elevators at 4:59. I need hard-chargers on my team, not a bunch of clock-watchers.

"That's ridiculous," I say. "That would mean that I would have been better off going home after my lunch meeting. This actually penalizes me for returning to work." I realize I shouldn't sound so pissed off, but there's something about Marge's voice that sets me off. Reminds me of my ex when he used to quiz me about why I got home so late and why I needed to travel so much.

I see my light flashing; another call is coming in.

"Can I get back to you later on this, Marge?" I say.

"OK, but like I said, I can't process this voucher the way it stands now, unless...." Her flat voice trails off, like she is thinking.

"Unless what?"

"Maybe if you submit it with the explanation you just gave me I can get it through." I feel her pause theatrically. "But then again, I don't see that you submitted any expense documentation for that customer lunch, did you?"

"That's because the customer picked up the tab."

"The *customer* paid for the lunch?" Marge says; I now think she is toying with me, like a cat with a mouse. "That's probably the first time I ever heard that. Maybe you should share your secret with your friends in Sales."

"The customer has some ethics rules he has to follow – I can't pay for his lunch." I'm scrambling; the words are out of my mouth before I realize I still could have vouchered my own lunch. Maybe Marge won't notice.

"Ok," she says, and I exhale. "So just identify on the parking voucher who you ate lunch with, where you ate, that kind of thing. Oh, and you will need Level 5 approval."

"Level 5? Are you sure?" Level 5's are AVPs. My light flashes again; I'm missing another call.

ISSUE 81

"Yep, the voucher protocols require skip level approval for these kinds of discrepancies, and you're a level 3 aren't you?"

"Ok, but for the record, this is not a 'discrepancy,' Marge," I say. "So Don Cochran can sign off, right?" I think of Don's long, patrician hands signing vouchers, stroking my face, doing anything.

"Mr. Cochran's a Level 5 all right, but he can't sign off on the voucher."

"Why not?" My assistant Lorrie opens the door and mouths "It's Don Cochran." I see the flashing light, indicating that the call is on hold, and then hold up my index finger. Lorrie closes the door.

"It can't be just *any* Level 5. It has to be a Level 5 in your reporting structure. You're in Marketing and he's in Legal."

"But the only Level 5 in Marketing is Marsha Davis, and she's in New York." Marsha used to work here with me, before she went to that Executive Women's Leadership Seminar and networked her way to New York. Now she's trying to get me transferred up there too. Some folks thought I was upset when Marsha got promoted, and I guess I was at first. After all, she was only one year ahead of me in grad school. But after the initial shock, I was excited to think it was possible, that a woman could actually get such a big promotion in this place. It made me want to travel more, do more Powerpoints, answer my Blackberry at 2 AM. Whatever it takes.

"That's right, Marsha Davis," Marge says. "Just fax it up to her." Marsha's too straight, I think, she would never sign this voucher. She would subject me to more cross-examination than Marge.

"OK, Marge. I've really got to go. This is ridiculous. It's not worth it. Send the voucher back – I'll just withdraw it."

"You can't do that," Marge says. Her voice now sounds like my older brother used to sound when I landed on Park Place and he owned three hotels. She's a couple of steps ahead of me in a game I didn't realize we were playing.

"Why not?"

"There's an internal auditing rule. Once vouchers are submitted, they must be resolved one way or another. Auditing needs to be able to track everything. You know – to detect fraud."

"So you won't process it, but I can't withdraw it either, is that what you're telling me?" I try to stay calm.

"That's right."

"So then what the fuck am I supposed to do?"

"No need to raise your voice like that. I'm just doing my job."

"Ok, I'm sorry Marge, but seriously, what am I supposed to do?"

"The protocol says that once you submit a voucher and a discrepancy is noted, you have to cooperate with any investigation until it's completed. I just went over the same thing this morning with Mr. Cochran." Don. The blinking light. He's still on hold.

"What exactly did you 'go over' with Mr. Cochran?" Just then, the blinking hold button light goes out. It is plain to me now – Don has been trying to reach me about this. I see my cell phone vibrate with a text message from Don. "Don't talk to Marge until you talk with me" it says. It's so like him – just because he's the lawyer, he thinks he's the one who should always be in charge, in control. "Don't worry," he always says when I ask when he's going to tell his wife about us. "I just need some time to figure out how to get out without my wife robbing me blind," he says.

But Marge is speaking again. "I'm not able to disclose to you the content of my discussions with Mr. Cochran. But I assume you know that he also submitted double parking vouchers at the same garage for the same day."

"Oh," I say, careful not to admit or deny. It occurs to me now that she may be taping this call. "Marge, I really, really need to get to a meeting. I do have a job to do, you know. Can I call you back later today?"

"I suppose so. But I have to warn you – do not discuss this matter with anyone, especially not Mr. Cochran."

"What? I work closely with Don Cochran. We talk every day." Talk – I guess you could say that. Even now, after two years, I still get a

ISSUE 81

tiny thrill when I hear his name or see him walk down the hallway, dressed – as he always is, even on casual Friday -- in a white shirt and pinstripe suit. I can feel the animal magnetism beneath that cool, tailored façade. Sometimes after meetings, after listening to Don's silky voice probing and analyzing, his raw intelligence making sales managers stammer like complete idiots, I'd be so aroused that I'd almost be unable to get up from my chair. A few times, we just closed the conference room door and did it right there, like two kids in the backseat of a Chevy.

Marge's voice continues. "Discussing the investigation with Mr. Cochran would be in violation of the protocols. And as I am sure you are already aware, violation of the protocols or falsification of a voucher could result in disciplinary action, up to and including dismissal." I hear the Colombo-like satisfaction in her voice, the vise closing around my neck.

"Over a $10 parking voucher?"

"Absolutely, if fraud is involved. As you know, integrity is a core value of this company. We take our core values extremely seriously." The nuns at St. Whoever's would be very proud.

I text Don. "Am on phone with Marge now." Then I speak to Marge again.

"I'm not following you Marge. If I'm taking my car to meet with a customer and for that reason need to park in the same garage twice, how could that be fraud?"

"Well if it happened like you say, there should be no problem. But let's just say that you didn't meet a customer, but instead that you and Mr. Cochran – say – met at the Embassy Suites Hotel on Route 55. And let's say that I had my monthly meeting of the Rotary there at the Embassy Suites that same day and happened to see your cars in the parking lot. And let's say that I followed you and saw the two of you enter room 225. And let's say that I was able to get a duplicate of the statement from the front desk as part of my investigation. Let's say all of that's true. Then the duplicate parking voucher would have no valid business purpose. Submitting the parking voucher would be fraud. Do you follow me now?"

My phone vibrates. It's Don. "Don't talk to her!!!"

ISSUE 81

"I think I understand where you are going, Marge," I say. Then I text Don. "She already knows."

There is a long pause. I look around my office. It's not a corner office, but there's enough room for a sofa and a conference table. The Stiffel lamp my parents gave me sits on the end table. "Fix up your office like you're already a success," my dad always said. I bought a small oriental rug to set off the mahogany coffee table and cover up the worn spots on the grey institutional carpet. Trinkets and plaques from successful marketing campaigns line my bookshelves. It's a pretty nice office for a thirty-something, – much better than the cubicles some of my buddies from the MBA program still occupy. And I am destined for more, much more, I'm sure of that.

No more texts from Don, but I'm as certain as I've ever been about anything that he has left his office and is on the elevator, on his way to my floor. I can almost feel his energy descending the elevator shaft, like a heat seeking missile, about to burst through my closed door in about five minutes.

"So," I say, "how can we move forward on this?"

" Well, if we can just get your full cooperation, then I'm sure we can put all this behind us," she says unctuously. "I mean, you're probably the victim here. Sexual harassment. You did say you work closely with Mr. Cochran."

The phone vibrates again. "I'm on my way down," he texts. When he gets here, I'll be putty in his hands. Again. But I'm not sure I trust Don to do what's best for me. He doesn't want me to go to New York, he says. But what has he offered in exchange? I put the phone in my purse.

I close my eyes.

"He said he could get me a promotion," I say. The knife goes in cleanly, between his shoulder blades.

"I'm certain this will clear everything up for you," Marge says. Then she adds, "Maybe your department will have another opening soon." She hangs up.

Someone is pounding on my door.

ISSUE 81

C.S. Ellis

Molotov's Dogs

May 26. We limped out of the badlands at night. Las Vegas was a million screaming lights. The car almost crapped out at the halfway point, the fuel pump is shot. I was worried that we would break down in the desert and die of thirst. Sand would cover our bones and nobody would ever know. Eryn said I was being childish. She has been talking nonstop about how we'll both get famous when we get to California. "The planets are aligned for us," she said. "Your negativity will fuck them up."

May 28. Tomorrow I have an interview at a print shop. Eryn already got a job as a waitress at a Japanese restaurant. It was the first place she tried. She walked in off the street and they hired her on the spot. Some luck. The place is lit with tiny oil lamps. Just enough light to give you a look at how well she's built.

May 29. The accident was one year ago today. I didn't mention it, and neither did Eryn. Our money is gone. It took the last of it to pay for a new fuel pump. One thing about Las Vegas is that it is a great town for finding half-smoked cigarettes on the ground. Everything will be fine.

June 8. Yesterday Eryn went to an open audition for models. The ad in the newspaper said models but it was really a call for girls to be in pornos. The guy told Eryn she had potential. "The way things work nowadays, you could star in two hundred triple X videos and still end up co-starring in a sitcom," he said. "The business doesn't carry the same stigma it used to." Later she showed me his card—Paul Maul, Eroticist. He works out of a warehouse that contains eight or ten half-built rooms, a couch or a bed in the center of each one and Klieg lights looking down from poles. I don't want her to do it. I told her I don't want to share her. But if she's ever going to be a real actress we need money to get her nose fixed. It will cost $5,500 for a rhinoplasty, which is the doctor-word for a nose job, and another $2,500 to cap her teeth. The plastic surgeons in L.A. are supposed to be the best, but she doesn't want to wait that long. Paul Maul told Eryn that her body was one in a million, like Ginger Lynn, but they couldn't use her as is. Back in Okemah people would wince when Eryn told them she wanted to be a movie star. The damage is bad enough that you can't not see it. She said the guy was a nice guy. He offered her some money. He said he wanted to try her out. I asked if he made her take off her clothes, and she said "Not really." I figured I was better off not knowing.

June 10. As a show of good faith I pawned my bass and my practice amp.

June 12. I hung around outside the phone booth while Eryn called her sister collect. "It's called the creepy crawl," she said. " The Mansonites did it in the Sixties. No, I mean, they killed people but they lived on pretty much no money. Desperate times and desperate measures, you know?" She's jumbled up Manson and Samsonite but I don't say anything. It started me thinking about Mansonic lodges cropping up across the country, all those Benevolent Moose and Lions and Elks from Okemah with X's carved between their eyes. Life would be like the cover of a Black Flag record. I drag Eryn out of the phone booth and we get started immediately on the Mansonite secret handshake.

June 17. Today I said to her: " The Buddha went for a whole year without eating." I'm not one hundred percent sure about this but I said it anyway. "So it's like method acting," Eryn said hopefully.

June 18. The sun in the early part of the evening is like the hot head of a match. Even when it finally gets dark you can still feel the heat rising from the asphalt like a wall of ghosts. You elbow through them. I'm ready to cave in but Eryn is talking about being barefoot on the carpet of an apartment that smells of fresh paint. How the living room will be echoey from no furniture. " We can get a leather sofa," she said. "When it gets greasy we just wipe it off." The light caught her eyelashes and electrified them. I coughed a little. I wanted better words but the pause did not let them settle. She had a pack of Winstons in her apron that one of her customers had forgotten on the table. Sometimes you get a break. "One of these days we'll laugh when we tell all this to a reporter," she said. I leaned and kissed her lightly behind the ear. We were like regular people walking along. Bums on Fremont were asking us for smokes and spare change. That's no way to live.

June 20. I stole some candy bars from a 7-11. We had to lick them off the wrappers because of the heat. It's almost unbearable. Three days of the creepy crawl have passed.

ISSUE 81

June 24. We need to relocate to a different parking lot. There is a Black Angus down the street and the smell of cooking meat hangs in the air until well after midnight. "God, I'm hungry. I feel like one of Molotov's dogs," Erin said. Eryn. I keep forgetting the goddamned Y. Molotov's Dogs would be a good band name.

June 25. Eryn won't shut up about this girl Melanie, her shift leader. She says Melanie has been watching her. I have a bad feeling. Neither of us has had a bath in a while and the car stinks like periods and balls.

June 26. The pawnshop sold my bass out from under me. The guy behind the glass shrugged his shoulders.

June 28. At work yesterday I made a pretty good score. There was a grand opening a few doors down, a new cell phone store, and the Hot 99 DJs came down in their party van. I walked over on my lunch break and managed to fill my book bag with a dozen or so bottles of Zephyr water. I also grabbed three bags of Doritos, two prepaid phone cards, and a Hot 99 t-shirt. We had warm water and Doritos for dinner. We've been in Las Vegas for three weeks now.

June 29. Just now I was thinking about those old Warner Brothers cartoons where two guys are stuck on a desert island. After a while one of them starts hallucinating that the other one is a Thanksgiving turkey or Christmas ham and ends up chewing on his leg. I stole half of someone's salami sandwich from the refrigerator at work and wolfed it down in the bathroom. At the staff meeting the assistant manager said, "There is a thief in our midst," and I felt my face turn red.

July 5. We had our anniversary. We borrowed from the surgery fund and got a room at the Frontier for a couple of days. We had a fight first thing. I was fucking Eryn on the big bed, the air conditioning cranked up. Her ankles were up on my shoulders and she was cursing at Jesus. I got hot. I thought of a bucket tickling the water at the bottom of a deep well. Just thinking about a deep well was enough to trip the wire. I tried to pull out at the end but didn't make it. She was furious. "You're selfish," she said. "You'll ruin everything." Down at the slot machines a woman in a wheelchair had this retarded kid who pumped in the coins for her. I tried making jokes but Eryn kept ignoring me. The slots were too slow for Eryn, she wanted the jackpot. She thought she understood blackjack. It cost us $20. Another $20 on craps. I was loafing. The waitress wouldn't serve me. I kept my mouth shut. The buffet seemed like a good place to hide.

There was a couple there who looked like just like my folks, only fatter. I freaked when I saw them. I thought maybe they had come looking. The parent clones did not speak, they grunted at each other. Just like my mom and dad. I made fried chicken sandwiches for later and stashed them in Erin's (I mean Eryn's) bag.

July 11. Eryn got a $50 tip today from a professional baseball player whose name I didn't recognize and can't remember. I accused her of doing other things for the money. Sometimes I'm an asshole. "It's all your fault anyway," she said. "If not for you I wouldn't look like this." She's right, but this only makes things worse. We were both drunk that night. But I was the one driving. It was an accident. You can only say you're sorry so many different ways. Today I chewed the same piece of gum for 12 hours.

July 17. In the middle of the day we drive down in one of the subdivisions off Oasis Parkway and look for open garages. "You remember how my stepdad had that fridge in our garage he kept beer and stuff in," Eryn said. "All we gotta do is drive around until we see a house with the door up and no cars in the driveway. We do it fast so no one notices." To me it seemed like a long shot, but we are backed up against the wall. The surgery fund has grown to $640, stashed under the spare tire. Only about $7,000 short of what we need. The first subdivision on Oasis was called Casino Royale and it was a bust. The only open door we saw revealed a garage completely empty of anything. Just three white walls, two oil stains, and light bulb.

July 18. We tried another subdivision. This one was more like a neighborhood. The houses were older and they weren't all identical. One of them was exactly as Eryn had described. The door was up and the garage was filled with furniture, bicycles and cardboard boxes. There was no room for a car. I felt kind of bad because I also saw a wheelchair and several oxygen tanks. A fridge stood in the far corner. The street was a dead end, so I told Eryn to go ahead and turn around. "We'll let this be our test run," I said. "For all we know that fridge isn't even plugged in." I trotted up the driveway, keeping an eye on the house. The windows were open and I could hear a television inside. Bob Barker was making big promises. A bird sang sweetly from above, calling me out. I yanked open the fridge and the whole garage rattled. Inside were cans of soda, hot dogs, lunchmeat and pasteurized cheese slices. When my book bag was full I ran back to the car and Eryn peeled out like we'd just robbed a bank.

July 31. When the manager was up front closing out the register I boosted a can of tuna and a can of sliced peaches from the break room. I think the kit press operator saw me. He gave me a look. "You better come up with an excuse now in case the boss asks you about it tomorrow," Eryn says when I tell her what happened. She's distracting herself with the rearview mirror, tilting her head, looking at her nose from every possible angle. Tonight I couldn't get her to eat anything, even though it's Friday and the steakhouse is working overtime. The sweet smoke of cooking meat was billowing from the chimney. Her poor nose is so crooked. I wish the sight of it was motivation enough to kill my appetite. There was a noise from my stomach that sounded like a creaky floorboard followed up by a thunderclap. I sat on the hood and ate the tuna, pretending it was grilled salmon that was just a little cold when it came to the table. No big deal.

August 10. Last night a cop caught me digging in the dumpster behind the Food Max. Just as I was climbing out his spotlight landed on me. He jumped out of his car with his gun drawn. "Stop or I'll shoot," he shouted, and I was hoping it was a bluff. I ran until I saw flashbulbs snapping in front of my eyes and hid in a ditch off Fortuna. When I came back empty handed Erin and I had a fight. She started crying and would not stop. I slapped her. It didn't help. I keep writing "Erin" by mistake. I keep forgetting she's a different person now.

August 16. My boss called me into the office and told me I needed to do something about my appearance. I explained that times were tough, but left out the part about living in the car and stealing food to save money for a nose job so Eryn can become a porn star. My boss said it was out of his hands. The district manager had asked him about "the wino in the stockroom," meaning me.

August 19. Last night I dreamt we were being chased by Molotov's dogs. Their mouths were like open furnaces. They were running alongside the car. Somehow I knew they wanted our gasoline. Erin was in the passenger seat, and her nose was made out of blue plastic. She asked me, "How does it look?" and I said, "It looks okay."

August 21. Things are better. After weeks of washing ourselves in gas station bathrooms, we discovered that the community college has locker rooms in their rehabilitation center, the place where they train physical therapists. The janitor opens the doors at 5 AM but nobody shows up at the front desk until 8. So we started sneaking in to use the showers. I wanted to break into some of the lockers but Eryn said we don't want to draw attention to ourselves, since we already don't belong there. She told me the mirror in the women's locker room is huge and harshly lit. "It makes my nose look like a mushroom," she said, about to cry. "It shows you everything that's wrong." I tried to put my arms around her but she pushed me away.

August 25. Yesterday I'm at work, and Brian tells me I've got a phone call. "Sounds like an emergency," he says. It's Melanie. She tells me Eryn's having some kind of breakdown. The same thing happened when we were in high school, and she cut herself up with her brother's hunting knife. You can still see the scars on her arms like white latticework. The rest of her is tan. I tell Brian my girlfriend is sick. He let me go early. The car is almost out of gas, the fuel light is burning bright in the dash, but I make it down to the restaurant. Eryn's out front on the curb with Melanie. Melanie's got her arm around Eryn and Eryn's eyes are wide and blazing. I realize it's not a breakdown, that she's been doing coke. I don't say anything.

August 27. Eryn is going to stay at Melanie's apartment for a few days. There's not room for me, and Eryn says it would be rude to bring me along. She promised to wash some of my clothes. Melanie, smirking, picks her up in a yellow Volkswagen with a fake sunflower attached to the antenna. Eryn gets in without giving me a kiss goodbye. It was 106 degrees today.

August 30. I haven't heard from Eryn so I went looking for her at the restaurant. They wouldn't tell me when she was working again and they wouldn't tell me where Melanie lives. I barely made my shift on time. My beard finally looks like a beard. I trimmed it up with scissors and it looks okay. I wrote Eryn a letter but misspelled her name so many times I threw it away. Why can't I remember to spell it Hollywood style?

September 13. Eryn calls me at work. She tells me we're finished and that she wants her half of the money. I can't really talk because there are too many people standing around listening. I ask her if there's someone else and she sighs and says: "No."

September 17. Today on my break I was watching this lady eat a McDonald's hamburger. She threw most of it away and she was barely out of range before I was digging it out of the trash can. The people at the shoe store were out front smoking and they looked

ISSUE 81

at me like I was a three-legged dog. One half pity and one half amusement. I am the scum of the earth.

September 22. Last night I cut an X between my eyes with a linoleum knife. I knew it would freak people out and it did. Everyone at work stared. At the end of the shift Greg took me into his office. He said, "Well, that's it. That's the last straw." I clocked out.

September 23. The sun was going down. Eryn was waiting at the car. When she saw my forehead she got upset. "What are you going to do now?" she said. I don't answer because I don't know. She's wearing a lot of make-up and a miniskirt made out of pieces of blue jeans. She tells me that she and Melanie have gotten stripper jobs but she won't say where. They do a baby oil wrestling routine together. I ask if Melanie is her new boyfriend, she just shrugs. She's about to start crying. I reach out and touch her face. She lets me because she knows this is goodbye. "I'm going to miss you," she says. I lean in and kiss my baby's raspberry lips. I see the yellow Volkswagen, and Melanie's silhouette behind the wheel. Eryn gets carried away; she closes her eyes and gives me her tongue. It's a sexy kiss, like when you're balling; I get excited like I never have before. Her eyelids fly up like window shades when I bite down. Then there is a piece of her tongue on my tongue. I swallow it whole. I think I read somewhere that tongues grow back, like lizards' tails. My baby sounded like she was howling around a mouthful of hot coals, her lips forming bloody words. "See you at the trial," I said, and Eryn's face elongates into a pale mask of disbelief. Melanie is shouting from across the parking lot. When I turn to look I see her simultaneously running and reading the directions on a can of pepper spray, a miracle of coordination, her hair blown out behind her like a bleached flag.

ISSUE 81

Elizabeth Green

ISSUE 81

Taste

It's the hottest day so far. I really like it here. I like the open lawns, the trees, the nurses in their white. How they stand out against the green grass. I like the big white building I get to eat and sleep in. It's nice not to fear the place I sleep in. To fear my own bed. But the nightmares bring me back.

When I was in prison it was different. Instead of a rolling green lawn, we were surrounded by wire in a dirt-covered pen. Concertina wire curling and writhing around the top of the fence. They brought me to the mental facility not because I was trying to escape, but because I was trying to eat the wire.

Most people thought it was funny. On my way up, the other inmates shouted, "Hey, Jack, where the hell do you think you're going?"

I had reached the top by the time the guards noticed me. I could have slid over, slicing myself up, but escaping all the same. Maybe landing in a heaping bloody mess on the other side only to be dragged back by the dogs.

But when I started to eat the shiny concertina wire, they stopped aiming their guns. I could see them peripherally. I watched them stare stupidly at me as I licked away at the gnarled metal shards.

See, I had to do something drastic. Earlier that day I overheard the guys planning something terrible for me. It was going to happen that night. And I had just about cracked already. Whatever they had planned, it was going to be worse than the gang rapes, the multiple kicks to the ribs, stripping me down and making me dance. Whatever it was, I didn't want to find out. And I'm not a big fan of suicide.

When they brought me down, my chin and neck were covered in blood. It's always one thing making new scars, but reopening them and making new ones in the same place is something special.

No one said anything as they walked me out of the yard. They just kind of looked on, dumbfounded as I smiled at everyone. It's not easy being a smaller guy.

Now I sit here under an oak tree. It's so hot that I've taken off my shirt. I see Nurse Judy walking toward me. She doesn't like it when I take off my shirt. Ben, this guy I talk to sometimes, says it's because it makes her "hot and bothered." He likes to use archaic phrases that don't really work in the here and now. I would have just said horny.

Nurse Judy stands over me, her white skirt swaying in the breeze. I look but I can't see much more than the tops of her thighs.

"Jack, where's your shirt?" she asks.

"Man, I don't even know." I laugh.

"Don't call me 'man,'" she says. "Where is your shirt?"

"You should go look for it," I say. "Do you guys have any of that pudding stuff left?"

"No." Nurse Judy doesn't like me because deep down, she knows I'm not really crazy. But if I don't throw in crazy sentences once in a while, they'll start to doubt my insanity. She returns from around the tree with my ugly white shirt in her hand.

Sometimes my psychiatrist asks me why I ate the concertina wire, and why I like to eat anything that might be sharp. They won't let me around anything potentially dangerous without supervision. I don't blame them. I'm not all that interested in cutting up my body. That's sick shit anyway. I'm no self-despising masochist. But if I see a pair of scissors, I can't help but spread those blades and drag them down my tongue.

I don't remember much about my past. Only the high points. Only those days in the bathroom with the door shut and the scissors, tweezers, and nail clippers all to myself. And it's all a lot easier to do than you think--that is, if you need to do it bad enough. My question is: how can you call it masochism when it feels good? Or when it's necessary?

Dr. Ritter asks me why I ate the wire. So I just complain about the prison food. How everything was just so fucking bland. And it's not

ISSUE 81

that far from the truth. There are practically no taste buds left on the surface of my tongue.

"You're not answering my question," he'll say leaning forward. He likes to pretentiously link his hands together.

I mirror him and say, "Well I'm fucking nuts, what do you expect?"

Nurse Judy holds my shirt in her hand and shakes it in my face. She throws it at me. "Too much for you to handle, Judy?" I ask. I like to think I have the torso of Hugh Jackman.

"Hot and bothered!" Ben shouts from half-way across the lawn. Her pace quickens, and I laugh.

The thing is, she would be pretty if she just relaxed. She's too tall, thin without the curves, about six foot something, with red hair and big green eyes. She's a monster. And when I first arrived, this schizophrenic guy Dan told me she had a thing for guys with Napoleon complexes. I told him just because I'm short doesn't mean I have a Napoleon complex. He didn't follow.

I have these nightmares. Sometimes they're about prison. Sometimes I'm stuck at the end of a long, concrete alley inside the prison walls, crouched down. My ass is facing the wall. There's Dirty Frank. He was named after the bar he used to frequent and pick up murder victims in. There's Hairy Joe, the red-headed child molester. There's Icy Fin. I have no idea how he got his name, but I remember the black tattoo tears running down his face and decided he must have been in a gang or something. The guys are really big, about six foot something. They reach out with their fat fingers and suddenly my face is to the wall. Just like that. And the pain comes back and it's so goddamn real. Like it's really fucking happening again.

Sometimes my dreams are about my dad and how he used to hit me. Sometimes my dad replaces the prison inmates. But most of the time, my dad is feeding me.

In my dreams, he's shoving the food down, but I don't taste anything. In my dreams, I've beaten him at his own game.

But in my nightmares...

ISSUE 81

Eat your damn peas, Jacky. He'll say, shoving a spoon deep into my throat. *You're too tiny, you gotta eat.* The peas always pass my tongue and make me gag. In my nightmares, my dad is shoving broccoli down, brussel sprouts, green beans...everything I hated--hate to eat. I can taste them in all their putrid, green vomit-covered glory and I just want to die.

I wake up screaming and the nurses rush in to strap me down. I don't need to be strapped. But they think it's the right thing to do so I let them. Sometimes it's just nice to have people around.

Sometimes Nurse Clara, a new nurse at the ward, stays beside me until I fall asleep. She looks to be about twenty-one. She's very pretty but I don't tell her. She only started taking care of me about a month ago. Everyone says she's a transfer from another hospital. No one says why she transferred, but it doesn't really matter to me. I just want to hear her voice.

Tonight I awoke strapped down again for the third time in a week. They've gotten worse over the month. In the dream I was young. There was a little girl with me but I couldn't make out her face. We were crouched down over a frog, trying to shove it into a little toy car. We were going to push it down a hill. I wanted to crash it into a rock and she wanted to dress it like a princess. We started to fight. I began to hit her with the frog until it fell apart. Then the little girl started to bleed from her hands. Icy Fin was smiling over us, five times our size. He switched to Dad with a spoon in his hand; green conglomerate ooze was slipping from it, but the spoon stayed full. It got closer and closer.

That's when I wake up.

I'm covered in sweat and I think I've wet the bed again. My bladder has never been so weak as it is this month. Not since I was four or five. Nurse Clara is sitting beside me. She has tears in her eyes. Other nurses are in the room too but they move so fast I can't tell who they are at first. I hope they can't smell the urine. I hope they just think it's more sweat down there.

"You okay?" I ask Nurse Clara.

"He's awake," Nurse Rachel says.

I ask her again, and she says, "I'm fine."

All the nurses leave but Nurse Clara. Her hand is on my forehead.

"Your hair is starting to grow," she says. "We'll have to shave you tomorrow."

I shrug.

"Why are you crying?" I ask.

"Nothing, it's nothing." She wears a smile that I don't believe.

"You can tell me," I say. She takes a clean white cloth and wipes my face with it.

"What do you dream about?" she asks.

"I can't remember half the time."

"What about the other half?"

"Prison." I say. It's not entirely true, but it's good enough for her. She smiles a little, looks down at her hands.

"Do you remember why you went to prison, Jacky?" she asks. She closes her mouth quickly, as if trying to catch back some words.

"'Jacky?'" I ask, "No one calls me that..."

"You're right." Nurse Clara stands up. Her eyes flick down my bed. To my legs. I tense. "I'll send in Nurse Judy for you."

"For...?" I didn't want to say the reason. I swallow. "I don't want her. Doing that," I say.

She looks at me for a moment.

"Nurse Rachel then."

"I'll be okay."

"I'm sending someone in."

She reaches for the doorknob.

"I'm not...I never used to do this."

She angles her head funny and for a moment, her eyes seem to sparkle. She leaves me in the room with the lights on.

"Mr. Flannery," Dr. Ritter says, "tell me about the concertina."

"I believe it's a musical instrument, like an accordion with keys--"

"The wire, Mr. Flannery," he says. "Why did you try to eat it?"

I look at him.

"I didn't eat it," I correct him. "I tried. It was too hard."

"Give me that."

"Give you what?" He looks at my hands slowly unwinding a paper clip I snatched off his desk. I pop half of it into my mouth like a toothpick and lean back in my chair. I smile.

"You're being very difficult today. I heard about your incident last night."

I shrug.

"That isn't an answer."

"There was no question."

"Jack--"

"That's Mr. Flannery to you." I say, "I'm a married woman."

"You're not funny." I really wasn't. There wasn't a quiver of a smile on his weathered face.

"You ever catch lobsters?" I ask.

"Excuse me?"

"You look like you used to catch lobsters."

"I fish on the weekends. Not in the ocean."

"Your face looks like a ship captain's. You would have been better as a fisherman."

Dr. Ritter looks at me a minute.

He lifts his eyebrows at me. "You should have been a guidance counselor." I laugh. Now *he's* funny.

"You're right," I say. I scratch my neck where the stubble is creeping down. I glance at the clock. "Time's up."

I stand, put his paper clip back with the others and head for the door.

"Stick out your tongue."

I stop and turn to him.

"Why?"

He stands. He never stands. "Stick out your tongue, Mr. Flannery." The man is shorter than me. He's fucking shorter than me.

I widen my eyes, bear my teeth, and stick out my tongue. "HAAAAAAA." I breathe. He recoils, probably expecting to see a torrent of blood or something. But I'm unscathed.

"Thank you."

Nurse Clara stands beside me with an electric razor in one hand. I can't take my eyes off it. If you break the guard and turn it on, it can do some damage. But I notice this guard isn't broken.

I'm wearing a wife-beater instead of my regular white shirt. She throws a dry white towel around my shoulders.

"You have little ringlets," she said, turning on the razor. It makes a sound like a hundred pissed-off bumblebees. She touches my hair with her hand, and something familiar flows through me but I can't place it. Her hand lingers on the top of my head for a moment too long and I turn to her.

"You alright?" I ask. "You're acting weird."

"Fine," she says, turning my head back to face forward, "I'm fine."

I look into the mirror as the razor edge begins to buzz off my hair. I watch some fuzz fall onto the towel. Nurse Clara has hair like me. It's blonder, but just as curly. I look at myself for a long time. I have big brown eyes. Clara has big brown eyes too. I have a straight, hard nose that curves up slightly at the end. So does she. I have a very distinctive jaw-line, as does she. I look at her. I look at me.

She continues to buzz off my hair until my entire head is one very short length of potential curls.

The razor switches off. She bends down, unplugs it, knocks out the loose hair. I watch her put it into an upper cabinet. She locks it.

"Safety," she says, when she catches me watching her.

"I know," I say.

"Two-thirty," she smiles.

I frown.

"Mr. Flannery," Dr. Ritter begins, "Why did you ask about the lobsters the other day?" I groan and kick my foot up onto the chair beside me. He watches my foot and continues. "Is it because they have sharp snappers?" I don't answer. "Do they attract you? Mr. Flannery? Do you find them enticing?"

"Do they *attract* me?" I laugh at him. "Look, I didn't climb the fence and try to fuck the wire, I ate it."

"I don't mean it in a sexual sense."

"Then be straight with it. Don't screw around." I put another foot on the chair, "I'm not attracted or *intrigued* (the better word) by lobsters. The only reason I asked is because you remind me of one."

"I do?"

"Well don't look like that. That just makes it worse."

"What am I doing?" he touches his chest, open palmed.

ISSUE 81

"You have poor circulation?"

"Why?"

"Either it's poor circulation or you're an alcoholic."

"It's...the circulation," he says. "How do you know that?"

"You're nose is as red as a tomato."

"Mr. Flannery--"

"You moved the paper clips."

He closes his mouth. Opens it. "Yes."

"Safety," I say.

We each take a breath.

"Some new detectives are coming by later."

I swallow. I must have gone pale because a sadistic smile grows on his face. "I don't care," I say.

"Just letting you know." He looks at the clock, "Time's up."

My feet are on the floor again but I don't remember taking them off the chair. My hands are gripping my thighs. I feel my bladder loosen a little.

"When?" I ask.

"This evening."

I stand up, head for the door.

The bathroom is just down the hall.

Please don't let me pee in front of him...please don't let him see that...

Just around the corner and down the hall.

Please, God, please...

ISSUE 81

I can make it.

I reach for the doorknob but it's too late. The warmth creeps down my legs fast, gathering at the cuffs of my pants, making a pool around my shoes. I can't look at him.

I'm playing gin rummy with Nurse Clara in the rec. room but I can't concentrate. Ben is watching us, giggling into his sleeve, whispering to his friend Carl. Carl is deaf, but Ben doesn't seem to care.

There are many different versions of gin rummy but Clara and I happen to know the same one.

Since three o'clock I've had a headache. Now it's five and it's only gotten worse.

"You look terrible," she says, placing the threes together in front of her.

"They're coming today," I say.

"I know." She takes my hand in hers. Our eyes meet. Ben laughs loudly and we break apart. "Let's go somewhere else," she says.

We walk into the smallest waiting room in the facility. It's hidden away in a tiny alcove in the wall. It's also one of the most private places. It would be completely private if not for the 24-hour surveillance camera.

"You need to tell me the truth, Jack."

"The truth about what?"

"Prison."

"The truth is, it was terrible." What does she expect to hear?

"No, not..." she sighs. "Tell me why you went to prison."

ISSUE 81

I don't say anything. She continues, "You don't have to tell them the truth. But tell me. Just...don't tell them anything if you don't want to, but please tell me. Please."

"Listen..." I can't seem to speak. My throat tightens. I'm very tired. "...do you know how many people have been asking me this? Did I do it? Am I guilty? Do you know what I've gone through? I've been through hell, Clara! I've been beaten by four cops because I couldn't tell them. I've been humiliated, denied food, put in solitary confinement for it." Her eyes widen, "Oh yeah. You don't think they torture people? Well they fucking do. And do you think for a goddamn minute if I knew what happened I wouldn't come out with it?" My words emerge in sputters, my throat is tight. My snot and spit is hitting her but I don't fucking care. This is two years of frustration coming out.

"And you know what?" I say, "I would tell you. I would. But I don't remember anything! All I know..." I sit down on the little blue couch and she follows me.

"It's okay, Jack." I meet her eyes. She's crying. She touches my hand again and I pull away from her. I rest my head in my hands.

"All I know," I say after a moment, "is that I hurt some kid. They show me pictures. I don't know who he is. I don't remember..." I wipe my nose with my sleeve. "I don't even know what my parents look like. I...I get these dreams but I don't know if it's memory or not."

"Do you tell Dr. Ritter any of this?"

I sneer. "He's a fucking tool. I don't tell him shit."

"Jack--"

"What are you going to say? That he's trying to help me?"

"Yes," she says quietly.

"I'm sorry."

She deliberately takes my hand, and puts hers inside of mine. Our palms meet. She asks, "See this?"

She shows me a tiny moon-shaped scar on the back of her hand, right between her thumb and forefinger. It's about two inches long and very thin.

"How'd that happen?"

"We were playing with dad's knife."

I laugh, "What?"

"Dad let you borrow his knife. The red one with the white cross on it."

"I don't...you're my sister?"

"You remember?"

"Are you fucking with me?"

"Jack, I would never do that."

"I feel like everybody's just fucking me up."

"I'm not lying."

"I don't know...you could...could tell me anything and I wouldn't know! You get that? What am I supposed to...?"

"Trust me."

I liked Nurse Clara the moment I met her. I felt no impulse to rag on her like I do to the other nurses. There was always something different about her. Maybe I do trust her. I give her a chance and listen.

"You caught a frog in the yard and you were cutting it up. So I ran at you to stop. You started to chase me around, and you cut me."

"I would never hurt you," I say.

"You felt bad afterwards. About the frog but especially me. So you threw the knife into the woods. And then Dad asked for his knife back and you couldn't find it. Do you remember any of this?"

"He hit me in front of you," I say.

ISSUE 81

"That's right."

"I wet myself."

"Yes."

"And he just got angrier."

"Jack..."

I look at her. I can't hug her because she looks terrified.

"Mr. Flannery." I jump. Dr. Ritter is standing behind me. "The detectives are here to see you."

"Tell them I'm sick."

"Clara, in my office immediately."

"I'm sorry, but I...I needed to know." She stands, her hands ripping each other apart.

"And you've broken the agreement." Dr. Ritter says. Nurse Judy comes around the corner followed by three men in suits. I start to sweat.

"This was a delicate process Clara. You've disrupted months of work."

"And I've gotten more from him in a month than you ever have."

"And what good is that? We didn't get to hear any of it, it wasn't recorded, there were no witnesses--it's useless! It was a mistake bringing you here!" he says through clenched teeth.

"Dr. Ritter--"

"In. My. Office."

"Yes, sir."

She wraps her arms around me. I don't remember the last time I was hugged. I squeeze her back.

"I'm so sorry, Clara. I'm sorry about Luke," I whisper.

"You don't need to tell them anything," she whispers. "I just wanted to know--"

"Ms. Flannery." Dr. Ritter stamps his foot like an angry child.

Clara and I let go, and she kisses my forehead. She turns a corner, followed by Dr. Ritter, and I think it's the last time I'll see her.

"We can do this here." A suit says to Nurse Judy. His hair is cropped like a frat boy. I sit back down on the couch, squeeze my thighs together. I can still smell Clara. Like vanilla, something mild and sweet.

I think about the last thing she said to me:

You don't need to tell them anything...

"Mr. Flannery," the frat boy sets a running tape recorder on the coffee table between us "We're here to understand some things."

"Like what?"

"This boy..." he takes a file out of his briefcase. I hadn't noticed it before. He sets it down, face open on the table and shows me a photograph. The same photograph they've been showing me since I was arrested. I had never remembered the kid until now.

And now, I remember everything.

"He looks like you," another suit says. This guy has red hair and freckles and reminds me of Hairy Joe. He's about as big as him.

"Has your eyes, your feature," the frat boy agrees.

"Your powers of observation are incredible," I say. My mouth is so dry. The third guy just stands there, clicking his tongue. He has a pen in his pocket.

I decide I don't like any of them.

"Mr. Flannery, why did you assault your nephew?"

And I make another decision.

I could tell them everything right now. That I was watching Luke one

ISSUE 81

day while Clara was out. I decided to show him something. Let him in on the greatest secret I'd ever discovered. I took a paring knife to my tongue and showed him how I did it. He was only six. He didn't understand. Things just got out of hand.

See, he wasn't doing it right. Cutting in deep enough. I wanted to show him. I wanted him to understand because no one else probably would. People have negative prejudices about things like this. They don't see what freedom it gives, they just see the blood. He was young, impressionable. It was harmless. And once you've fucked up your mouth enough, you can eat anything. Anything at all and no one will have to force you to eat. You wouldn't know the difference between Big League Chew and a brussel sprout. You're invincible. Immune.

But when I saw how much blood this kid had in him, and how gray he was, I panicked. Blacked out.

I decide to keep them guessing. Keep myself here, in this safe, clean hospital. Away from the prison, away from being just another bitch. Am I sorry? Of course I'm sorry. But it hasn't sunken in yet. I think it will soon. Tonight when I'm sleeping, maybe. I'll have a new load of nightmares to deal with from now on. I'll scream into my pillow, hate myself, I know it. But I can't break now. Not in front of them.

And I say, "Did Dr. Ritter ever show you his toy ship collection?"

The suits frown. I can feel the control coming back to me.

"It is really really something," I smile at the clicking guy. I see a pen in his pocket.

"Can I see that a minute? I want to write something down."

He hands it to me. They all lean in with incredible curiosity.

"No!" Nurse Judy takes a frigid step forward. I click the pen open and take a sheet of paper from inside the frat boy's file folder. There is a black and white picture of Luke on it before it all happened. I write:

Time's Up!

ISSUE 81

I hold it up to them.

"Jack, give the pen back," Nurse Judy says.

I smile at them and slowly drive it downward into my tongue.

ISSUE 81

Mariko Nagai

How We Touch the Ground, How We Touch

As usual, another season of betrayal must follow the harvest.

During the harvest, we are safe. On the field, we whisper half a phrase and hum fragmented sounds of words amongst us, messages of the Carpenter-Son hidden in broken phrases of weather and harvest. We bend our backs to cut the stalks, huddling as close to the ground as we can, but not falling. Even the strongest of us bow our backs as low as the translucent stalks of rice, golden skeletons bowing with the autumn bounty. Cutting the fistful of stalks in the rhythm of gravity, hoe against the bundle, fist around the bunch, we gather this year's harvest slowly. Then, after the harvest, we will turn the earth upside down to dig out roots that have clawed their way down, deep into the soil. But until then, we drag the harvest time out as long as we can, and time becomes elastic, easily moldable in our hands.

The harvest is good this year, and because of that our season of betrayal follows immediately afterwards.

All hours are hours of apostates for us who must live through the season of betrayal. All hours are a litany of passion, though our passions are invisible, less obvious than those of the Carpenter-Son. In this hour of apostates, in the field, all of us are alike: men take on the slender napes of women, bobbing up and down with the northern wind that signals the arrival of autumn, and women take on tree-like stumps for legs because we are so near to the ground, because our days are measured by how close we can get to the ground without falling. As we rhythmically cut down the harvest, the Elder starts a hymn, a chant unlike the one Domu-niku had taught us, but the one we have cut out from the original to bury the message into songs more familiar to us. The Elder sings of the *paraiso*, of the Carpenter-Son, the promised land and of ourselves, who amongst us will carry on the season of betrayal. And who amongst us must die. It is decided: this season, the Elder will die because De-us our Father has given the permission, to him and his family. We will carry it out, we sing out. The Elder sings in praise of De-us, in praise of the sun and the rain that give, that destroy whatever tries to ground itself to earth, he sings of De-us and His mysterious way, of the sweet revelation, the little *lamb, lamb*, of the paraiso, yes, the paraiso.

Abruptly, his song turns into a hushed hum of one note, suspended like the body of the faithful, as we hear of the procession of our landlord, steps and grunts of horses on the mud road, that ground that sounds softer than it really is, and no one can say that the mud is soft when they have been thrown into a hole filled with mud. The cold kills; the slow oozing of mud clogs the pores until the flesh begs off, when the flesh begs off the soul it encases. And we have all done that. We have betrayed De-us in those moments when we were encased in mud, confessing the crime of believing Him.

The Third Elder sings one note, and one note only, as his face masks into empty indifference, as our faces take on the faces of the apostates.

We call it season of betrayal. *They* call it cleansing. *It is a law,* they tell us, *why do you only want one god when there are so many amongst us. Why believe in a god when so many of you have fallen, and He still remains quiet to your prayers?* They tell us many things as they line us up and tell us to step on the face of our beloved, and we, one by one, step on the face, step on the face of the Carpenter-Son and His mother, Maria of the miracle, Maria of the Stabat Mater. After each harvest, we line up one after another, the procession of all the apostates before us, all the apostates that will come after us, even after our bodies have been rooted to the earth, after our bodies become another element to feed the bodies after us. We step on their faces to prove we do not love them, though we do. Our hearts break. It has been going on for twelve years, ever since Domu-niku fell.

The hours of the apostates started out one day when a man with sky in his eyes appeared in front of us from the cave by the edge of our village. He spoke our tongue in fragments, but when he spoke, he spoke of the Land, of De-us. In his halting tongue, he pointed at his tattered sparrow-brown robe, said. *Domu. Niku.* Domu-niku, we called him. He spoke of a world better than this one, about the world where hunger was kept at bay, where the tilling of earth was as forbidden as the utterance of the real name of gentle Father in this world. *De-us.* Domu-niku told us, he told us many things and we drank his words greedily as if we were thirsty, as if we never knew we were thirsty until we drank the first word, and we became thirstier and thirstier the more we heard him talk. *See,* he told us, *your hands are not used properly. See,* he told me as he gently cupped my hands with his, *see how your palms are like slightly eroded maps with so many rivers running through? How they have been telling you that your palms are a map of your life, the life you must live? Press them together*, like this, like this, he said as he pressed his hands together and pressed my hands as if he were pressing a flower between pages to be kept, *there, your life disappears. This is the life you are meant to have, a life in prayer.* He gently pulled me into his arms, and he smelled of a cow, a pig, something so earthbound that if it were another man, I would have thought that he could never be a man carrying the words of De-us.

Pray, and De-us will respond.

Pray so that the land will parch, cracks opening for the rain that would never come; pray so that the water will submerge the land, so that people will be covered in boils and scabs, so that the faithless will die and the Gates of Paraiso will open up to spit out winged men. Pray so that we can be delivered to the arms of De-us.

Pray so that our palms will erase all the foredoomed lives we must live; pray so hard that our palms will blister from the pressure.

Only then will the Man-Bird listen, only when all the faithfuls' palms are bleeding like the hands of the Carpenter-Son, the hands of the holy as he bled from his hands in order to purify the land.

But not until then.

They came at night and caught Domu-niku with three of us. One of us betrayed us though we do not know who. When three of the villagers were bound together in the shape of a rosary, their torsos and strong arms bound, when they whipped them forward up the mountain as we followed, slowly, when they stood at the mouth of the volcano mountain, Domu-niku cried out once, then twice. *They* did not hold him down; *they* only asked that he watch, and we watched him as we watched with these three martyrs. *All you have to do is to renounce your faith, and you will save these people*, a voice emerged out of the forest as if it was not a voice of a man but the sky itself, *but if you don't, then they will have to die for your faith.* *They* first kicked the old Elder into the broiling mouth, and held the next-in-chain by the lip; the Elder bobbed up and down mid-air, unable to go down, unable to go up, burning, but not burning. The Elder cried out the name of De-us, only to be erased by roar of the

ISSUE 81

volcano. *Foreigner, your god tells you not to kill, but you are killing them.* Domu-niku, unable to run toward them nor run away, kneeled and turned to us for prayers, but we did not offer him prayer or consolation. We just looked down, making ourselves unnoticeable. We could be next, but we did not tell Domu-niku that we feared dying, we feared that we have not seen De-us as Domu-niku has, but we believed him. We believe him so that we can dream of a better world. And mostly, we feared that after all the prayers, all the praises and all the dead bodies, we feared not finding De-us when we crossed over to the other side, that all our prayers were made in vain.

The elder's rope burned. He fell into the mountain, disappeared. The next one in the chain hanged from the lip of the mountain, his scream as loud as the boar fighting back during the hunt. The woman at the end of the rosary jerked forward, and *they* held her tight, Domu-niku's refusal held her to the top, she was at the mercy of one word, but it was only a mere word. *It's your last chance, Christian man – say you will renounce, and you're saving these lives.* Domu-niku kept shaking and praying, pressing his palms together, praying for guidance, for mercy, *God, God why have you forsaken me at this time of need, I am only human, God, please, tell me what to do*, and he raised his arms toward the sky, kneeling on the ground, digging deep into the sand. He raised arms upward, his palms still pressed together.

Last chance– where's your god when you need him?

God, Domu-niku shouted, *God, what can I do?* His hands still held in the form of a prayer, he yelled, his face upturned to the sky, and not even a bird replied.

The voice, in a startlingly sad tone, almost a wail of a gull's before the storm, crooned out of the water, *Well, so be it. I'm sorry.*

The last bead of rosary disappeared into the volcano; they all looked at the place where the three of us fell. They turned to us. We kept our eyes to the ground.

Still kneeling, Domu-niku's hands flew apart, some force greater than the one in his heart, pried his hands apart. Palms orphaned from each other. He clawed, he would have clawed out the sun, the eye of De-us, if he could have. Veins grew on his upturned arms, fists grew at the end of his upturned arms.

He collapsed to the ground; he fell to the ground and cried.

He became the first to fall.

Domu-niku the apostate.

He now carries the cross on his face, though he is no longer the Domu-niku who stood straight, his legs firm on the ground as he taught us about paraiso, of the Carpentor-Son, his Mother, the Domu-niku who had held my hands, the Domu-niku who had traveled three years across the ocean in order to spread the words of De-us. He is of the outcast, orphaned from his Father, Ada-mu outcast from paraiso, orphaned and left to live in a country so far away from the origin of his faith.

Domu-niku the man, a mere fallen man who has thrown away the frock he had arrived in and has taken on new clothes, a new name, and many new gods. He no longer hold our hands in the dark night, listening to our confessions; he no longer talks of his paraiso, the Land kept behind his shut mouth, and now, he talks of the starry sky and of the lands we have never seen nor believed to exist.

He became the first fallen one, and our season of betrayal began that year.

And I hold on, as we all do, on to the words of Domu-niku, as we cup our hands around the rice husks, the golden husks standing out radiant as Domu-niku said about the ray of god and the beloved, and each harvest, we hold the god in our hands, our private god, our own because Domu-niku said that he is in our hearts, because He is the only thing that is ours, because the land is not ours and our lives not our own. The husks, brilliant, as our love for Him. Then clouds cover the sun, always at our moments of illumination, and the golden husk returns to this ordinary earthiness, the rice which measures our worth, and our lives which have no meaning.

De-us the god of the golden husk has been silent all these times.

We pray in vain, late at night, when no one is around, when it is only the apostates awake, uttering our prayers into holes in houses where no one can hear. We carry our faith as all apostates do, and we call it the *hours of apostates*. And for apostates, all hours are

ISSUE 81

hours of apostates. Our lives are measured by all these hours we must live as apostates.

And this year, at the late hour before the gathering of harvest, a week ago, our Elder gathered us, because we no longer have Domu-niku to call us, because the season of betrayal will start soon. He said that he had a dream, a dream so beautiful that if what he saw was paraiso, he'd rather be there than where he was. *Maria the mother was there, the Carpenter-Son, and all the 26 martyrs who died, they told me that it is my turn to be the apostle. He told me that my job is done, and I can do nothing more. In the dream, he lifted my robe and touched my cross,* and he unrobed his tattered robe, *one for each season of betrayal, I have cut myself deep, and I carry twelve lines to show,* the black welts as thick as worms, twelve fierce worms wiggled vertically as he breathed hard, *it is my turn, they told me, I no longer have to step on Their faces. I have been carrying the weight of our burden.* His wife and daughter clasped their hands together in prayer.

You are now the leader, he turned to me. *You are now the leader; you must lead these children as I have done, hiding our faith, hiding who we truly are so that you can deliver them to paraiso. Your path will be hard, but remember that it is not as hard as the Carpenter-Son. You know what you must do.*

Harvest has been good. We will not eat what we have worked hard at. The earth itself is full of bounty, golden and already luxurious before it must sleep during winter in order to repeat the cycle all over again. The harvest has been good. And the season of betrayal will start soon. It has been like this for twelve years now. They test us, to see that we do not believe in De-us.

We go to the temple, as we always have done. We stand in the line with our eyes downcast, not betraying us yet. The Elder is the only one who looks straight at *them.* At Domu-niku, who stands with his back stooped, down to our heights, not looking at anyone. Domu-niku who is no longer Domu-niku; who now has a new name, new wife, and new role. The line crawls forward as one by one, we step on the faces of Maria and the Carpenter-Son. It is quiet, though our hearts are breaking inside, though we are wailing as we step on the faces of our beloved. And suddenly. The Elder calmly steps away from the line. His wife and daughter step away from the line with him. He announces that he can not lie, no matter what, not anymore, not ever. The Elder says that he is too tired to live the life of a lie, an

ISSUE 81

apostate, and he is an apostle, he has been the apostle who has had to live as an apostate. Taken by surprise, *they* ask him kindly what he means. Domu-niku does not look at the Elder.

And the Elder recites what all of us hope to recite openly, the names of De-us, the Carpenter-Son, the glorious triangle of mysteries; he pours forth the forbidden stories and glories of De-us. *Paraiso, paraiso*, the Elder sings, *Deus, deus, deus,* he sings, and his daughter and wife join him, their voices weaving into a triangle of songs in the fall sky of the harvested earth.

Do you understand what you are doing, Domu-niku asks quietly, *do you understand what they'd do to you once they know you are believer of a foreign heathen god?*

The trinity of voices does not quiet, but insistently push themselves forward to their end. They are bound there. *They* tell us we must watch as a punishment for harboring these "Christians," they tell us that in order that we will not protect any more of these people, we must participate in the punishment. *They* say that they'll tell us what, later, what we have to do. We already know what we must do.

They coax him, holding his daughter and his wife, telling him that if he does not renounce De-us, *they* will have to make him submit. He shakes his head with a smile, *See how foolish you are. De-us is closer than you think, He stands here, with me, and understands that I can no longer lie, even if I wanted to.*

They, too, shake their heads, *Do you understand what you are saying, this is your daughter and wife.*

And the Elder stands firm in his faith, in his conviction, telling them that He does not allow His children to take their own lives, but if He gives permission, we can leave. And He has given the permission, glory and mercy.

They do not touch him. But Domu-niku steps up in the front, bind the daughter and wife. *They* pour cold water on them, Domu-niku jabs a dull knife under the finger nails, they scream, they scream, they pray and called out the names of De-us, and the louder their screams, the more joyously and loudly the Elder sings of paraiso and of De-us, and we watch with our closed faces. Domu-niku's face is closed as ours as he jabs the knife one by one, twenty in total; he keeps his eyes away as he slices off their noses and ears, slowly.

And it does not end. Domu-niku makes the daughter and the wife dig two holes deep enough and wide enough so that a body can sit in each; the Elder sings from the cage like a domesticated finch. He stays like that for a week while the wife and the daughter sit tied to the tree with their faces branded with burns in the shape of a cross. He watches his wife and daughter poked around with hot rods while he sings of paraiso, never once wavering in his resolution. And we watch with him. We watch as Domu-niku stares at the ground.

Finally, *they* make the daughter and wife sit so that the Elder can throw the dug earth back around and *they* make him stomp on freshly earthened holes and he stomps wildly, almost a dance, a passionate dance. Two tired heads poke out of the ground as if someone had gently placed two beheaded heads on the ground. *They* hand the Elder a rusty saw taken out of someone's shed and command him to saw off their heads.

It's because of your foolish faith, they yelled, *you don't have to kill your daughter. We hate to do this, we do, you understand, we never want to harm you people.*

The Elder's head pops up and down as if his head is held only by thin skin, as if it is his head that is getting sawn off with a rusty saw. And he sings and sings, his voice breaks, cracking, so much like Domu-niku's that day, anguished, breaking. Domu-niku wailed out questions; the Elder wails out songs of De-us. We stare at the ground, unyielding ground. The Elder sings and, following the rhythm of the saw, he begins to saw off his daughter's head, and the wife joins him, singing joyously, wildly, insanely, rhythmically with the movement of his arm. They sing; he saws off as quickly as he can, as energetically and as fast as he can, first the daughter, then his wife.

Now, turning to us, *you have to punish this man for killing his wife and his daughter in a brutal and cruel manner. The just punishment is to kick this man to death. Kick,* they tell us, *kick this man until he dies. And remember that you will not harbor any more of these foreign-god worshippers.*

And we kick, I kick as hard as I can, quickly, swiftly, we claw and kick, so that the Elder will die quickly, so that he will be delivered to

De-us quickly, so he can tell Him that there are many of his believers still waiting, still praying for Him to release us, to give us permission to return to His arms, that we are still waiting. We cannot wait for the harvest to fail, we cannot wait for the faithless to die. And we kick, tear, praying silently, *please take the message for us, for prayers have been lost somewhere between the ground and the sky, please take the message,* we punch, pull until the Elder is nothing but a heap of tattered flesh, tattered meat, and he whispers, *thank you, thank you,* and we kick for easy deliverance, for mercy, for forgiveness, and for many things and he is no more. And our season of betrayal ends finally.

Catherine Parnell

Sirens

My father calls twice from the small hospital in our town – the first time he says: "They are working on her." The second time, less than three minutes later, he says: "Your mother is dead." I tell him to stay where he is, that I will come and get him, that he can't drive after a shock like that. Then I hang up on him. The thermometer outside the kitchen window reads ninety-two degrees, but a chill spreads across my chest and down my arms; my legs shiver beneath my skirt. My coffee cup shakes in my hands, and I drop it in the sink with my cereal bowl. The mug breaks, shards of porcelain ricochet in the silver apron-front basin. In the cereal flakes and milk and coffee there is one perfect slice of banana. At the front door, I clutch the brass doorknob, because if I walk out of my house it will be true. I'd talked to my mother last night. She wasn't sick, but withdrawn and quiet; we both knew something, but we didn't speak of it, because she had begged me never to call my father a bastard again.

I have to go. She's waiting for me. No, he's waiting for me. She's dead.

Suddenly I am eight years old at the beach and my father holds out his arm, flexes his muscle and shouts *Hang on*, and my brother and sister and I do, the thick bulge on his upper arm hard as a rock and he holds us up high, swings us around, and drops us into the water. Like little fish they swim away. I can't swim and he knows it. The sand lifts around me, the water bright with sunlight and dark with his shadow; I'm flailing, reaching for him, but his legs push against the water, away from me.

My mother saves me; she lifts me out of the water and pats my back while I spew sandy water.

I have to leave my house.

I grab my bag and open the door. I drive to the hospital. My father stands by the coffee machine, staring at dirty pennies in his palm. When I put my hand on his shoulder, he cringes. "Let's go home," I say. He closes his fingers around the pennies and shakes his hand.

The coins rattle; his body rocks.

We don't go home. I guide my father to a chair and shove him down on the grainy seat. I sprint to the ER and see the silver gurney where my mother lies, her long silver hair in a tangle. Blood on the floor, tubes, the monitors, syringes, blue paper sheets. Discarded latex gloves. They are inside out. A nurse steps around the gurney, walking toward me; her mouth opens.

"Dr. Gordon."

That can't be me, but it is. I've been in this room many times, my patients young, trusting, and sick. My pediatric brood, my little friends.

"Amy, I'm sorry," and I turn to the nurse. Her eyelids flutter; her face is gray with worry.

"Leave me alone," I say curtly, and she leaves the room.

I wipe the blood from my mother's face, examine the neck collar and the discoloration on her cheek. We're a small hospital, more interested in care than paperwork, yet I stare at the clipboard. Time of death is duly noted; cause of death is blank.

When I return to the waiting room, my father is twisting my mother's lavender scarf in his hands. He cocks his head and smiles weakly. "She could use this to tie her hair back when she's better." Untangling the scarf from his grip, I wrap it around my throat.

"Get up," I say. On the short drive home, he hangs his head out the window, his mouth open against the rush of the air. His mouth is not a mouth at all.

I call my brother from my parent's house. "Kenny," I say, "pick up the phone, I know you're there, it's Saturday, have you had your coffee yet?" (He's thirty-two, but he will not leave the house until the coffee has done its job, and it's not to wake him up, it's to kick start his intestines, and I have asked him not to tell me this, but he thinks it's funny.) I call three times before Kenny picks up and I say, "I don't know how to tell you this, but Mom is dead. I've got Dad here and he hasn't said a word to me; and the hallway has been tossed, the tables turned, and there is a cereal bowl and orange juice on the floor. Should I clean it up?"

ISSUE 81

ISSUE 81

Kenny says, "Don't."

Then he says, "Let me pack a bag, and I'll be there in an hour." I say, "Don't you want to know what happened?" and he says, "Please don't tell me," and I hang up. My father looks at me, and he opens his mouth as if to answer a question in his scholarly manner, and I walk away, and last night when I talked to my mother she said this: *A boy should love his father no matter what.*

I call my younger sister. It's not yet noon, and I hear the ice in her glass, she giggles and says, "Iced coffee," and I say, "Julie, I don't know how to tell you this, but Mom is dead."

She says, "No way."

"Yeah Way," I reply.

And Julie asks, "Are you sure?"

And I say with some exasperation, "I saw her body, they cracked her chest, and there was a tube in her mouth."

"Did you take it out?" she asks me.

"I think you had better come home. I have Dad here and he's not talking."

Julie laughs, "Do you really think he wants to talk to you?" and I say coolly, "He called me."

"But did he talk to you?"

"No," I reply, "but it's going to be me or the police," and she panics and says, "Don't do anything stupid before I get there." She forgets to hang up the phone, and I hear her howling like a baby locked in a room in the dark. I scream, " You forgot to hang up the phone," she throws it against the wall, and we're disconnected.

My father sits on the couch in front of me as I dial Paul's number. "Paul," I say, and Paul says, "I heard, I'm on my way, and I'll take care of it." Paul is my best friend from high school; he is my best friend in this small New England town. He runs Doherty's Funeral Home with his father even though Paul wanted to be a doctor.

I say, "Paul, I'm counting on you," and he sighs. "I know," he says, and for the first time that day I know someone understands what I have to do. "I'll see you soon, Amy," and he hangs up.

My father stares at me, he has not cried, but his eyes are red.

"Amy," he says, and the cinnamon swirls in the carpet start dancing.

"Not now, Dad," I say. I pick up my mother's address book and I call her secretary at the college where my mother teaches History, and I break the Saturday news to Sally, who weeps uncontrollably as she sits in her apartment decorated with glass frogs. When she pulls herself together her voice is firm and dedicated, and she says she will inform all Joyce's colleagues at the college, which takes care of at least twenty phone calls. I don't know who to call next, and I excuse myself — from what? — and I go into the bathroom, and I throw up, all over the place, but specifically on my father's toothbrush that he left sitting on the side of the sink as usual.

I call Annie, my mother's sister. She makes everyone laugh; when she picks up the phone she says, "Hello, Darling." She is one-thousand miles away. I say, "Annie, I don't know how to tell you this, but Mom died this morning."

From the dark mouth of the phone comes the sound of heavy wind, and I am swept up in the air and I find myself sitting on the floor, my hand and the phone all one piece. "That bastard," she says, and I say, "Yes," because we three, Joyce, Annie and me, have no secrets, and from the roaring phone I hear Uncle Doug's voice, "Annie, you look like your best friend just died," and Annie whispers to no one in particular, "She just did."

I say, "Annie, I can take care of things," and she says, "You better keep me away from him or we will have a double funeral." She starts to cry, great gobs of hiccups punctuated by dry rasps; then Doug is on the line.

"He finally did it," he says.

"We don't know that, she had a bad heart." (Already I have started the lies.)

"He had no heart."

"You've got to trust me, Doug." And Doug says, "You get him, you hear me?" And I start to cry, because my mother is dead, and there's no changing that, but maybe there's a way to set things straight.

In walks Kenny; he needs a haircut and a beard trim; otherwise he looks as consumptive as a Yoga guru, which he is in these parts. He heads for Dad and hugs him and holds his hand; my father warily looks at me out of the corner of his eye. While Kenny pats Dad's bald head, my sister walks in carrying a jumbo bottle of Cutty Sark and a small overnight bag made of leopard-spotted fabric. Julie looks like a hooker with her platinum-streaked hair, green contacts and little spandex skirt. The three of them go into the kitchen where my sister solemnly pours three glasses (although there are four of us in the house) of Cutty, no ice. She puts the glass in my father's hand; my brother stares at the counter as if snakes were slithering on it, knowing his three sober years are over. The three of them drink; within an hour they are on the back deck telling dirty jokes and singing. The neighbors bring food, and I explain that grief takes many forms. They nod, because they saw the ambulance take my mother away, they saw my father's car rush after it, they tell me all this as they quietly place deli platters and baked beans on the counter. (Did they start cooking at the first sound of the siren?) Someone brings a honey ham; I tear off a sweet slice when no one is looking, and I chew it so long that I start chewing my tongue.

My shoulder is the place where the mourners rest their heads when they hug me, but I can't cry with them. "She went quickly," I say, and I hope it's true, but I'm a doctor and it's never that simple. When Paul enters the crowded kitchen where I am pouring glasses of water and passing tissues, I wonder how far I will go to take care of things; Paul whispers to those he speaks with that my mother had heart trouble. Even now he cannot help but emphasize *heart* because we both know how my mother loved my father.

Paul wraps his arms around me, and asks, "Are they at it already?"

"Yes they are," to which he replies with a wink, "No Way."

I wink back at him but my right eyelid sticks and I can't see. Paul touches my eyelid, it pops open, and I say, as I lose my balance, "Yeah Way." Paul holds me up, because my legs have buckled and the one little piece of honey ham I ate is on its way up.

"I'm right here, Amy," Paul says. He raises his finger to my lips, and a hush falls over the neighbors. All those eyes are on me as Paul walks me to a chair. Someone offers me a sweater and I wrap it around me. Paul kneels before me.

"Have you decided?" he whispers.

The neighbors lean in.

Paul's hands are on my knees. I place my hands on top of his and pat them.

"I need some time," I say.

Paul removes his hands. The neighbors sigh.

Evening comes. The first wave of mourners have left their offerings everywhere. I think I will open a soup kitchen to get rid of all the food, but then I see my father standing by the ham, ripping slices of meat from the bone. He drops the pink ham on a plate as a siren wails in the distance. He flings himself against the kitchen wall and the telephone falls off the hook. When he turns around I am standing there. Our eyes meet. I narrow my gaze. He doesn't move, not one single inch, not a breath raises his chest, not a blink closes his eyes, and I walk towards him as if I am taking my first steps. My balance is off, but my head is clear, and to him I say, "You have to tell us what happened."

I clamp my hand around his thick wrist and walk him into the family room where he sits in his gray Laz-Y-Boy chair that he bought off the back of a truck in a bad part of town for twenty-five dollars. His fringe of hair touches the towel-covered headrest. Kenny and Julie see us through the glass door leading to the deck; I motion for them to come in, but my sister shakes her head with vigor.

Kenny drags Julie in; she screams, "You just ignore her, Dad, she thinks she's so smart, but she doesn't understand, does she?"

Closing his eyes, my father asks, "What do you want to know?"

"How did she die?" I ask.

"Don't do this, daddy," my sister whimpers.

My father's left eye twitches; the stubble on his face beads with sweat. He sips his drink; he chokes. Clawing at the air, he bends over and a thin line of scotch comes from his mouth. I smack him between the shoulder blades, and he straightens up.

"Sorry," he says, wiping his mouth.

"So," I say, leaning over him, "What happened to my mother?"

He pales. Out of the corner of my eye I catch my reflection in the sliding doors leading to the deck. My thick blonde hair, my height, all six feet of it, and my thin white t-shirt – I've grown into my mother's form. My full lips tighten. They will never touch my mother's soft cheek again.

"Daddy," Julie pleads. "Come on out back. I'll pour you another drink."

"Take it easy, Julie," Kenny says. His face is creased with fear.

My father's not going to speak to what I know, that my mother's neck was broken, and I know Paul, with his mortician's skill, will be able to hide the welt on her cheek.

"What happened?" I ask. I am the only one in town who will ask. The law, the doctors, even Paul, will not ask, because my family is The Family.

Julie snivels, Kenny hands her a tissue. The air is thick with Cutty Sark and sweat, and I shove old issues of *National Geographic* and *The Economist* aside and I sit on the coffee table directly in front of my father. Julie and Kenny move so that they are on either side of my father.

"She couldn't breathe," my father says.

"How did the mirror get on the floor?"

"She pulled it when she fell."

"And?"

"She couldn't speak."

"You shook her?"

ISSUE 81

He nods.

"And the ambulance?" I ask.

"I called the ambulance. The paramedics took her away. The ambulance stopped at the top of the street and I raced on to meet her at the hospital."

"Then what?"

"I arrived before the paramedics. I waited." He looks at Kenny and Julie. "They worked on her heart," he says.

"Was she alone?" I ask.

"Damn you, Amy," Kenny cries out.

My father waves his hand. Kenny shuts up.

"Blood," my father says. "I saw the blood. It's barbaric what you doctors do," and his face contorts with rage, his hand is in the air, the chair flips back and he's kicked the coffee table out from under me. "My baby is dead," he howls as he raises himself to his full height.

"Oh, Daddy." Julie touches his shoulder.

"She was mine," he bellows, and the pictures fly off the walls as he tears past them, and he's gone.

I'm flat on the floor; I check myself. Kenny hugs Julie; Julie hugs Kenny.

"Go get him." Julie pushes my brother. Kenny looks at the floor.

"Go get him," she says again, only now she is pouting her best little-girl pout, the one that she used to make me do shadow puppets on the wall in the dark of the bedroom we shared as children. "Please," she says to me, and the word sounds like a zipper coming undone.

"No way," I say. "You two take care of him."

But in the end it's me my father comes to. He slips out of the dark study as I straighten up the house. Tapping my shoulder, he walks past me into the bedroom he shared with my mother. I follow him. He flicks on the light, and strips the sheets off the bed: the bed they bought at the PX when he was in the Air Force; the bed where I slept between them when I was sick; the bed where passion and heat outstripped reason; the bed that cushioned my father as he sang *Baby It's Cold Outside* and my mother sang *Shine On Harvest Moon*. My father dumps the sheets in the hamper. He walks to the linen closet and pulls out crisp white sheets. Silently, he makes the bed. You could bounce a dime on it. It's dark outside and the hydrangeas under the window glow in the moonlight. I scratch the screen; a woman walking her dog looks at the house and hurries past.

My father's hand is on my shoulder. "I'll sleep in the study," he says.

"Oh no," I say. "Sleep in your own bed."

"When she comes back, I want her to find you."

Tears run down his face.

"She was so proud of you; I think maybe she loved you best. Those two" – he twists his head – "are mine. But you belonged to her." He wipes his face on his sleeve.

I scratch my cheek. Her fragrance is everywhere. I decide to sleep in the bed.

"You always hated me," he says.

"I don't want to hear it," I reply. "Go to Julie. Go to Kenny. Go to hell."

He leaves the room and I hear the door to the study shut. I kick off my sandals and feel the dense mauve carpet between my toes. Above the bed is the watercolor by Annie, a picture of a woman on a rock, her hair wrapped in a thick auburn coil around her head, her eyes the color of water on a sunny day, her body languid, naked and thin except for her pooch of a belly. Her glasses rest on a hump of moss. She holds a baby, pink, naked, and sleeping. This is my mother. This is me.

I take the picture down and wrap it in fluffy white bath towels and I take it out to my car where I put it in the backseat. On my way back in, I pass Kenny and Julie in the family room; they are playing rhyming games.

"Amy," says Julie. "What rhymes with head and begins with 'd'?" Julie laughs so hard she blows a sliver of ice out her mouth. "Dead!"

ISSUE 81

ISSUE 81

She screams hysterically. "Don't you get it? Dead, dead, dead," and then she's rolled up in a ball on the floor while Kenny kicks her with his bare foot and calls her "Hedgehog," because she always does this, rolls up in a ball when she's afraid, and once I rolled her down the hill out back when it snowed, but she stayed curled up tight, and my mother made me go and kiss her.

There's brown sugar and garlic and yeast in the air. I step into the kitchen. The neighbors have been too good. Not only did they bring food, but they brought paper plates, plastic utensils, napkins, Styrofoam cups, plastic cups, and the silver urn from the church. If I turn it on I will have thirty-two cups of coffee. Instead I pack up all the food and put it away. The refrigerator won't shut, so I pull out the orange jello mold and start eating. There's so much food, and then I remember that Saturday night is potluck at church; they probably cancelled and brought all the food here. I look at the wall calendar and see that it was my father's turn to lead the informal discussion group that follows the meal: "Education Priorities in Our Town" and I laugh, because it's just one more attempt on my father's part to garner votes in the fall election. His campaign button, "Re-elect Brian Gordon for School Committee," is stuck next to the list of emergency numbers my mother kept handy.

The jello tastes fabulous, so good that I eat the entire ring including the maraschino cherries. Kenny wanders in and I hand him a spoon. While Julie whimpers in the other room, we dig into the baked beans.

"Think he'll win?" I ask, pointing to the button.

"Yeah," says Kenny, "unless you make a mess of things." I glare at him. Kenny looks at the floor.

"He never hurt me," he says, sipping from his scotch.

"That," I say, "has to taste like sewage after eating baked beans."

Kenny raises his glass to the campaign button. "Cheers," he says. "Cheers," he says again as he clinks the glass against my forehead. "May all your dreams come true."

Suddenly I'm exhausted. Leaving Kenny in the kitchen, I walk to my parents' bedroom and kneel beside the bed. I reach under it and pull out my mother's journal. It's nothing but a spine of fabric; all the pages have been ripped out. I stuff it under the bed and stumble into the master bath where I puked earlier. Someone has cleaned it up, probably one of the neighbors, and there are fresh toothbrushes on the sink. I grab one and brush and brush and brush until my gums bleed. I rinse; I drink; I strip; I pee; I pull out my mother's peach-scented body lotion and rub it all over me. I'm so naked.

I lock the bedroom door. My mother always did when things got wild.

I crawl into bed; I finger my eyes for tears, but they are dry and sandy. My mother's glasses are on the nightstand; I try them on – I had no idea her vision was so bad. With her glasses on, everything is blurry and I find I like it that way. My heart races; I can't breathe; I count to one-hundred and I realize I am having a panic attack. There's a low moaning coming from the walls and then a dog-like howl; it's my father, and he's definitely not sleeping. I hear Kenny knock on the study door; when there's no answer he walks away. I hear Kenny and Julie talking; then Julie marches down the hallway. Her knock is shrill and demanding; it, too, is ignored. I wait until I can breathe again; I pull on my underwear; I pick up my jeans; and I pull out my cell phone and dial my father's business line. It rings in his study; my father picks it up.

"Hello," he says.

"Knock, knock," I say.

"Who's there?"

"Boo," I whisper.

"Boo who?" He catches himself. "Who the hell is this?" he roars.

"Boo hoo," I say. "Now quit your crying and go to sleep."

"Amy," he says slowly. "That's not funny." And he hangs up.

But I hear my mother laughing. It's a howling, snorting, raucous laugh, the one she never could hold in even when she should have, the kind where she held her hands in front of her mouth to stifle the snickers and the shrieks. Once she laughed so hard her fingers shot up her nose and she bloodied it with her carefully manicured nails.

I'm laughing now just thinking of all the times she laughed: the day I bought little snap-its, tapped the tobacco out of several of my father's cigarettes, stuffed the snap-its in, and packed in the rest of the tobacco – my father lit a cigarette and it blew up in his face, and my mother laughed so hard she cried, and then her tears of laughter were replaced by tears of fear when she saw he'd smashed me up against a wall, his hands against my throat (*Brian, please don't kill the girl, she wanted you to quit smoking, it was just a joke, let her go Brian, damn it, let her go*), and the freefall down the wall, the cool cloth on my throat; the way she mimicked my father's religion whenever she saw one of the red, white and blue road signs indicating High Church was nearby (*Look, Dear, an Episcopal Church!*) and my father blushing deeply, caught between her laugher and his pride; the time my father went waterskiiing and his bathing suit dropped around his ankles, Uncle Doug looking back at my father, still upright, and saying, *Tell me again, Joyce, just why do you stay with him?*, and Annie saying, Doug, Darling, Put on your glasses, and we all laughed so hard that we nearly drove the boat up the shore. Oh, I'm laughing now, laughing so hard I'm crying, and then I'm pounding the pillows and tearing the sheets off the bed, right down to the mattress cover, and I huddle in a corner staring at the bed like it's quicksand. If I touch it I will be sucked down by memory. But I silently repeat to myself in my best medical voice, *There's no need to panic*, and I crawl back on the bed and close my eyes.

My cell phone rings.

"Dr. Gordon," I say.

Silence.

"Hello," I say, and now I'm angry.

The phone crackles and my father says, "She was going to leave me." I hear him waving paper. "She wrote it down."

I'm spinning away now, back in time, to the day I graduated from medical school, when my mother turned to me and said, *Now you can really help people*, and I asked her if she would please let me help her, and all she said was, *I'm fine, darling, I'm just fine, you need to move on*, and I said to her, *I can't leave you like this*, and she cried till her face turned pink. She hugged me and whispered, *Promise me you won't make the mistakes I did*. Then she laughed, and I nearly wet myself.

ISSUE 81

Which I have just done. My father is crying so very loudly that I am not sure if I hear him through the cell phone, or through the two thick doors between us. I reach for the box of tissues my mother keeps on the nightstand, but I'm still wearing her glasses and I knock the Kleenex off the nightstand onto the floor. My hand plunges down to the carpet and I reach and I swipe and I come up with what I think are Altoids. My mother loves Mint Altoids and I pop one into my mouth, carpet fuzz and all. It's sour; it's bitter; and I spit it out. I pull off the glasses and stare at the scored pill. It's Trazadone. And there are more of them on the carpet.

"Dad," I say into the cell.

"What is it, Amy?" His voice is sharp.

"Would you like a sleeping pill?" I ask as I finger the Trazadone.

"What?" he asks, and his voice is tinged with fear.

I hang up. I hear him pacing in the study across the hall; he settles on the creaky leather couch; and I'm suddenly touched by silence. I blot the mattress and spread a towel over the damp spot. I remake the bed. I step out of my underwear, kick it into a corner, and step into my jeans. I'm careful with the zipper. I open my mother's top dresser drawer and yank out a soft white t-shirt and pull it over my head.

When I step into the hallway I smell sour milk. My watch reads ten o'clock. I keep walking, past Kenny sleeping on the couch, past Julie curled up in the Laz-Z-Boy, and out to the back deck. My toes curl when I step on the wet grass.

Flipping open my cell phone, I stare at my directory. I call Annie.

Annie's voice is hoarse. "I've been thinking," she says.

"Me, too," I reply. "You tell me first."

"I never was one for heaven. Neither was Joyce."

"And now?" I ask.

"She can't be gone," Annie says staunchly. "A person can't just up and disappear like that."

She can't see me nod, but I do. Annie sighs.

"Wherever she is, she's better off without him. Maybe that's heaven."

There are probably stars in the sky above me, but I refuse to look at them. An owl hoots and I kneel before my mother's butterfly plant. Tiny night moths, attracted by the long reach of the porch light, flutter around the white petals. I blow them away.

"I can't do it, Annie." The words fly out of my mouth. "It's not up to me."

"I suppose it isn't," she says quietly. "It never was. You're a doctor, not an executioner."

"I don't know about that," I muse. Before she can answer, I say good night.

As I walk across the lawn, I think of all my patients, all those I've saved, the one that died – the hundreds I've stitched, poked and prodded, the ears, noses and throats I've peered into, and the training, the promises, the oaths, and quizzes, exams and tests, and all the way back to the pigtails that strained my scalp.

I knew all along I couldn't save my mother. Less than twenty-four hours ago I asked her if she regretted marrying my father.

No regrets, she'd laughed. *That's no way to live.*

ISSUE 81

Elizabeth Thorpe

William Tell

Tell me, William, was it worth it? Do you remember the
long shadows in that square, the way your shoes scuffed on the
cobblestones, the way the multitudes cowered at the perceived
authority of one man? Not you. You walked on by. So many of us
work and work to make a legacy, but when push came to shove,
doing nothing was your spark.

Of course, you had worked. Hours and hours in the woods
with your bow had made you an expert in things of this nature. In
shadows and light, with live prey and imagined, these skills were
your greatest power. Your punishment tested what you did best.

And so you went to another square, another day, this time bound
with your son in tow. Your son was scared, of course he was. You
worried he wouldn't keep still. At the dinner table, in church, and
with his own bow raised, he never kept still. This was a test of his
bravery, maturity, as much as your confidence.

The crowd assembled, the same men and women in somber colors
that had bowed not to the emperor, but to a symbol only, his raised
hat. Did you wish at this point that you had just gone along with
them, knowing it was stupid but doing it anyway? Did you see the
way the sun shone on your boy's hair and regret your stubbornness?
Or did you relish this chance to show your skill, to bite your thumb,
as they used to say, at the powers that were?

The crowd went quiet, and you relied on them, too, not to distract
you. Everything had to be just right, this golden moment: Boy,
arrow, apple, string. Did you pause as you sized up the target? Were
you proud of your boy for standing so perfectly still, still like the
alpine air on that cool autumn day?

Yes. You pulled the string back, you took aim at the apple, just above
the spot where your son shone brightest. You took aim, you let go.

The look on your boy's face when it was over, when he stood flecked simply with apple juice and not with blood. The pride you felt in him, in yourself. The way the crowd cheered.

Later Gessler shook your hand, and it seemed he had decided to make an ally of you. But you remembered those little indignities, the new things the teachers were told to teach, the unfamiliar lessons your son had come home repeating. The new colors on the castle walls and the new taxes at the farmers' market. They called Gessler a military man, but his hand was small and he shook softly. He smiled and asked about the second arrow in your quiver.

If he had been a sporting man, a working man, he would have known. Nobody relies on one arrow alone. Nobody gives himself only one chance. You looked at your son, gave him the old family signal, a nod of the head and he made himself scarce.

"If I had killed my son, so help me God," you said, still grasping Gessler's hand, "the other arrow was for you."

Meena Alexander

Stone Bridge

I went strolling over a cold stone bridge
Beside the Fondamenta degli Incurabili,
A child went ahead with a cat on a leash
An old man traipsed behind, a fedora on his head
The clouds were pink with giggling cherubs.
I saw you at the window of a second floor room
Filled with sickness no one understood,
Your hair brushed back and your elbow taut
Against the wall; the Russian plains hung in a print
Gathering darkness and the snows of Siberia
Boiled on the gas stove, in a simple pot you bought
In Rialto market -- and everywhere the sounds
Of the alphabet grating against fine paper,
The whispers of those forced against their will,
Cold fists of infants on death's hill.

(In Memory of Joseph Brodsky 1940-1996)

ISSUE 82

Meena Alexander

Wind Song

He loaded me into the wind,
As if I were a dragonfly, blowing softly.
Under the slurry wall swallows were mating.
My thighs bruised:
Threads of silt packed into vesicles
A man's arm, a boy's kneecap
A girl's milk tooth, a slip of silk curling.
On Lispenard Street I heard wings beat
A man and a woman in love's flood.
There was something in her eyes, a startled music.
On lowly ground, I knelt
A mute thing, watching a slit of blood
Inside the ruined columbarium
Where lost hairs sing.

ISSUE 82

Arlene Ang

Analysis of Shipwreck

the dead spitting up the future
the dead recurrent in seated positions

heads tilt toward
                the music sheets on the chandelier

attached to the cello
a hand a leg & blue-bottle light from windows

hypothesis: the distribution of the dead
           depends primarily on their correct simulation
    of seaweed & lovemaking

the body is held together
        by an intricate web of skin particulates

discussion points—

    (1) what are the habits of the dead?

    (2) do the dead follow the insomnia of their constituents?

    (3) who are the dead in relation to what is unknown about
        them?

                there's a mother to all this
arranging her red hair over the knife wounds in her body

fish eating the eyes of the dead
recurrent hunger in all physical things that are undead

obiter dictum: when the dead walk
        their left shoulder is slightly higher than the right
    their left elbow is raised

        as if in drink

ISSUE 82

Arlene Ang

Process of Forgetting

When Mrs Kovacs upstairs left the door open,
we brushed it aside as carelessness. After three days,
we began to think of burglary, or worse, maggots
hicupping their way into the body. Mrs Kovacs was absent
from her home at the hour of death.
When they found her in the river, they had to find
someone to identify her. What did we know of our neighbors—
it takes less than ten seconds to forget a dream.

We didn't attend the funeral. That night we lit a candle
and stayed until it burned down a whole forest
of shadows from the walls. Every day we stood in the park,
smoking, until the shade of an oak—shaped like a brain—
slowly filled with gaps as the leaves were snuffed
out by the gathering cold. That's how we knew mortality
is all about forgetting. Even as we observed each other,
the holes were already in place: the skull is structured
around them, the senses merely tenants
who might suddenly choose to go for a swim
in something as absurd as ballet shoes and plastic gloves.

ISSUE 82

Erin Bealmear

False Prophets

You'd think
that the owner
of a cool pair of vintage polka-dot pumps
would be the number one
senorita
in town
bouncing her lips
from girl to boy
but let me fill you in
on a little secret
vintage polka-dot pumps
won't perform miracles
like a tiny leprechaun
or an evil talking doll
they'll just sit there
mocking
your arrogance.

Erin Bealmear

Miss You All Fucking Ready

I know that I don't have any musical talent,
never learned to play an instrument
can't sing without making the dog run,
but if I had written "Nothing Compares to You,"
which I didn't and I'm not claiming that I did,
but if I knew anything about manipulating strings
and had composed that song, it would be about you
and I would sing it with the full force
of my romantic interpretation,
as Prince intended, and think about you
wearing your favorite, old wool beanie
and not imagine my mother being gone
because that would make me even more depressed
than I am right now.

ISSUE 82

Madelyn Camrud

Animal

The night's been one of interrupted sleep,
you, having forgotten

we've moved our bedroom
to main floor.

How ridiculous we've become,
me chasing you

around the house, up, down the stairs,
2 AM, urinal in my hand.

It hasn't been a night for good dreams,
not even a night for shadows

that pick and poke at the person
I don't want to be.

Tonight I am the shadow, picking,
poking at you

from the side of me I don't
even want to know.

Where is the lovemaking so important
fifty years ago? Animal then,

animal now with far different habits,
you claw at me.

I fight back, the urge in my groin
no longer there, you,

the clumsy bear, stronger than I,
the hunter

having forgotten about love,

my best weapon.

ISSUE 82

Alex Dimitrov

An Offering

Outside the dream
I heard your voice and rose.

Sat in the light
between fog and the gate,

waiting to be taken.
Touch me without knowing

how you'll hold on, you said.
Feel my hands move across yours

and into this lightning
we'll quicken, like gods.

ISSUE 82

K.E. Duffin

Patience

Wind snaps the reins of the telephone pole
and giddy-ups the day. Cloud herds brightly
run before the sun as one long cable
dances with its shadow on brick, politely

mimed by a faded partner. Maybe a bell
rope so a noon of robin's egg blue can ring
in the tide? The land on its crumpled side is shelved
down to the sea, a miser of warmth. Spring

is only a dim thought in the mind of December
as plates of waves shift like a lizard's scales.
A robin out of season is a rust-colored sentinel

atop a tree. I half expect it to spin in a gale
like a weather vane, but instead it glides in a blur
to the dead lawn, tut-tutting, "Wait it out. I will."

ISSUE 82

Joe Fletcher

Age of Holes

I push along a dirt road slicing through a cold russet meadow of spiked wheat, littered with wren twitter and the dried corpses of voles. Then a forest where the road bends left.

Then a wooden series of poor shop fronts joining ramshackle buildings. Within: languor, mothballs, clothes dangling from racks like slaughterhouse skins. I move through that tawdry museum. Ladies behind counters watch with indifference, eating orange food from styrofoam containers. My mother sadly picks the flesh of a herring from its bones. Her head is bowed, as if not wanting to reveal to me her shame, her disappointment. Children push parents into their graves.

Then a shelf of photographs of boys at various ages. I am told that all of them are me, that I leave a trail of photographic husks in my wake to be marveled at by a wave of identity pushing through flesh. But those boys are a lie. They are impossibly small and in the landscape of the photographs light passes through them; they cast no shadow. Nor do the photographs themselves. I reach behind one of them and feel something warm and flowing.

The cheap dust on the trinkets. The make-up on the women stinking of berries. The mannequin whose head turns to follow my exit, not before I glimpse the cord that connects it to the wall socket and snort. It calls my name. The door bangs shut behind me.

Outside among the winds. Shredded clouds hurl across a sky wiped smooth and gleaming like tar. Prey to a violent sickness, one that reverses my rivers and wrings me like a stale chamois, I am carried on a pallet by some unknowns. I lay—a field of cramps, of exhausted twitchings, a bad sweat drying to me. I am carried to a house that was also carried there by men with different faces. I swallow some arrowroot powder. Winds shake the earth. Through the window the stars blink. There is little to protect.

ISSUE 82

A violent thud against the house and I leap from the scattering continent of a dream, creep across the darkened floorboards, past the quivering heirlooms. The toppled candle.

Outside at the hem of woods: chilled meadow and wet dirt road beyond. At the corner of the dark house a shattered boat. The gables sag toward the splintered collision site. Oars and crates and tattered, musty canvas collapsed in the prickers. Dark bodies lay strewn in the grass. They are punctured and dripping. I swim among them in my disease. The waves...

Joe Fletcher

Gardenback

When the sun is eaten by night
the soil is blue and dense vehicles
glisten among the elderberry.
A rubber-scented vapor seeps
from charcoal-colored puddles.
Sitting on a flower is a kind of
apostle or apostate, thinking
toward a corner of his mind,
his tongue pressed against the
roof of his mouth, his spine an
arrow pointing down through
the green beetle-traced epidermis,
into the tunneled clay, below the
axe-blade lodged in the skull
of a child, to the face of a diving
god who blows life into the seeds.
The man is Gardenback and his
eyes are flowers and he sits so
still his fingernails grow into his
palms and woodpeckers drill more
holes into his head and bacteria
doze in the languid rivers of his
blood. He sits so still the cameras
forget him. He watches as they
breed in their aluminum hives
and go roving through the stalks,
their probes blinking in yellow fog.
Like everything, he has to move
sometimes. He creeps, low to the
ground, a mute knuckledragger,
through the jimsonweed, across
rain-slick asphalt, past the rusting
pipes and frayed cables. He passes
an amphitheater in which a black-
haired girl eats a butterfly. He passes
a helmeted man speaking hurriedly

into a box of wires mounted to a
post that juts from a riverbank.
Gardenback has a stick of blue chalk.
On the ground he traces labyrinths
which the cameras enter, clicking
and churring, wandering circuitously
while above them lightning loosens
vast black chunks of sky. Atop
another flower he sits to soak in
cloudspray. He is heavier than
twelve suns. There he waits for
no one, forgotten among the bloom.

Joe Fletcher

Larval

A band of hurricane weather splashed through and soaked the
Morning Glory mound humped over a bean trellis. Then a rinsed
blue broke, pierced by sun. I sucked a wedge of pineapple and was
read to by a child who was later taken away in a van driven by a
camera and an orange braid of wires. When everyone had left I took
off my shirt and hung it on a nail in the goat pen. I looked down at
my chest and imagined my heart in the space mother had told me
it was in 1949, in Jefferson City, at a faded picnic table on whose
edge I wiped peanut butter from my palm while watching a yellow
hickory leaf fall at an angle through the shade cast by a freight
trestle. I imagined that heart as a hole which pulsed, and when it no
longer pulsed (as one day it would) it would widen and I and the
world would be sucked through. The air smelled of wet burlap and
tomatoes. On an outdoor table that was really an unplaned pine
plank set on two rickety sawhorses I saw Tom cut into a flounder
that reeked of ocean. He'd sell pieces of it to migrants trudging home
from their shift at the cement factory. Tom made a living that way.
He was in his own cloud and I couldn't lift a hand to him. He opened
his mouth to me and might have said a thing, but a jet roared over and
pummeled our bodies with sound (from the jet a general looked down
at our carnage, flipping a lighter and sipping a glass of cranberry juice
that was handed to him by a black arm that reached through a curtain
slit). I removed my pants and stretched them on the lawn. I walked to
where I could no longer see Tom. I walked away. It's best to be hidden.
Beneath an eave or the sill of a leaf, but I won't tell you where, lest you
find me. Upside down, I fastened myself through my feet and curled
my meek head up. The green storm grew within. It split me open,
enveloping me in a savage green tongue of mucous. It's from in there,
where, very still, I'm calling you.

Caledonia Kearns

For His First Wife
para Adriana

The winter after he left, my mother
took me to Sanibel Island.
Selena was four. Offshore —
         black blurs of dolphins.
Every afternoon I walked
down the long beach, reconciling,
  noticed no one.
     At a sandbar we disturbed pelicans

to collect sand dollars,
wrapped them in tissue to take home
to Brooklyn,
     you were dying in Manhattan.

***

You, beautiful,
fierce and thin, told me once
I was better suited for him.
One night half-asleep he said,
        Que sueñes con los angelitos,
the only time he confused me with you
  in bed.

***

I hear your voice the day you called
"I have gossip!
It's about me."
  Telling the second wife
you were in love again, a woman.

***

Years before, when you came to get the rest of your clothes,
retrieved your cats, from the apartment you'd left
  and I'd moved into
— he found it too rough, being alone —
picking my underwear out of the dryer
you said to him,
"I'd never wear these."
    I never learned why.

***

Months later, in the tub, letting out
the slow water, I reached deep into the clogged drain,
unearthed a wet clot—
                your long black hair
kept coming and coming out
of that drain
                slippery and dark.

ISSUE 82

Nancy Krygowski

All the Words We Want

Still the man's
tongue flaps
between
his lips, though he's clamped
his teeth down
gently.
The tongue is thick
and long
as his short
chin. In
and out.
He can't seem
to hide it,
which makes the tongue

his mind,
exposed.
We learn to keep
fingers out of the body's
holes
(at least in public),
to not say
all the words
we want, to keep
chewed food
hidden.

As my mother's brain
made her
the same stained
shirt, fried chicken
in the cupboard,
the *I don't know*
I don't know I don't know,

ISSUE 82

ISSUE 82

she wanted to show
me more.
After years of wanting
to know, be known,
she showed

the thin clear mucus
running from her nose. *See?*
The soft
white beads
she'd pull from her eyes,
squish and rub.
She'd wipe
those small private clouds
on the rich public
burgundy
of restaurant chairs.
Look, she said. *Look.*
And I did.
Until I looked
away.

Nancy Krygowski

I'm Shouting at The Man

in the left turn lane,
Be nice! Be nice!
as he's calling the woman
in front of him an asshole

for not cutting off the cars
whose right it is to go straight,
who's not shoving her car-heavy way
in the world of Friday afternoon Pittsburgh traffic.

Earlier today my friend and I were talking
about kindness's root—
how behind the kind thing you choose
to do lies a lack of ego,

 a void dark and fertile as organic potting soil,

and we were amazed to find another case
for what's missing
being more important
than what's there--
it seemed so newly scientific.

Asshole? Asshole? Who is really
the asshole? I scream, punching

the *walk* button,
but the left-turn guy's
not paying attention to me
and the alleged asshole woman
isn't paying attention to him
or the cars, her eyes settled

on the big patch of Conservancy flowers
decorating this gray intersection on this gray day:

ISSUE 82

Deep red haze of gladiolas,

orange celosias posing as fire,
electric popcorn of yellow coreopsis,
squat, humble marigolds fencing them in.

The asshole-yelling man pounds
his steering wheel, stuck at the light again.

I doubt he'll catch a whiff
of the marigolds' sweet mustiness,
see the garden's planted beauty—
this act of kindness--

but I do. When the word *walk* shines—
a line of windblown daisies--
quietly I go.

ISSUE 82

Tony Mancus

Bars

Now it's a streetful of them—and it's my head
they're talking in. Take the weather away, take all the nights
where the moon could be a streetlight, could be a bare bulb
with a red fade, while under it tiny cars move around, wavering.

The taste of stale gin, a bottle tipped and *You* they keep saying
You only know so much about one thing—Kenny's Pub, and The Bog,
Danny's, and Jack 's and The Garter—
gaping, they all garble together.

They shut their mouths.
They moth.
They stop up oil, voice, lower back pain.
They stand in the moonlight aflutter like questions.

One word in neon spits its color
out on the street like curdled milk.
It's an invitation. It's temptation, this early hour.

The sounds of a guitar neck, tabletops
dripping, a crowd wet with its gathering breath.
Consistently the cash drawers open. A mirror
splashed with light, with all the happy customers.

A man of hazy outline sits, stilling his hands at a bus stop.

He waits to hear a night bird warble him home. Other
passengers come off the late shift. They file like paper:

A pack of kids with their bodies and voices aching
from a sporting event. A small woman with a creased face

runs her fingers slowly over beads. A mother with her tiny daughter
in tow from the grocer—their plastic bags drag behind.

They can smell his breath from ten feet at least. No one
whispers decently. So he sings:

You know if a bird come home,
you ain't have to worry 'bout them

going off again. They trained
to be still, they trained to sing,

sometime you can train 'em to stop
talking, but that's not a good thing.

The girl's eyes lift up at him, she points a tiny finger.
Her mother swats it back.

I don't know   silence too much

His voice gets crushed by the exhaust
from the bus.

The song he waits for etches itself along the floor,
the sound of a door opening.

The last thing he hears each night
is her cage, its rattle.

Empty lock, empty living-
room. Outside nothing
but bars for miles and miles.

ISSUE 82

Tony Mancus

Big Rock Sinks

The body gone
down. Whatever use it had—

Now, in the dark, the lights play.
One splash. Another.

No parapets or skittering heart shapes. Broken, the water
bandages itself. Strips of light

unwind right through the lines that mark its edge.
White are the notes struck by certain reeds there.

They are never alone. Beneath them,
water laps against everything.

ISSUE 82

Suzanne del Mazo

ISSUE 82

At Four

i fractured my skull

i hardly even felt it
and i was more afraid
of the twin nurses
with stirrup pants
curly hair
and mean upper lips

the nurses call me big
brave girl but
i know it was more
than a busted head
it's practice
to face the hard moments alone
cause my parents are out
of the office

give grown ups
a smile 'cause i know
they need it
feel my own ugliness
in 16 stitches and a huge gauze pad

that is the day
i learn to read pity
understand that no one will touch me
after being broken

Kyle McCord

Galley of the Beloved in Torment

And we are given into the hands of the First Beloved that
the broken lifts might light again. That the slave ship leaves
port. That the mercantile act might again act.
As a replacement. That the gift given might not rest
lightly in a mind's given dust. In the lift called monogamy.
Not break nor give in to fits of epilepsy. Like rain or one left
in rain.

The Beloved to whom we are given offers neither tibia
nor tongue. To replace those we have lost.
Each error, individually, (even the act of the error accessed)
must be taken as a gift, in stride. The lethal act of the
Beloved to I, or I to mosquito, or mosquito to skin cell,
or the lethal act of literacy to slavery, the trade of arms.

The First Beloved preens above the neon grave of the heart.
Scientists soon will unlock the mind. First Beloved, your gifts
of rain, of truck overturned, turned over, returned. Of tongue
unfolded like laundry, humps of sand above breakers.

The sky's cracked heart is lightened and pressed
open to the multitudes. A broken elevator opens
in the mind of the epileptic. And one is given into the hands
of the beloved in fire, and in sickness, and in a great boat where
one rows toward the Beloved, unarmed, dreading, aflame.

ISSUE 82

Erika Meitner

Inconsequential Alchemy

It's predictable summer again, the sun frosted
and glaring like a cheap Home Depot light fixture
when it shines on the garden center rife with
landscaping plants nobody loves but everyone

buys as yard-filler: pachysandra, rhododendron,
euonymus, groundcover along with festive pansies
in black plastic six-packs that die by mid-July.
There's no substitute for the figure of a sunflower

on a hill wilting past its stake, head drooped, body
crucified. The neighbor—the minister's wife—tried
to fill in the barren clay on the ridge our houses share,
but nothing thrives there—not even the guaranteed

grass seed she bought that claims to grow on rock.
But she's out watering anyway, her chemo crew-cut
glinting silver and ambiguous. Last season she offloaded
ziplocks of heirloom tulip bulbs from her freezer,

asked us to put them in our yard since she was too weak
to plant them. We buried them at the requisite depth,
but they never came up; instead, a scourge of Yellow Trefoil
entwined with the lawn. This week she offers me three jars

of home-preserved beets from their congregants.
Everyone must be praying for her, so that even
those beets glow fuchsia on our counter,
countering the TV's ready-made alchemy.

The local news is a strip-mall fire: remains of an
irreplaceable 1950's tricycle from the charred bike shop
that had been in the family for years. The form was
recognizable, but the vehicle was literally a shadow

of itself, isometric charcoal, long and difficult.
There are disruptions, and there are disruptions.
The news is always brought to us by Oakey's Funeral Home
& Crematory, and then on Sundays paid programming follows:

Millennialist news that trumpets the New World Order.
Prophecies of the ages converging. Specific details
of the return, the eternal state of both the saved
and the lost. These exciting last days in which we live.

Dante Micheaux

Vis-à-vis de Rien

Chaos is a hanging thread—*minor*
but out of place, insignificant in infinity,
says the keeper of Shangri-la.

On the corner of Trinity and Church,
a small girl offers me the sun for a nickel
and I'd gladly take control of the solar system

but do not have a nickel.
The sun, with its watery-urine yellow
and burning stench, is bitter; its rays are loud.

Give me the moon, free and great pacifist—
a showstopper when it wants to be.
Even Clotho spun at its pace.

Fear the insignificant, says the
keeper of Shangri-la. *Because there is one,
there are many.*

Consider the infauna
that will someday rule the world,
their benthic plots.

Life is? *Six eggs in one basket,
half dozen in the other.* It's the soft bottom
of pride that gets in the way.

That which surrounds has its own trickery.
Don't be fooled by the butterfly;
it would kill if only its mouth were bigger.

ISSUE 82

Zachary Pace

Pastoral

Observation is all we're allowed
aboveground, where interminable
durations govern eruption—each
dormant seed an eventual
otherworldly gift intended
to halt your burgeoning heart—
particularly this bundle of violet
orchids I'm holding in the audience,
your performance of uncontainable
viscera & poise—my organs pause
when our eyes lock—a gesture laden
with Possibility, which I've already
diminished by repeating aloud.

ISSUE 82

Zachary Pace

Werewolf

Though he is totally toothsome, little
remains of my old bestial appetite:
reduced to this dog yapping
at the wrong backdoor.

Across unmarked property
lines we sniff from one haunch
to the next. What fray!

I keep a needle in my sheepskin
girdle should someone find the sole

gold thread in me & snip it.

Allison Power

12.04.09
from December Poems

The day's almost over and I've put on
my last clean shirt. Can't leave the apartment
till I write a poem. Adam calls to tell me
he met Jane Freilicher and aren't I jealous?
I just want to write a fucking poem.
But he goes on about JA and Shapiro
and those collages: "Remember what your
analyst said? People don't know what to do
with those pieces of paper." Later I meet
Adam at MOMA for a showing of *The Last
Clean Shirt* and apparently Alfred Leslie is there
but I'm hungry and Adam's snoring and
there are too many speakers and not enough
film. We cross Fifth Ave singing *Bad Romance.*
I go to a birthday party and drink too much
Prosecco and when I get home I pass out
with the lights on and the curtains open
and I didn't even write a goddamn word.

Matt Schumacher

Drinking Song

The Miraculous Alcoholics think
Boozed-up snobs and yuppie fops
Less festive party guests than cops.
Cops, at least, shout and start, wave guns,
Flail frantic at Bacchanalian antics.
Such bourgeois duds, such punks
Smug as fuck, could put them in a slump.
Champagne be damned. Slammed Pabst
Spiked by 151. Blurred vision forcefed Thunderbird
Until bedspins send them churning to the head.
Better yet, send them on beer runs to bad neighborhoods.
Tap the last keg, that glistening beast of foam,
Oceans of gushing suds, tidal pint after pint--
That rainstorm in their throats, sloshing its way home.

ISSUE 82

Matt Schumacher

The Miraculous Alcoholics Drink the Great Lakes

The miraculous alcoholics are tipsy from Oconomowoc to
    Poughkeepsie,
for every heave of the sea, from boom to lee, is lost
    on these gloating stowaways,
these shot-to-hell sailors, soaked with dripping chasers.
Look at their drinks swirling like nautilus shells.
Their ferries merrily trolling the great lakes of bar and tavern,
slaking thirsts as multifarious as flathead catfish whiskers.
Most slowly they drink, the way toothless spoonbills
scoop plankton, but when they capture their second wind,
their chartered steamboats and drunk captain startle the harbor.
When the miraculous alcoholics deem to put on their Captain Nemo
    routine,
the bartender's submerged as a drunken Jules Verne.
He leaves the bar open as Michigan, Superior, Huron, and Erie.

Britton Shurley

In the Story Concerning the Ice Storm

In the story concerning the ice storm
the trees are dripping crystal,

& the wind snaps their branches
like glass. There are ink-black birds

pecking pinholes in the puddles,
& an early, purple crocus

huddles frozen in its blossom.
The evening sun sets its pink on the yard

while a swollen, brown-mouthed river
waits patiently to rise.

ISSUE 82

Sean Singer

Elvin Jones Jazz Machine

Elvin, a marvel in a vice, vying.
Reveal each torsion in a vial of gold and hyposulphite.

An iron shadow and a sterling dome.
On the doorstep its lit fuse and wires.

Brushed plantation crimson; torpid promenade.
The saxophone yellows under the petrol metropolis—

The piano like peeled peaches—
The drums torture us with their torture.

I've finally decided jazz has a pink side.
It enlarges the sincerity of the room.

ISSUE 82

Sean Singer

Love Song

Sizzle and calibrate: white curtains hanging heavy –
a pasteboard match and the purple rim of mist:

illusions of silver are all gone, sugar and a spouted jar.
What has come to pass again, what they done me wrong.

There is another city and beyond the glass floorboard:
this pelagic mollusk swallows arrowworms and jellies.

Cluster here. . .a cardboard cello and bone castanets.
What is scattered gathers in a fork on the grooved road.

There's a sandcastle mixed with sea salt and a wooly ear.
I'm going to burn this moat and wring the towel on your neck.

ISSUE 82

Ed Skoog

Big Chief Carpetland

Do they mean magic, the flying carpet
speeding to our other lives?

They have their Indians confused, then,
India confused with Persia, reality with story,

also my problem, as I drift summer's
green fantasias, documenting.

I need what the late sun is alert to,
not a heavily pentametered anguish

drawing sense from station to station,
but tender proof that flight is real,

and my hand holds the line that chiefs
the soaring fabric, and keeps me on it.

ISSUE 82

Ed Skoog

Go

Motto of the precipice, vast periphery,
more go than gone, there is no center only

the lover on the couch saying don't go,
that old game. Tack a go sign on me too.

Preference is made for going away,
raised hand from a pale king who shakes

the midnight pillbox calypso, so I say no
to gong-song of drip faucet nobody fixes.

The building is tired of purpose and sags.
I am not Go. "Go" call itself scatter like groan,

ghost alias drifting aria through dahlia dust
gods would play in, were there gods or ghosts.

ISSUE 82

Ed Skoog

Whole Personal Melons

My dear, entire, and here hear
my entreaty for your humble entrée

true, already on display for abusers
to test for aisle ripeness, for *thunk,*

still to me undisputed your melonry
whole and personal I wish preferred

and tendered, *tendres boutons,* untitled.
For I would be entitled to their pursuit,

apertured perturbers, traffodil lunge,
agitated caroming in antique anorak, O

tropic encirclements, I beg you,
hear me adore, heave close, and divide.

Joannie Kervran Strangeland

When It Is Blue

First she found a lump no bigger than a pea
or a preposition—a small verb: to be.

The danger lies in conjugation
and the tenses—

is, are, would, could.
Will. She kept the will, a world.

I will, we will.
A synonym for tomorrow.

The shape of here is loss,
or a trade—flesh for life.

Her new body: built now for water—
sleek, streamlined—

a seal or a porpoise
(think of dolphins around the bow

as a schooner races along the coast
and the sails are full).

The wind makes a web on the water.
The body makes a plot.

The pain makes her tired. When
it is blue, the sky makes her sharp.

ISSUE 82

T.M. de Vos

The Pirate Father

Any port, he said,
not one where he would be loved,
or well-received.

In the legend, the stuck man
grows into his ship, the models he worked
collapsed in their bottles, masts clean
as whitefish bones.

It is lightless; he filters the tobacco-sluice
of his own swallowed water.
Around him, his boat turns to paper;
his signatures in his books
leak out like cuttle ink.
The decks he mopped are shored now,
their circuits snuffed. He walked on insulators
over those floors, a live grid.

His son comes for him:
there are polyps on his face,
he will not come to bed.
The weeds on his knees
are a soft afghan; his drowned dog,
diamond-eyed, whines for his hand.
Caws from land scramble, half arrive.

Here, only the ear-percussion of water
and the burped words, *Do not choose me.*

ISSUE 82

Jason Zuzga

Bog Man

Flowers pull from mouth, tongue to tulip,
back of head thrust back:
there is no empathy tool fashioned
to rub a tell from your tummy.

The peat shovel slides right down
through your leathered arms held
horizontal to your sunken standing.
More peat cubes to burn stack
by trucks fueled behind homes.

A pink stick exclaims your site.
Disarmed body extracted
with brushes and tiny steel tools.
Your mane gathered tightly to a ponytail.
Not now, but then, what you did.

Your orange throat is still if
pursed open. The frayed skin discloses
a stone blade's degree of serration.
Eyelids wrinkled in what and shut
puddles of dark matter. They
contrast with your glamorous eyebrows,
their delicate liquid swirl intact
unlike your thighs, torn loose to bone.

Your oblonged skull bears
your whole face free to now
travel down this then that fast route.
Not in your now, to stop at a rest stop.
Not in your now but then we shall face you,
a we that wills not us.

Jason Zuzga

Thrift Shop

I can put an "it" into this and a "was."
I could put you through "this."
Or is "this" just a rehash of the same old plot and
any dawn's dumb tint, any discount trick to make a sale.
Wait and see with me anyway what might find us
sewn behind into our one spam tin of time.
We can still leave here with a bag of what looms.
If two locked male buck can't detach from fight
they will starve, become something else after their bodies balloon.
We flesh things through, we can work things out.
But you can't sound, you can't see the stop watch
alarm hand meshing our live flesh, sloppy seconds
Zipping the hole back before us like singers sewing fast.
Dress up but don't wait for me. I'm already over there
Waiting for you to shut up, I mean, keep talking
as the prices continue to fall.

ISSUE 82

The Woods

I have always been afraid.

In my childhood bedroom, streetlight against sycamore trees created frightening shadows on my walls: men, I imagined, breaking into our home, creeping soundlessly. Huddled under heavy blankets and bedspread, I waited for the creak of a loose floorboard, sounds of shattering glass, gunshots. These were not reasonable fears. We lived in a safe town. Thirty-five years now the doors of my parents' house have been unlocked. But my Catholic school days bloomed with images of Christ bleeding out on the cross; and at night, my sleep was shattered by the swelling fury of a drunk father. On every floor the cabinets shook—pills clamoring, china rattling. In the basin of my small mind, fear rose. I couldn't watch scary movies. I was afraid of pitch darkness and short heights, like ladders and spiral staircases. Terrified of crossing sexual borders, I lost my teenage boyfriends to more willing girls, and carried that fear with me in an already overflowing pocket.

Most of all, though, I was afraid of people disappearing. When Matt died, his sister Jenny and I were on our way into sixth grade, our lives filled with the buzz of summer locusts and the wistful crooning of Donny and Marie. One hot Fourth of July afternoon, long before the scheduled fireworks, Matt lay down in the grass forever. Blood vessels exploded in his brain. Of all the fears I have, I know that Jenny shares this one: that the ones we love will suddenly and inexplicably leave us.

It is Jenny who I hike with the summer I move back home, a small New Jersey town two miles long. We are almost thirty; we have been friends since we were four. We drive out of town, held in the comforts of air conditioning and conversation, passing indistinguishable strip malls, blank-faced suburbs, and glittering Jersey diners until the roadside buildings thin and the pitch pine trees rise. We talk about the lives we've led while we've been apart. Jenny is engaged to Lou. I have met him once. Lou is raven-haired, olive skinned, with a gentle smile that easily erupts into mischief. He is kind and dependable, and when he met a woman full of fear and loss, he responded with a patient steadfastness. Jenny is happy. The reasonable side of me declares that I am happy for her. But beneath the grid of my smile, I think, *How can she marry a stranger?*

Of course, I'm afraid to say such a thing out loud.

Jenny follows the signs to Batsto Village. Here, we will intercept a piece of the 49-mile Batona Trail. It is a Saturday in August, windless. A shelf of humidity hangs in the air. The Batona Trail snakes through New Jersey's Pine Barrens, the most hidden expanse of wilderness on the Eastern seaboard. Here, rumors of the Piney people abound: tales of incest, of children spawned by the devil, of drunken and violent misconduct in the woods. I was nine years old when I heard nothing about the passing of the Pinelands Protection Act, but this piece of legislation would save the landscape while Jenny and I glued dioramas of the Vietnam War, while we slipped on our first unnecessary bras, while we snuck into the woods and applied mascara before heading inside to homeroom. It would take us twenty years to get here, to this moment, and by this time, we thought we could survive anything.

Jenny stops at one of the rare back road traffic lights. There, we see a wild looking man, thickly bearded, with darting eyes and filthy clothes. He is crossing the road at a dangerous place, standing right next to the road sign reading ANCORA. We don't know anything specific about Ancora—we have never been there—but we remember that when we misbehaved in high school Latin class, Mr. Tremolo would look down his long Roman nose and shake a knuckled finger at us. *Behave,* he would say, *or I'll send you to Ancora.* We gathered that Ancora was the sire of a jail, an insane asylum—or something worse.

"He's escaped," I say, waving to the man.

"*Semper ubi sub ubi.*" Jenny watches him in the rearview mirror until the road curves and he disappears from sight.

At Batsto Village, a weather-beaten trail map tells us that these flat lands will offer no hardships. True enough. We hike easily through the sandy soils, through strands of fire resistant pitch pine grounded by a thick understory of wild huckleberry, dangleberry, blueberry. We pop sweet highbush blueberries into our mouths, giggling like girls. We slap at flies. We are mildly surprised that no one else is on the trail. We are new to this place, and there is much we don't know. We don't know that small ticks carrying Lyme disease are now leaping from blades of grass to legs, crawling to our warm, dark places to feed. The yellowthroat warblers, pine snakes, and white tail deer have fled at the sound of our crunching footsteps. We don't realize that the sandy soil beneath our feet is all there is, as hostile a growing environment as there is, arid and acidic. When rainwater falls on this sandy soil, the water filters through to a subterranean aquifer beneath us, a body of water equivalent to a lake 75 feet deep and one thousand square miles in area. We walk and walk across this shaky ground, oblivious to everything but the chattering of each other's voices.

When I remember this day, I see the cloudless sky and sharp pine trees. I see two young women trying to reclaim a friendship, passing an icy bottle of water back and forth, wiping sweat on the shoulders of their t-shirts. But from the dark thicket, a gray fox spies. A turkey vulture circles, waiting to strike. A shadow passes and disappears over those poor, unsuspecting girls who dare to cross this sandy raft, this trembling sea.

Three years pass and the sign ANCORA is now covered with tangled greenbrier. I am a new teacher with a superficial grasp of history and ecology, arriving at the ghost town of Batsto Village on a glaring yellow school bus with fourteen students. I ask them if they think their town could have all the businesses and people disappear, like here at Batsto. This was once a vibrant place where workers populated the land and dredged the pond for iron bog iron to make cannonballs for the Revolutionary War. They built furnaces, leveled trees, and prepared charcoal to fuel the furnaces. Trees fell and the sky opened up. Each furnace's blazing fires swallowed a thousand acres of woodland each year. Then, Pittsburgh's iron industry was born, and the few remaining trees believed they had been spared. Not so. The lovely sandy soil made fine glass, and the forests fell for fuel again. When the last tree was cleared, the glassmaking industry collapsed, and I suppose the tired workers walked west, to Philadelphia.

Remarkably, my students listen, studying Batsto Village's only remaining buildings: the mansion, the sawmill, the gristmill. The trees have come back: Virginia and pitch pine, scarlet and post oak, sassafras and swamp azalea. After the collapse of the iron and glass industry, I tell them, wealthy Pennsylvania businessman Joseph Wharton arrived. He purchased Batsto Village and the surrounding land with a sly venture: his wanted to pipe the pure water submerged under the Pine Barrens across New Jersey and into Pennsylvania for *them* to drink. Luckily his plan failed, and his 109,000 acres of disappointment—now the Wharton Forest—is where we stand now.

Beyond the village is the Nature Center, filled with the labors of an energetic taxidermist. A scraggly beaver is about to sink its huge brown teeth into a piece of wood. There are turkey vultures and egrets, killed and stuffed back to life. Michele, a student who has one blue glass eye, stares into the eyes of an owl. She matches the owl moment by moment—a contest she just might win. Beyond us, a square passage is cut through the wall so visitors might speak to the naturalist in his office; but Gilbert Mika is nowhere to be found. In Mika's office, you can see a litter of paper everywhere, blanketing the desk and chairs and floors. A poster hangs on the wall, dogeared: KEEP YOUR PLACE FIRE SAFE. Well-worn books tilt along shelves; a tray of slides is perched precariously on an orange Uncle Ben's box. On top of a file cabinet, there is a murder in progress: a stuffed owl has a mouse in its talons. Cobwebs connect the owl's wings to the flowered blue wallpaper, and I feel strangely sorry for these creatures: the owl, salivating over its furry meal, is in eternal anticipation; the mouse, forever dangling, is trapped in its terror forever.

The students murmur and point, and I remember Jenny and I, young like them, our heads bent in whispered secrets. All those years ago, we sat in Catholic school classrooms beneath portraits of haloed Jesus and Mary. Like me, she woke to the nighttime thunder of a drunk father and desperate mother. Shattered little girls, we woke on weekends, roller-skated through the empty schoolyard, and somehow emerged from our young lives whole. I like to think that we took each other from the stillness of cobweb and capture into the fearless surge of the world.

Outside the Nature Center, the bright sunlight makes me blink. Clouds skate across the sky. Michele and I follow the others to the dim nature trail, bordered by wild rice on Batsto Lake. We hear distant buzz of a circular saw. As we hike to higher ground, we pass cedar stands and murky water, shaded from sunlight by white oaks and sugar maples. Greenbrier vines tangle around the scaled armor of pitch pines. I tell my students you can dig a half mile deep here and not hit bedrock.

When we reach the Batona Trail, I recognize pink hashes painted on trees marking the trail where Jenny and I hiked three years ago, when she was newly engaged. The trail is still thick, overgrown. I am telling my students about prescribed burns in this forest. We reach a section of the trail where the greenbrier drapes across the blueberry and heather underbrush, then climbs the tall oaks, the sturdy pines, the sassafras with its lovely leaves. Above us, oak leaves flutter like confetti against the sky. A match dropped here would smolder and rise, flames licking the length of the vines, climbing to the treetops. The thought of such a wildfire? Terrifying.

I take my students further into the woods, to the park service's most recent controlled burn. Here, the light is brighter; there are no oak trees, no climbing vines. Nothing to stand in the sun's way. The understory grows in threaded shrubs; only fire-resistant pitch pines stand tall. At the base of the pine trees there are rings of charred black—evidence of the park service's care and intention. A lit match dropped here? The gentle fire would rise to waist level maybe, feebly fueled by the weak kindling of recent grasses and shrubs. The brown pine needles would burn briefly and die.

Controlled burns prevent huge disasters, promote fire-resistant pitch pine succession, enhance the complexity of the acidic soil.

Michele recommends a controlled burn of Gilbert Mika's office. Then, she turns her still blue eye to me. "Where would you go if you were trapped in a wildfire?"

The air is hot; the breeze has faltered. Michele swats a fly. There is a story of a man who dug himself into the earth, I tell her, covered himself with the bark of the pitch pine, and prayed as a sky-high wall of wildfire passed over him. He survived.

I'm not sure if this story is true.

Michele and I walk together, the same trail I hiked with Jenny three years ago. I have not seen her much lately. She has settled into marriage with Lou, adopted his fierce conservative views. Her days are spent with a newborn daughter and endless, enthusiastic in-laws. I stop walking. I look up to the bright sky and blink away the suffocation of a sudden longing. I cannot look down. My students slow and wait. They think I see something in the air.

I don't know why I start. I begin to tell them the story of the day I hiked here with Jenny.

We pass the sign for ANCORA.

We drive past the man on the roadside, filthy and fearful.

We are walking on the Batona Trail that hot August day, slapping at flies. I carry Jenny's cell phone in my waist pack, along with an apple and a bottle of water. We see no one. The trail is empty.

"What would you do if that man showed up here?" I ask Jenny.

I am joking, of course.

Would he chase us?

Jenny smiles.

Would he catch us?

Kill us?

Each step, each joke becomes heavier.

"Seriously," I say, "what would we do if a man—dangerous—showed up?"

"Does he have a gun?" asks Jenny.

"Yes."

We are quiet, our steps crunching in the sand. We imagine the same scene. A man steps out from the thick of lambkill, wild and dangerous. He holds a gun. The cell phone, zipped securely in my waist pack, would be no help.

"We run," Jenny decides.

Easy for her to say. Jenny has always been agile, quick, a Division I athlete. I imagine her darting away, me lumbering behind, a dead woman.

We stop walking.

"Do we split up or stay together?" I ask.

We look at one another. We agree.

We split up.

Our chances are better that way. One of us will survive.

"Then what?" I say.

"We run for help."

We look around. The forest is thick, the wild understory dimming any escape route. We are in an unfamiliar place. Once off the trail, a person could be lost in these woods forever.

Now we have scared ourselves.

"This place is creepy," I say. I look at the empty, wide open trail in front of us, behind us. "I've never hiked on a Saturday—"

"In the summer," Jenny adds, understanding my point immediately.

"Where *is* everyone?"

*   *   *

My students and I near the end of the trail, and through the trees we can see picnic benches, a parking lot, the park office.

"What happened?" Michele asks. "Did you see the wild man?"

"We scared ourselves silly," I say. "We ran back to Jenny's car and drove away."

We are disappointed by my story. No blood, no gore. No crazed escapee chasing two innocent girls.

I don't tell my students about my fears. I worry that my father will pick up a drink after 22 years of sobriety. I worry I will be attacked when I am alone, and that I will be too weak to save myself. My mother worries that I will fall asleep during a nighttime drive— that's how her father died.

ISSUE 82

Here, in the shelter of pine trees, hours can pass without hearing the trill of a warbler, the touch of cool wind, or the sight of another human face. It's easy to disappear. In our big wooded world, no one speaks about broken hearts between best friends, the most submerged of sorrows.

Ahead, Jon and Vijay carry a green cooler over to the grass. Lunchtime.

I walk slower, not wanting to leave these woods.

No dangerous stranger crossed our path. No man with a gun. I have feared the wrong thing. Jenny and I never asked, *Do we split up or stay together?* One of us darted off—that was the plan, right?— legs pumping through the tumble of blueberry and lambkill, while the other lay waiting, fearful and faithless on a bed of pine needles, waiting for the wall of flames to pass.

Clouds appear and disappear. My wounds have made me stupid. I blink away the sun and wish with all my might for something I cannot speak. This afternoon's glare will surely soften, I tell myself. But I'm afraid it won't.

ISSUE 82

Emily Fridlund

Lake Arcturus Lodge

It wasn't my husband that wanted the bear, it was me. Erich
has always been so generous, so optimistic about people. When
we opened for business, the lodge was empty as a lost castle, but
he just said, "People will come when they do." He talked like this
sometimes, which is one of the reasons I fell in love with him. He
sounded like he'd given the world and its problems a good once over
and made up his mind without regrets. I admired his peace, because
I was always getting trapped in thinking one way about a thing and
then the exact opposite. For instance, when we came up in '23 to
this forsaken woods, I felt punished, first, then blessed. The snow,
especially, was a blankness I craved, not a blotting out, but a nursery
for us. That first winter we were here we were born. I can't tell you
how beautiful it was. We saw trees grow wooly as beasts with snow.
Let me tell you what else: we saw a moose with a beard of ice drop
through the lake's crust and disappear altogether.

Funny, I don't remember exactly what Erich looked like then —
though that was only a few years back, no time at all. I can remember
what I did to him, but not what I saw. I held the tea kettle with a
damp cloth when I filled his cup. Sometimes, I broke ice from his
moustache so he could talk, tiny corkscrews like claws, which melted
in my fingers. He had a moustache, that much I know, though he
was barely twenty — a boy still! — and now I remember what struck
me then: his eyes were two different sizes. I used to wonder if he
held one eye open wider than the other, if it was a matter of muscle
rather than structure. I still don't know. My husband was good at
everything else, so what did I care if he wasn't good *looking?* He'd
learned English in two years flat, the way other people learn cards or
knitting. You could hear his determination in the way he talked, how
poised he was in everything. From the beginning he spoke in a way
that made me ashamed to have spoken English all my life. He was
elegant as a diplomat, but more sincere.

Of course, he has always been good with his hands as well. He
built this place with a crew of three in just two summers. During
that time, I stayed in Duluth and scrounged up nice linens. Also
carpets, couches, drapes. The third summer he put on a blue suit and

ISSUE 82

I put on silk stockings and a hat, and we sat down to wait for guests in the lobby. I remember how miserably we chatted through those hours, our legs neatly crossed, our fingernails white. We had never courted properly (we met as teenagers, ate chicken, got married), but those first days at the lodge had all the ceremony and panic of a long date. Was there no future at all? we wondered. No guests or children to verify our efforts at contentment? We said many foolish things in our wish to escape such awkward circumstances. We talked of Chiang Kai-shek, of butterfly migrations, of stew.

"There's something in your hair," I told him one lonely afternoon.

He lifted his hand cautiously.

"Here," I said, rising. But I was lying, and he was already at the mirror in the hallway, turning his head. I remember his bow tie was crooked and looked something like a badly plucked flower. I couldn't help smiling at him. Even then, I was always getting kindness and cruelty confused, so I can't be exactly sure why his dishevelment made me so happy.

We had to coax our first guests to us. The locals were suspicious — you know how logging people are — so territorial and shifty. They couldn't understand why we made such a show of everything, why we carted in candelabras and pickles. I admit we didn't know why we did these things either. After mamma's inheritance was gone, we spent a great deal of time washing things down, fluffing pillows, pressing napkins. We made an earnest effort to be as grand as possible. Can you imagine? We had ideas about hotels from Davenport and Redwing; we expected weekenders, not hunters and fishermen. But who rides the train to Duluth, then takes a steamer to Marais or a pontoon plane to Ely for the *weekend?* The longer the lodge sat empty, the harder we tried, until everything started seeming like an instance of decoration. In those first days, I floated lupine petals in the water basins, arranged butterscotches in bowls. I knew cosmos would die, but I planted them anyway, in a daze of hopeless opulence and inevitable waste.

We didn't know the first thing about lake country. I grew up on cobbled streets, with sidewalks and gas lamps; my husband had escaped as a teenager from a nail factory in Bremen. I admit I thought of our lake primarily as transportation to town and scenery through our windows. I was bewildered to see Erich so charmed by it. I remember watching him sink an arm into the depths, splash up a bit of water into his mouth, flick his face dry. He took the boat out at night and rowed to the logging camp on the far side of the lake, where the rocks were as wide as automobiles. He learned to trap from the logging people there, who kept him some nights. He learned to bring down a pine without fuss and float it across the waves, slim ship bound for furniture.

The lake yielded up our tables and chairs in this way, and other surprises too. That first summer after we opened we found a floating broom, a fox pup under our canoe, and Noah Williams. Noah was our first real guest, and he just capsized his boat during a storm, so we didn't charge him anything. We were nervous as new mothers around him. During the night, we argued over whether we should leave a lantern burning in the hallway for him, whether we should wake him for breakfast or let him sleep. Noah was a good sport, a middle-aged fisherman with a cabin out west, and we convinced him to stay a few nights after the storm dissipated into occasional columns of rain. With his pale blue eyes and black eyebrows, Noah had a shambling, uneasy, angelic look about him. He said his mother had died in an avalanche in the Rocky Mountains. After a few glasses of Canadian gin, he confessed he'd clawed his way out of the snow and left her buried beneath him. He kept saying, "I just wanted to survive, but now I can't do nothing. I'm a napkin. I'm rust."

We kept him for three nights. We gave him pies and towels, a boat ride to the falls, a kite. By the time he left, we were disconsolate and proud. We felt as if the very best of ourselves was rowing off towards Canada, the only useful thing we'd ever done.

Goldie came next, and she only came because I asked her. I sent her a simple but pleading letter, and she arrived at the logging camp across the lake with two trunks, a kitten in a cage, and a hammock from Mexico. The hammock was a gift for our porch. Goldie was my second cousin, tall and frizzy-haired, unmarried. The first thing she said to us was: "I'm so, so sorry!" She gripped my arm, almost painfully, explaining she was late, she was unkempt, she was tired. I told her "Nonsense!" but in truth her apologies were charming, inventive, almost intimate, like confessions. When I told her to stop apologizing, she apologized — warmly, enthusiastically — for that.

She settled into one of the rooms on the second floor, shyly, hanging her frocks on the bedpost, and stayed for a long time. When her kitten left stools like crusty larva behind the drapes, Erich swept them discreetly into a basket. I saw him do this, so I knew how much Goldie meant to him. I never told him that I asked her to come.

My husband wanted babies and I gave him guests instead. Should I be ashamed? By the time the lodge opened, we'd been together five years. I was the only married woman I knew without children. We didn't sleep well at night there were mosquitoes, heat waves, other lonelinesses but it wasn't that we didn't, as they say, *try.* I should revise that a bit. I had nightmares in which I was sick, blistering with tumors, malignant as death: I was pregnant in every one. I woke up with my hands on my breasts, my arms crossed, my own fingers harassing my nipples like mouths. In my dreams, I lived in a pit of children. Their hands were the same size and texture as their gums, as their earlobes and faces. Everything could gnaw in a hideous, painless way without teeth.

I won't pretend I wasn't chastened and relieved to wake up empty, myself. Organized. I really thought I might be able to avoid that kind of grave forever, if I tried. Erich grew melancholy after a time, but I grew industrious. I made up for the vacant house by filling it with people.

"Her name is Sugar," Goldie said of the kitten one night. I remember this specifically. We were feeding Goldie pike caught two lakes over, the gin Noah left us, and imported jelly. The kitten was on her lap, humming unremittingly. Goldie made a face, then put her hand on my husband's arm when he stooped to retrieve her plate. "Isn't that terrible? Isn't that just the first thing you'd think of?"

I saw him sit down and put his head in his hand, as if thinking the matter over very seriously. Since Goldie had arrived, I'd seen something new in him, a tolerance and almost gift for inanity. It was like hearing him speak in German, seeing this ease with something so alien to me. I knew him only as hard-minded and grave; with her, he lifted his eyebrows. He grinned in a way that parted his moustache.

"Will the cat understand his name? Or is this name for you?"

"It's how I feel about him, I guess." She took a curl from her head and placed it absent-mindedly in her ear. "He's stupid, of course. He won't know Bob from Pumpkin."

"Stupid's a good name."

"Stupid?" Goldie asked. She lifted the cat up under the armpits and stuck out her tongue at it.

Erich was beaming. I was impressed by his ease with her and, at the same time, irritated. He grew up in a German factory town, worked like an Indian to stay alive during the war, snuck away on a boat when he was sixteen. He always seemed to me like a wizened old man under his young skin, his soul worn to the point of serenity. Who was I to forbid him whimsy?

Later that week, I told Goldie my husband needed help in the garden, and out she went, apologizing as she left for not helping sooner. I was half in love with Goldie myself for years, so I knew what it meant to be around her. She was five years younger than me and so thin she was always bent forwards or backwards at the waist, as if unable to fully support the upper half of her body. She believed she was ugly, which made her lovelier than she was. Even I liked to watch her in humid weather, pulling hair from her ear in a perfect coil, like the tendril of a newborn plant. She was superficial, an oddball with nice teeth, but we couldn't get enough of her. We gave her meals we couldn't afford, grew severe and nasty to each other in our guilt, came from our quarrels clean, as if they were a form of hygiene.

Goldie stayed so long, we went through all the pickles and scented soap in the pantry. With these amenities gone, we spent days on the dock, shoeless, Goldie and I playing cards, Erich reading about fishing lures in out-of-date magazines. It felt a little like I imagined university might feel if we'd gone, all that indolence and talk, all that lazy thinking. In July, we watched a hornet hive form high in a tree, bulbous and sound as a football. In August, the lake started to smell and dry up a little, leaving strangely punctured fish on the shoreline. When the muskrats came for the fish, I started to worry that Goldie had misunderstood my invitation. She had been with us for almost five weeks; she was kind, but not rich, and Erich knew it.

One morning around that time, he woke up and put on old trousers instead of his suit. I could only guess he'd picked up part-time work across the lake, chasing or climbing, whatever grunt jobs they gave foreigners. I watched him work a soft leather belt through the loops, cinch it without looking down in resignation. He was just about to leave the room, when I bolted up and yelled, "Wait!" He turned around.

"Why don't we talk?"

"Sure," he said.

"We don't have to have everything work out," I told him. But you know how people say things to convince themselves, how every word is part lie because it crosses out and denies one quadrant of truth. Of course everything had to work out.

"It *won't*," he assured me, coming back, putting his hand on my forehead. Forgiven as I felt, I disliked how he needed so little from me.

I started to cry. One half of my body was under sheets. The other half, like a figure on the prow of a ship, arched mutantly towards him. What was wrong with me? I kissed him, resentfully. I held my lips over my teeth and bit him until he came back for me. I *wanted* him to wear trousers he was a clown in his suit, an imbecile but I didn't want *him* to want to, you know? We were far too young to stop pretending.

Later that day, I went into town and telephoned Grace Wilson, an old Chicago acquaintance who (I knew from rumors) had married well. I made her agree to come to the lodge by reminding her that she owed me. In high school, I'd covered for her when she accepted marriage proposals from two boys at once and needed an excuse for one when she saw the other. It was a sacrifice of my dignity to do this, but Goldie wasn't going to pay our bills, and we had hornets in the pantry. My mother's good silver was tarnishing, and I couldn't get myself to polish anymore what no one used.

The Wilsons flew in from Duluth on a chartered float plane. The plane sent waves knocking against the shore, drenching the steely rocks, overturning Erich's cedar rib canoe. When Grace stepped out onto our dock, I saw she was wearing white gloves and a funny type of moccasin. She held out a booted foot and said, "Look what I bought in Duluth! Indian shoes. What do you call them, Harold?" She touched my sleeve. "Good for *creeping*."

She took a few tiptoeing, warrior steps across the wet planks.

Two nondescript boys in raincoats lumbered onto shore and commenced digging a hole beneath some pines. Harold (who was not one of the fiancés from high school) surveyed the lake, stepped

ISSUE 82

gingerly over an invisible hazard on the rocks, and made his way towards the woods. Erich called after him, "Can I take your bag?"

The man turned, sulkily, imperious, and then a shift went over his face, as if running into an old friend in a crowd of strangers, and he said, "I don't believe in packing much, thank you. Look here, I have all I need in this hamper." He opened one hinged lid and pointed out the contents, obviously delighted by his own thrift.

Grace put her arm in mine and whispered, "Harold's writing a book, but he hasn't actually written anything yet because he's rich. Would you believe it, Midge?" She affected a pained expression. Behind her, the chartered plane gutted the lake and lifted over far trees. "I'm *moneyed* people."

For the first time that summer, the lodge was nearly full. We put the boys in one room and their governess (a yellow woman with a Texan accent) in the room next door. We gave Grace and Harold the room over the porch, with a view of the lake at sunset. Unlike Goldie, the Wilsons were loud and busy guests, inexhaustible. The boys brought turtles to the bathtub, pebbles to the dinner table, an antler to bed. They had an idea about the physics of air and were determined to build a craft that could float them over the lake like a balloon. I talked with them about this at length and could never determine the extent to which they knew they were playing. Jasper was six, and he became furious with his little brother, Jake, at any suggestion that the venture was not possible. On the shore there were complicated arrangements of thistle and jars. For days, they claimed their failure was due to sabotage by locals: sometimes Indians, sometimes wolves. Then one morning they came to the dining room before breakfast almost sobbing, saying they had done it, they made it to the other side.

"Why are you crying, then?" their mother pointed out. She was mocking them because all of us were watching, and I think Grace knew she was better at winning a crowd than raising children. Jasper reddened at his mother's words, clearly crushed. He explained, putting his face into his armpit and taking it out again, "Jake's crying because he's a *baby!*" Grace turned to scold the yellow governess for negligence, but the boys were sopping wet, breathless, and I believed they believed that they had done what they said.

ISSUE 82

I told them this. That night I went to their bedroom and touched their heads. I said "Good job, boys!" but they looked at me in a sickened way, barely tolerating my presence. I realized I'd made a mistake, but I had trouble sorting out what it was exactly.

I won't say we became friends with Harold and Grace, but something else happened that was a little more complicated. A week after they arrived, I ran into Harold smoking a pipe and he asked me to help him out of his marriage. He was sitting in the woods under a line of laundry I was drying, and he spoke simply, his mouth around the neck of the pipe, so his words sounded lazy, offhand, almost unintentional. Then he took the pipe from his lips and put the warm mouthpiece against my ankle.

That night, I lay with my husband in our bed and gently stroked his throat. He liked that, and it frightened me a little how vulnerable he was with his chin thrust back how bony and ridged it was there, like the spine of a small, extinct reptile. "We should think of ways to draw more people here," I told him, fingering the hump of his Adam's apple. "We should advertise in the paper. We should make signs for the road."

That's when he said for the second time, "People will come when they do."

"But what for?" I felt a lurch of desperation. It was as if he refused to understand the basic machinery involved in being human, how one thing led to the next. He had a fixed notion that all lives were as pure as his own, borne of unqualified, disciplined intentions.

In the next weeks, I took pains to avoid face-to-face conversations with Harold and Grace. They were spoiled and self-involved, and though I didn't approve of them at all, I found I enjoyed watching them from a distance. I grew interested in their diets, for instance, in Harold's taste for slightly soured milk and the way Grace picked at her fish. She slid her fork between the bones as if performing surgery, totally absorbed, frightened whenever she took a bite. I kept serving fish so I could watch her at this task, which made her seem vulnerable like nothing else, which made her appear strangely animal and vital. I grew fascinated by the way Harold and Grace derided each other, rarely speaking to each other in public, but always lightly narrating the other's faults for audiences. They seemed pleased rather than discomfited by the disorders they pointed out, announcing them like accomplishments: "Grace thinks books are for propping open windows," or "Harold, bless his heart, never learned to leave his mosquito bites alone. Look! He's like someone with pox." I liked best to hear them in their room at night, shouting. "You're unnecessary to my happiness," I once heard Grace say, and though I didn't hear the context, the phrase struck me as so poetic and ruthless, so wonderful, it ran through my head whenever Erich's disappointment in me showed. I imagined him saying it to me, the clean shard I'd become when he hissed in my face, *You're unnecessary to my happiness.* Of course, my husband was tender and formal most of the time. After the Wilsons came, he wore his suit every day again, like a man at an everlasting funeral. At night, he almost begged me to get pregnant; touching each other was like sitting in the empty lodge waiting for guests who never arrived; we were humiliated to find the other always present for our personal failures.

He kept saying, like a man purchasing milk, "Thank you!"

"Don't say that," I scolded, annoyed because I didn't want to be held accountable. I wanted his anger or forgiveness, but not his gratitude for this: the baby I refused to bear.

Once, the Wilsons wanted a picnic excursion, and when I went out to untie the canoes, I saw something beneath the dock. Not a broom or a fox pup, but Noah's kite, the one Erich and I gave him. It was caught beneath the planks like a sea animal, a thing from school books, not from lakes: yellow, red, and green. I got down on my knees to fish it out. For just a moment with my hands in the water, I believed that Noah was down there with it, floating white beard and blind newt hands, but then there was a gulping sound and water streamed down my arms. The kite was a wet heap in my hands.

"What you got there?" Erich called from the bank.

What could I say about this? I suppose we could have laughed together —what had we been *thinking*, giving a *grown man* a kite? —but I still felt something of Noah in my arms, which was disconcerting, unbearable in fact, so I lowered the thing back into the water. I didn't want Erich to see it, to worry about what had happened to our first brief guest.

"Nothing," I said. "Just a shirt, someone's lost laundry."

He called, "Bring it up, we'll dry it off," because my husband had industry enough to cast on any object at hand, wayward guest or washed-up trash, any irrecoverable article.

But I said, scolding, guilty: "No, it's ruined."

I went to him myself. I climbed the rocky bank and smoothed his moustache with a finger still wet with lake water. He lifted his eyebrows but did not move his face an inch, his breath coming through his slightly parted lips, like the minute, barely discernable current through two logs in the lodge. Gently, I put my mouth over that fragile draft, kissed him. His lips were papery, desiccated. They didn't seem like lips.

Was it then that possibilities began to dawn on me that hadn't before?

I'd been so certain for so long that it was some failure in me that kept Erich from the family he wanted.

Of course that day's suspicions were only confirmed much later, long after the Wilsons left, so it's possible I'm rearranging the order of my feelings to justify what I did to him.

ISSUE 82

The circus in Duluth was Grace's idea, and somehow she got us all to go with her. It was a long day's trip six hours in a hired car on the logging roads, and another six hours on the Superior steamer and I'd grown restless, I suppose, weary of the barren lake, the immaculate order of pines. I craved some adventure and disorder. Goldie wore her hair in yellow ribbons, and the boys put on shoes again for the first time in a week. Even Erich went along with Grace's plan, though he got carsick on the drive and had to sit with his head hanging out the window like someone's forlorn dog. We all stayed two nights in a ramshackle Victorian hotel in a residential neighborhood. The place had running water and electric lights, but Erich and I could not help but feel a vague competitive dislike for the rumpled maid and diminutive door man. I'm not proud to say we colluded in disparaging the place whenever the Wilsons were around, affecting a businesslike scorn of every attempt at convenience. We took pleasure in pointing at a crusty orange formation beneath the porch and making Grace put her hand to her breast. "Yuck," I lamented. "What on earth could that *be*?"

The circus was a few miles out of town at the county fairgrounds. We sat together in bleachers under the sun, balancing our hats on our heads and squinting like people who'd lived for a long time underground. I couldn't tell if all that squinting and sweating behind the ears made me feel oppressed or ebullient. I remember Goldie spent the day with the boys, shunning the governess who was reading a book and eating a snow cone. Grace and Harold settled in next to each other on the bench, argued for a moment about whether the seats were any good, and didn't speak to each other for the rest of the show. Erich and I sat on either side of them.

If you've been to a circus, you know how they manage to make preposterous things seem ordinary, even dispiriting. We saw three midget children riding hounds, for instance. They had shiny leather saddles and clown noses, and though everyone clapped, I kept expecting something more thrilling to happen. It was like a trail ride, the way those big-boned dogs lumbered their figure eights, the way the midget boys gripped their tiny pommels. Then a portly man in a wedding dress rummaged in his sleeve for a crumpled bouquet of daisies. After dancing about on his toes, he plucked the bouquet, petal by browning petal, and ate it. I felt like I was watching something I'd done myself — though in private, abashed — and I admired his shameless regurgitation. The bouquet came out of his mouth whole, reconstituted, wet. When he bowed and gave it to a woman in the audience, she held it far away from her body with two fat fingers.

Beside me, Harold offered me a piece of popcorn. I set the foamy, tasteless thing on my tongue and let it dissolve to its kernel. He positioned his knee so it lined up with mine.

"That's disgusting," I told him, stoutly, pointing out two scantily-clad obese women doing the polka. But it wasn't at all. It wasn't disgusting or even strange, but just one of the ways the universe worked. If you were very fat and a twin, you learned at a young age to dance for audiences.

During intermission, Goldie took the boys to look at the horses, and the governess stayed absorbed in her newspaper. The rest of us wandered over to the auction set up in a tent across a dusty field. Circling in silence the tables of linens and bicycles, I had a curious, nervous feeling, as if we were waiting for something to happen: as if we'd all set our marbles rolling down a ramp and we were now just watching to see how they'd collide. Grace and my husband were discussing the merits of putting a bid down for a painted wicker throne, which Grace thought would look good on the porch of the lodge. They were almost bickering over it, actually, the way Grace bickered with Harold, and I was about to join in when a man in suspenders distracted me. "What's this?" he kept saying, a little too loudly. I followed his gaze until we were both looking into a cage of sorts, but what was inside perplexed me for a moment. I wanted to say, *bear*, but it wasn't exactly. It was a couch, an old man, a wilderness. It was the first thing that had really surprised me in a long time, and before I even realized it was dead, I knew I could use it.

"Is that thing *for sale?*" the man asked.

Harold took my elbow and tugged it. "Do you want to take a walk outside?" He was not suave so much as needling. I looked at him impatiently and saw his hair was greasy. It was flat as a swimming cap over his eyebrows.

He started talking about his book. It was to be an exploration of the rift between loggers and conservationists, he said, a lesson on, no, a love letter *to* the wilderness. This was a new idea, something he'd discovered while sitting on a rock in our woods, and he'd already come up with many good metaphors for pine needles. *Rodeo tassels*, he said, shyly now, as if offering me a choice delicacy from his plate. *The fringe of a lady's dress.* For Christ's sake. Why was there no machine to lift boys over water, never any real artists, but always some fop of a husband dreaming his commonplace dreams of adultery? Rodeo tassels could not interest me, could interest no one.

I looked him square in the eye and said, "You're unnecessary to my happiness." I meant it to be kind, honestly. I meant it to release him from whatever responsibility he felt to impress me.

But it was only after I had said it — and felt its correct and appropriate violence — that I realized that the comment was neither original nor true. Of course, I needed him: it was childish to think otherwise. I needed his money before the end of the month; I needed him to tell his wealthy friends about the lodge and its comforts; I needed his wife to cheer my husband when I could not. I looked over at them assessing the wicker throne, Grace sitting in it like the queen she was, Erich rolling his eyes like a man who knew exactly what she was and was not bothered by it.

I pulled a strand of hair from Harold's shirt, apologetic now for what I'd said. I knew how to flirt as well as anyone. I said of the strand of hair, holding it up and leaning in: "Hers or mine?"

He was relieved and smiled, almost winningly. It was then that I let him grope for and take my hand. Of course, I didn't outline any plan for him, nor promise right then to be his mistress, but you how the human mind works. What is logic, anyway, but the way the mind takes control of facts and arranges them to suit its own interests? I wanted some measure of control over my husband's and my circumstances. I wanted that most of all. And Harold? He wanted to be flattered.

We got the bear carcass for almost nothing. I thought we should stuff it right there in Duluth, as the thing had been dead a full day already, but Erich said he knew a good taxidermist outside Grand Marais. We found an empty logging truck that was going up north that afternoon and paid six dollars for the bear to go with it. It took three men to sling the thing onto the palate, wearing leather gloves and cloths around their noses. Flies were already distorting its face, nursing its rear end. Grace was horrified, but the boys were ecstatic, absolutely jittery with love for the thing. Both these reactions pleased me very much. Before it drove off, the boys kept skipping around the truck, stroking the bear with sticks and touching its clipped, coral claws.

I could not stop talking at dinner that night, working out the details of my idea for the bear's new life as a feature in our lobby. I thought we could hire a photographer to take a picture of it, put ads in papers in Minneapolis and Chicago, draw rich, outdoorsy people with the very spectacle their unexceptional imaginations desired. I drank a lot of coffee, and found my hands were shaking when I lifted my mug, as if my body had been starved and was finally being fed again. Everything was so pleasant and unnerving. I wanted Erich to feel this as well, wanted him to see how things were going to work out for us now, but he was too worried about how much dinner would cost. I saw him peering at the bill over his spectacles, ever innocent. Very tenderly, I corrected his math.

Our guests that summer were our children, I raised every one of them myself: Noah Williams, Goldie, the Wilsons — though the boys were always just beyond me a little. By fall, we had other types of people, drunk fishermen who were stand-offish and strangers to me, but that summer the guests were mine. On the last leg of our journey home from Duluth, paddling across the lake, we sang impolite logging songs the boys had picked up over their weeks in our woods. *Fellows at the grand-'ole gates, say hello to your bosomed fates!* We pitched in our canoes, but I don't think I was alone that day in feeling vouchsafed against danger. Even the moose in our garden was hard to take seriously. We stood with our bags on the dock, a little uneasy, yes, but then Jasper and Jake went up so close they could have touched its black muzzle. They raised sticks to prod its hindquarters.

"Stay back," Erich warned them, but the moose was docile as a donkey, knock-kneed, a circus pet. For an instant, I confused him with the bear we bought and felt sorry for what we had done to him. His obdurate gentleness made my heart sink, because I knew there was something sick in him we couldn't see, a malignancy that softened and destroyed his nature. A wobble of mucus moved in each eye. He walked in a nice circle, very aimless and staged, and then everybody clapped when he took a step back and shambled into the woods. My pounding heart grew too loud, and I had put my hands on my knees, prevent a spinning sensation from pulling me down, and then pretend it didn't happen, pretend I was fine, and the moose was just another entertainment, and the bear — a thing that walked on a leash and balanced a ball — was once a vicious beast. And who was to say they were not.

All that winter Erich split wood till dusk. Nights, he held onto my strange, new body out of practical necessity, for warmth, teeth chattering in my ear. I could feel his worry going through me in shudders. But under that worry, I sensed how pleased he was, I swear to God. He *must* have been happy in his way, grateful to have the future coming so uneventfully, or else why did he fall asleep before I did, giving me up to the cold, forgetting everything? I lay awake night after night, waiting. Waiting for the ice to pull away from the shore, for mallards to return, waiting for our guests to come back for walleye.

I felt I just needed to get to spring. The doctor promised I'd be fine by then, but he was country people and didn't even bother to shave properly, so it was hard to trust what he said. Whenever he bent over me, I could see the stubble on his face like dirt. I didn't tell that doctor that I barely felt any kicks. I felt I understood the baby's quietness. I had prepared my own silence for her, after all. She would have her life and her father, her future with its fine logic, ah, maybe even my good skin, my small, dark eyes. But her secrets, those were mine.

Todd Jackson

The Story of Eugene,
from The Nickel Gospels

A great number of attempts exist to capture the story of Nickel and the days of William St. I hold a bead on this also, but will for the first time, properly compile the story of these events, as they occurred correctly, from the start.

During the days of the William St. Strip there was the Brooklyn Supreme bar, the degenerate center of the strip, and the tragically drunk youth saw this and struck there and drown themselves into the next generation.

And everyone knew the names of the scenic wrecks: Lil Sally, Johnny James, JB, Nicole, Josephine, Mikey, Sarah, Geraldine, Josephine and Nickel. Then it happened on a certain day that Nicole asked Josephine if she wanted to hit the Supreme and Josephine in turn asked Nickel to come along. And though no one knew or cared that Nickel was there, and though Nicole and Josephine did most of the talking Nickel saw in his silence that this was a good bar, even at that late hour.

As it came to pass Nickel had a dream that night and when he woke he described this dream to Josephine, "Last night I had a dream again of a man standing beside his truck in the foothills of the Rockies, at a station pumping gas. In fact, I'm certain that I saw this actual scene once when I was out west. And each time I dream it, the mountains are silhouette grey at exactly the same angle and at the same distance. And though I find it hard to describe, the dream does fill me with the same spirit or feeling each time: in the sense that this has me full of trouble and I feel something is out of place or a profound disconnection of some kind has occurred and that something is at least lacking. And the mood then passes."

Nickel then said to Josephine, "Perhaps this just needs to be rolled or kicked. I think I'm going to return to the Supreme and have a drink this afternoon. I like that bar. And Josephine heard this declaration and answered by nodding."

And as soon as it was afternoon the next day Nickel arrived at the Supreme, earlier than the rest of the drunks. And it fortuned that Sadie was behind the bar — Sadie, the owner of the Supreme — which collected Nickel into the heart of the William St and the Supreme itself. Then again the next afternoon and compulsively now Nickel returned to the bar of the Supreme and in the company of these drinkers and degenerates rolled and they together got loaded. This behaviour reinforced by Sadie's need and pull and the culture of instinct that idled at the Supreme. And it came to pass that there grew a fame of the Supreme and its people through the William St strip and to some extent around the city also.

And it became known that Nickel would arrive at the Supreme most days in the afternoon and sit and champion until dusk.

In the right hands the early effects of alcohol on the body are subtle and culturally significant: when the first thought that spills out of the drunks without control are better thoughts and the confidence results in new kindness and creation. And it fortuned that a pocket of the weak willed stumbled onto this secret and Nickel found the civility of this solution also. And so he found also a response to his anxiety, the source of his re-occuring dream, and hovered and sparked, drinking and carrying on.

And yet some that were in the Supreme heard Nickel and were filled with astonishment and cast him long looks, or turned their backs to him. And they asked him loudly, "Why are you still here?" Their chagrin born because they were wary of new drinkers or they were just angry drunks and uncomfortable talkers. And Nickel rebuked them saying like he did once, "Go fuck yourself Butter Bill." And satisfied, Butter Bill turned and finished his drink and Nickel was satisfied also. And the degenerate generation stayed loaded and received their lonesome crookedness and were pleased with themselves.

But the burden of drinking is well known and Nickel's compulsion to respond to each afternoon by training his barstool did test his health. So that Sadie noticed that his stories would repeat and she said to Nickel, "But I've heard that one already. You told me that just an hour ago." And this slip would roll the crowd. Then when Nickel saw his repetition and porous attention it angered him and he began to notice the randomness of his actions.

And it came to pass that Nickel's corroded attention corrupted his responses and he became surly and unkind. When Josephine saw this she asked him, "Nickel do you think you may be drinking too much? When we started your afternoon would end at seven or eight and now you hold on much longer. You were once the sun burning and rising but have changed into a limp muddler." And Nickel heard this and looked at Josephine and did not respond.

And he returned to the Supreme the next day. And Sadie seeing that he had arrived poured his pint without asking since compulsion is reinforced by routine. Then it came to pass that Nickel drank enough for himself and several others. Then Johnny James said, "Let's all go and see My Daughter's Surprise at the Pretty Fool." And Nickel nodded and they all cheered and rambled down the strip.

There is an eventual burden to this solution. The initial effects of alcohol become overwhelmed by confused reflexes and mistakes of judgement become more likely. And as he entered the Pretty Fool where the band is corralled by the door, it chanced that a harmonica was on the floor and so as he stepped he saw this and adjusted his lead foot in a way that left him leaning. He then fell quickly toward the plate glass window of the bar's front and grabbed a microphone stand on his way down. Then falling with the stand and the live microphone he split the window into pieces with his weight, and the speakers resonated this collision so that everybody heard the loud collapse as he crashed and Nickel landed face-up to the night sky outside, while his feet stayed inside planted with the harmonicas in the bar, his back stretched over the sharp edge of the remaining glass, and the final piece to fall remained in the frame above his neck like a guillotine. The alcoholic youth shouted, "Call 911!" And, "Jesus, Nickel are you OK?" Then they carefully eased him up off and back into the bar but he was not hurt. And Johnny James and JB helped Nickel into a cab and they decided it would be best if they had one more drink at the Supreme.

And when he left the cab they walked right back into the Supreme. And though it was now late Nickel ordered a whiskey and sat on the sofa instead of at the bar and quietly passed out, as he leaned slowly forward, until his face pressed into the armrest. And the bartenders saw this and because they were closing soon, and just wanted to leave, they considered what would happen if they locked the door and left Nickel alone. But they asked Johnny James and JB to carry him home. And he left the bar on his side, in their arms. JB managed to lift his legs at the knees and Johnny James raised him by the shoulders. And as they travelled their burden down the street to Josephine, his arms dangled, his waist slumped lower and his head rolled. All of this making their duty awkward as he wallowed.

And after nearly two months Nickel finally returned to the bar and he declared to Sadie, " This place is like no other and knows everything that paradise knows." Then Sadie answered and said, "It's good to see you. We miss you around here." And Nickel once more proclaimed his love for the Supreme and was rarely seen there again.

Peter Nichols

America's Oldest Living Published Poet

He had a reputation to uphold. There were two books of his poetry and a play, the latter still occasionally studied at a college or two. He'd survived to the age of ninety-four, so far. On the Maine island to which he and Eleasa relocated twenty years ago, they'd bought the defunct town library, and made it their home. In the perfectly square building with four-sided red tile roof and tiny cupola, the library's sign-out desk now held their kitchen crockery. It was comforting to be an old couple with a reputation, and his wife still did her part: Eleasa went out almost every day and did watercolors, and her doing that-- being so active and talking to people-- somehow kept their story alive. She was insistent on always telling anyone she met-- locals and visitors to the island in summer-- that her husband was, in fact, America's best known, oldest living published poet.

The only problem at the moment was that a relative of Eleasa's, with her husband, was arriving on the island on a vacation and expected to see them. It might require a performance, so to speak. It might be only the urinal story, which niece Matty no doubt remembered hearing from Eleasa. Some years ago Jacob had made a bit of a joke of it. The former library, used mostly by students, had a lavatory for the boys, of course. With two urinals side by side, rather than tear them down, the old boys' room became a kind of tabernacle, a room into which Jacob would invite a male guest as a kind of island secret place, for men only, to show off: stand at the urinal and talk about the art of poetry and invite the other male, whoever he was, to pee at the other one. The urinals were tall, wide and perfect, a style no longer built. For many years it was a kind of diversion, to see how the young male pup—particularly if he had artistic ambitions—would react to the side by side peeing while Jacob talked to him about the art of writing poetry.

"Going out?" he asked Eleasa this morning. As though he didn't know.

"It's all out there, the world," she said, her wooden paint box under one arm and her easel under the other. "I look, I breath, I paint. While you sit in your study and think. You old fart, don't worry about it."

"Can't they stay at the motel?" he implored.

"The motel had a fire. And she's my grandniece," said Eleasa.

So Jacob went to his study, under the eaves of the four-sided roof of the library with the cock at the top, and he didn't have to go outside to see from the weathervane that the wind was coming from the northeast because the water pattern told him so. He sat down with pen in hand. He couldn't write a word. So he went out after all, and walked around the house five times, through the windblown high grass that threatened to trip him. At 94, five times around was not bad, but he got no new ideas for a poem or play out of it. Meantime his wife, who was not a particularly good painter, was out feeling alive and productive doing a bad watercolor. He had no idea why her jumpy, colorful paintings of island rocks, sea, and birds sold out in her annual late-summer show on the island. Perhaps it was partly because, when they attended the opening every Labor Day, she was the 91-year-old artist wife of America's oldest living published poet, and the little pony act they put on for the tourists visiting the island affected her sales.

Predictably, long after he'd had an apple and a piece of chocolate cake for lunch, at around four Eleasa arrived back in her flurry of enthusiasm. Her long gray hair, once red and curly, was tangled by wind, wound up behind her neck. "I think I caught it!" she breathed. "The wind above the rocks at the Point." There it was, her new effort, a large piece of watercolor paper with a sweep of color and some kind of angles of dark rocks underneath—positioned on the table so the young guests could not avoid seeing it later. Then Eleasa began to prepare a salad and baby lamb chops from a local raiser so that the meal would seem like something very special for the guests. Show time.

"You're in charge of the drinks," she said.

"I know," he replied.

Their green Landrover—what a cliché choice of car, he thought—pulled up a little before six.

"Aunt Eleasa, it's been so long!" said the woman. Big hug. Everyone hugged now, it seemed.

ISSUE 82

"I hope we're not imposing," said the large young man, who, bizarrely, wore a blue blazer, as though he'd come to a yachting event.

Named Vernon, the young man turned out to be a very poor conversationalist. He was a bond trader working in New York and apparently felt rather out of place on a nowhere Maine island. No doubt his wife, niece Matty, had dragged him there after many years of telling the bond trader that she had an eccentric aunt who lived with America's oldest living published poet. Eleasa and Matty carried the dinner conversation, for which Jacob was somewhat thankful. He poured the wine, a claret, and no doubt his slightly wavering, jiggling performance—he did the same joke, pretending to almost pour where there was no glass—got a delighted laugh out of Matty but a dour look of fake concern out of her boorish husband.

The after-dinner liqueurs—artichoke from Sicily or Madeira— softened them up for the "tour" of the house. The switch was that, to Jacob's surprise, the young man backed off from the urinal challenge and almost insisted—preferred-- to rise prematurely to their prepared bedroom and bath on the second floor, where Eleasa would show him, out their window, the view past the roof eaves of the Point in the distance.

Left with Matty, Jacob found himself getting more enthusiasm from her than he wanted.

"I read—my class read—your play in college," she said. "I've read it over several times since and it's wonderful."

"I should hope so," he said.

"I wondered if you might help me a bit with my own... writing efforts before we leave tomorrow."

"What do you write?" he asked, not really wanting to know.

"Very bad poetry," she said.

Most young females, he thought, aren't aware of how bad their poetry is. He had to admit that her answer was a relatively good sign.

She leaned closer to him at the table to tell him her secret. "I talked my husband into going out with your wife tomorrow morning to see how she does her painting. That way you and I might have time together to talk about writing."

There was no point arguing with a young woman like her. It was obviously a done deal.

"So humor her if you have to," said Eleasa at bedtime. "What harm can it do?"

"She managed the whole thing," he said, settling his head into his pillow. "Do you think that thug gives a rat's ass about your painting?"

"You're such an old coot, as cynical as ever," she said.

In the morning the art couple were ahead of schedule, and Vernon would drive them to the Point, where, no doubt, Eleasa would give him some kind of art demonstration, and maybe even shame him into putting down some color himself—his "feelings"—on the extra pad that she'd convinced him to carry under his arm.

"You two have a literary meeting of the minds," she told them before exiting the kitchen door into the bright, breezy Maine weather.

He invited the girl into his writing room, with the window that looked east out to the Atlantic. No doubt she'd have a sheaf of her poetry to ask his opinion about. But to his surprise, she'd brought none of her scribblings. He was at a loss. She sat in his guest's chair by the window and said, "I hoped you'd show me some of your new work."

He had no new work, to speak of. His hand, as he put it up to the shelves where he kept his published work and the thin manila folder where he'd put a few lines of inevitably false starts, looked so old. There is a point when what are called "age spots" overwhelm the color on one's entire hand. And it was not shaking on purpose. He glanced back at this rather bullying young woman, who wore a purple-and-white-print summer dress and who kept smiling at him as though she expected something special to spew from his mouth. Some advice about writing.

He pulled his hand down from the folder. "I'm afraid we are at an impasse," he said.

"What I'd really like," she said, "is to see your famous boys' room. Is that allowed?"

"That was, and still is, the boys' room," he replied.

"Oh, who cares," she said. "I've heard about it for so long. Please?"

"I suppose you'd want to smoke a cigar in there, as well," he said. "That's how it used to go."

That was true. When Jacob had still felt proud of his published work, he'd offer a cigar to the man-- or men-- who'd come over for a cocktail or dinner. The two urinals were really just a joke, a kind of excuse to act in a writerly manner, to have some fun.

Matty rose to her feet.

Well, there was a first time for anything, he supposed. He gave the woman his best old man, cynical and writerly grimace, but she would not desist.

He lead her to the door of the boys' room, which still had the library, grammar school-style simple metal plate on it that said "BOYS." She followed him in. Jacob tried to think of that witty remark he used to make about that piece of art in the '30s, the found object urinal put in a museum by...but he could not remember the name of that famous surrealist artist. He felt tongue-tied, as nervous as a child.

The woman laughed, bent over at the waist with her hands over her face, and said, "I heard about this from Eleasa so long ago. You're going to think I'm so silly, but I imagined being a man writer and coming here and being able to stand—just there. Do you mind?"

He was thunderstruck, felt a bit light-headed. He could only shrug and then mutter, "Not at all."

She stepped toward the urinal on the right, right up to it. And then looked at him. "Come," she said, "humor me."

Well, he thought, you only live once. At least this was something new, something unanticipated. He could attribute it to his dotage, if necessary. So he slowly stepped up to the urinal beside her. Perhaps if he could think of something literary to say at this moment?

What happened next was too real to be a dream. Somehow it reminded him of his wife bubbling over about the breeze and the world out there that made it so easy for her to put paint on paper. For, after he'd placed himself at the urinal, this woman looked at him. She unbuttoned a button on the thin top of her dress and pulled down the print pattern, letting her bare left breast completely out. "I have a gift for you," she whispered, lifting her breast, and to his own amazement, Jacob bent down his old head and accepted her gift.

Lisa Heiserman Perkins

Tanner's First Deer

For five days running now, ever since I gave Tanner a 30-30
Winchester for his eighth birthday, my wife, Fleur, has been acting
furious with me. I explained to her that all the Derochers got their
first rifle when they turned eight, going back to when we lived in
Perrier, France. Lately, because of the expensive water, usually when
I mention Perrier, Fleur pretends to polish her nails on her lapel,
and when I tell her that's cheesy, she says it's cheesy on purpose,
which makes it not cheesy but "ironical." This makes no sense to me.
"Ironical" is a word she uses a lot, now that she's taken Expository
Writing at Bowditch Community.

She said, "It's ironical that you choose to celebrate the birth of
your son with a gun."

"I'll tell you what's ironical," I said. " That first night you and me
really got down to it? Do you not recall that also just happened to be
the first time I told you I'm a hunter?"

This turned out to be a big mistake. For starters, Tanner was
listening in the hallway and decided to make his presence known by
booming out the theme song to *2001: A Space Odyssey*. Also, Fleur is
now writing a column for the Seneca Weekly—"Parent to Parent"—
and so is all of a sudden quite the expert on all matters relating to our
son, and I had to listen to how, in this day and age, we have to protect
children from violence in every way, shape, and form, and on and on.
And then, total silence.

So last night when I got home, she couldn't hear the truck pull up
because it was snowing. I sat and watched her through the kitchen
window fixing dinner at the sink, laughing on the phone. Now,
the way that phone was propped on her shoulder made her look
like she has a double chin. This got me going in two directiohons at
once because that little double chin struck me as sexy. Most people
wouldn't see that, but one thing about Fleur is the way the flesh
sticks to her body, if that makes any sense at all. . .what I mean is, the
old masters would've had a field day. Still, I wanted to scare the hell
out of her, go bang on the window and let her know I've seen her,

ISSUE 82

and that she couldn't possibly be so very brokenhearted as she makes out. Instead, I slammed the truck door. She looked up, and there it was, the ol' sourpuss. So I went in the front.

Tanner was in the den lying on the carpet. The map I'd made of the trails starting from the Jerome Bridge was all spread out. He'd pulled the lamp over so that the room was dim, and someone could trip on that cord, which if Fleur saw would somehow be my fault.

Tanner's hair is straight like hers, but it sprouts up cockeyed, and he has no idea how goofy he looks standing there all serious, explaining everything under the sun. And especially now that he's got these enormous new choppers, it's just about impossible to keep a straight face, and he has been getting away with murder.

I am moving the lamp when he pops up and throws his arms around me so that I lose my balance, and I'm a big man too. Fleur makes a potato onion pie on Fridays, her grandma's recipe, and when I can't help but polish it off, she gets that wicked little smile, and I remind her that she has only herself to blame. But Tanner, not an ounce on him. It's like he's on springs, always flying off in a direction you don't expect, so that you're constantly worried about an accident.

The night before my first time hunting I'd hardly slept, so I'd stopped at the Video Hut to get something distracting for him. *Bambi* first came out when I was a kid, and I got all confused. Most of the guys my age around here with kids have the sense not to let that one in the house, so I doubt Tanner has seen it. I'm tempted to ask him, but then again he came out smarter than me and Fleur put together, so maybe he wouldn't have the same reaction and I'm worried for nothing. After I'd won the debate over whether *2001: A Space Odyssey* was "age-appropriate" for him, I was the one wound up with the nightmares. That black sky, like an abyss, and the air supply, just snipped off like an umbilical cord, and you float away. I couldn't shake it, still can't, which Fleur and Tanner think is pretty damn funny. Anyway, I picked *Butch Cassidy and the Sundance Kid,* but he'd fallen asleep by the time they jumped off that cliff together.

Me? I hardly sleep the whole night it seems, for thinking about how, on our way up to the camp, we used to stop at the Bridge Bakery for blueberry muffins, still hot, with two pats of butter. Tanner would have gone for that, and I am either wishing that bakery still existed, or I'm worrying that the camp will seem like nothing but a smelly old shack. But then again there is that whole mile of dirt road after the Jerome Bridge leading up to it, and any boy would love that, all twists and turns. It is one wild ride.

When it's time to get him up, I can see him by the light in the hallway with his covers kicked off. He looks like he fell dead asleep in the middle of his jumping around. My mama always liked to tell about how my first time, I'd gotten up in the night and put on my checkered jacket. It had belonged to my cousin, Petey Latangue, and already smelled like the woods. When they pulled back the covers, there I was, all ready to go, right down to the rubber boots.

I don't want to snap the light on—it has a loud snap to it—and I remember not waking up until Grandpa was carrying me to the truck, holding me face-up like you'd hold a baby, and that when I opened my eyes the sky was full of stars, swarming with them, hardly room for one more. This I will not forget until my dying day.

Tanner is in his PJs, of course. It's cloudy this morning, anyway. He senses me looking at him, jumps up, and snaps the light on himself. He's getting dressed so fast, whipping the clothes out of my hand, wriggling away so that I can't help him. He says nothing. I say, "Hey, buddy, where's the fire?" and try to grab him but he's in no mood, and is out the door before I can finish my coffee.

In the truck he sits forward in the seat, his eyes fixed on the yellow stripes like he's hypnotized. This goes on till we're 20 miles north of Montpelier, and it's nice and quiet. Usually he's going a mile a minute, until it's hard not to want to shush him up. But now he seems not asleep exactly, but not awake either. There, and not there. When I ask him if he's okay he says, "Huh?" and then nothing till I'm getting almost spooked and start wondering where in the hell his thoughts have gone to. Finally he comes out with, " The only reason deers don't bite you is that it's so much easier to stick you with their antlers, and what Mom doesn't get is, that's no fair, and that's why we need to have a rifle, right, Dad?"

I say, "I've never heard of anyone getting bit by a deer, Tanner," which does not register at all.

Sorely tried, he says, "*We* have no antlers, but if we had some—well, not antlers, but spikes, built in—we wouldn't have to shoot them."

"I never said we have to shoot them."

"Well, they run a whole lot faster, if you hadn't noticed." He's in a sarcastic stage, giving me all kinds of lip. It's natural, I guess. "He's *testing*," says Fleur. "Keep your shirt on." Yeah, well I'd've got a good smack in the mouth from my mother. Then she'd go stand over at the sideboard, dangling her rosary over my photo to cast out the spell.

What I'm really worried about is the way Tanner rolls his eyes at me and pushes out his upper lip like a dunce. When he does that he's a dead ringer for Fleur when she's had a few and decided that pretty much everything I have to contribute to any given conversation is beyond the pale stupid.

"How *long*?" he says, like all of a sudden he's being tortured.

"Figure it out for yourself, why don't you. The map's in the side pocket, and I put fresh batteries in the flashlight."

"'Fresh batteries,'" he says quietly, in the voice of a soap commercial.

"I thought you liked maps."

He looks at me and decides to be nice. "I just want to get there." He drags the flashlight out of the glove compartment, holding it like it's so very heavy, and slumps back with his face turned toward his window. His neck, lit up by lights of the dash, looks so small and round.

"You're not worried about that ol' deer," I say.

"What ol' deer?"

"The one we're gonna get!"

"Dad," he says, holding his hand out, palm up, "do I look worried?"

"I don't know. I can't see you in here."

He puts the flashlight on under his chin and makes a scary noise, flashes it at me to make sure I'm smiling, then wiggles it around so that the light jumps like a wild thing.

Like a dope I say, "It's Tinkerbell!" Exactly the kind of babyish stuff to set him off. I'm braced, but he just makes the light jump faster and in a high-pitched, terrified voice says, " Tinkerbell! Tinkerbell!" and keeps this up until I say to put that thing down, it's dangerous.

"Dangerous? You call this '*dangerous?*'" He's snapping it on and off. " This is boring!" he says, and kicks the dashboard.

I want to smack him, but instead I grab the flashlight and throw it in the backseat. He just looks at his empty hand. No protest, no nothing. I accelerate and he has the sense to keep quiet.

We're three miles now from the Jerome Bridge, and I can't help thinking about how I'd planned to tell him about the time we got a flat tire right in the middle, and now I don't even trust my voice. The sun is coming up, which I thought he'd like, but he has that blind look again. After awhile I think of him saying, "spikes, built in," and smile.

"Look at that," I say, pointing out the window. "Sunrise. You've got the sun and the moon both."

Tanner squints at me, gauging me for sappiness. I raise my eyebrows at him as if to say, "I'm clean, kid. It was a statement of fact."

He cranes around, then sighs. "I hate to tell ya, Dad, but it's the same as the sunset."

"OK."

Then he yells, "Hey! It's the opposite *and* the same!" He puts out one hand—"Opposite," and the other hand—"Same! There is no other thing that's opposite *and* same, is there, Dad?"

'Uh, let's see...."

He holds still, like he's wracking his brains, then comes out with, "I gotta pee."

" Well, how's about we pee off a bridge?"

ISSUE 82

He tips back his head and lets out his laugh. "Really?" he squeaks.

"Yep."

"You gotta pee?"

"Yep."

He glances over his shoulder like someone might see us being naughty.

The Jerome Bridge is wooden, one of the oldest in Vermont, nothing but a hundred yards but spanning a gulch maybe thirty feet deep over where Whitetail Creek falls. Couldn't be prettier. I pull over and I can tell Tanner's racing me. He gets his little squirter out first and lets fly with a whoop. I'm right behind him.

"The Golden Arches," I say, but he's distracted by the steam from our pee.

"Smoke! Hey, smoke!" He waggles his butt and wails out the refrain from that song, "Oo-oo-oo, I'm on fire!"

This hits me wrong, all wrong. I tell him to settle down, at which he jumps into a Rambo stance, and sprays his piss around, making like he's a machine gun, and I really yell and he just zips up, and cool as you please says, "Well, what's the point of bringing a kid out hunting and yelling at him to settle down?" He squints up at me sideways and saunters back to the truck, muttering, "I mean, what did you expect?"

I stand there, with the sun turning everything gold and pink, and the water sparkling like in a fairytale, and I'm holding onto the railing and I'll be goddamned if it isn't all I can do to keep from bawling. I start thinking about standing here, how we always stopped to eat those muffins on the bridge because somehow it reminded Grandpa of Perrier, and I'm remembering that one time, watching him change the tire, watching his stumpy hands, which were so cold and brown and hairy on the back. And the face he made while he twisted off the lug nuts, struggling, a wild face all full of rage, and I'd wanted to yell, "Stop!"

But suddenly he looked up at me and smiled. "She's a bastard!" he said.

ISSUE 82

Tanner honks the horn, and my heart about pops. He ducks, smiling probably, probably scared. I walk back to the truck, moving slow to catch my breath, get in, but just need to sit there. He's fiddling with his door handle. When he speaks, his voice is like a caress so sweet I was already wishing I hadn't felt it. "Don't worry, Dad," he says. "I won't tell her."

"*Tell* her?"

Now, he makes that dunce face. "Peeing off the bridge?" he says, like I'm demented.

"Whoa, whoa, whoa," I say. "We've got no secrets in this family, Tanner."

Tanner dusts his knee and, as though speaking into a microphone attached to his left shoulder says, "If you say so." Then he gazes at the wind shield, his jaw hanging down. I am afraid to move.

"Can we *go*?" he says in a soft voice, but also plenty whiny. I turn the key. The rumble of the engine eases my pulse. When we hit that dirt road, I take it slow. Out of the corner of my eye I see his little head, looking big on his little neck, bobbing along, and imagine how I'd pictured him, wild-eyed, gleeful, and then I imagine him bouncing so hard he smashes his face on the dashboard, over and over. By the time we pull up to the camp I feel like a crazy man. I cut the engine and ask him, "Are you all right?"

"Yep," he chirps.

"OK then."

Still, we sit there, though. He sighs.

"What it is, Tanner?"

He holds up a finger. "I do have one thing."

There's this rack over the door to the camp. I keep my eyes on it. It is one gorgeous rack.

"And what is that?" I ask.

"Well, it's just that, in case you're thinking that *you* have to get

ISSUE 82

'im instead of *me* because you don't want Mamma knowing that it was me killing a living creature."

I can't quite make out what he's saying. His eyes have gone so big and gentle that I can't quite see him, either. But I can feel my face, swelling, and as I'm wondering if he's able to detect that I hear, "I'm not saying you are thinking that, but in case you are—well, let's face it. She's gonna think you're a wimp."

"A *wimp*?"

Tanner squirms, turning red. "Yeah! Dad, come on!" He slaps both hands on the seat and freezes. "OK," he says, and slides his eyes up at me like now *she's* beyond the pale. "A *bigger* wimp." Shaking his head oh so sorrowfully, he says, "And then it'll be, ya know, the ol' story 'bout Tanner's first time, and how you wouldn't even let me pull the trigger!" He kind of chuckles, waggling his head. Then he turns to his door handle and says, "Dad?" "Dad?" he says again, not to me but to the handle, and nestling his little fingers around its crook, "*Are* you gonna let me?"

Kristin Dombek

Monkeys Might Fly

(An Adynaton)

My husband and I have made a quiet and comfortable life together in
Brooklyn. I teach at a university and he has his own business down
the street from our apartment building. Most evenings, we arrive
home from work around 8:00 or so, and order Mexican food, sushi,
pizza, or deli sandwiches. If there are any episodes available of the
four shows we both like—*Project Runway, Lost, So You Think You
Can Dance, and True Blood*—we'll watch one as we eat, and then
another, and end the night there on the couches, resting. Or we'll
take in a *Simpsons* or *Southpark* while we eat, and then Alex will
watch a movie and I'll lie in our pillow-top bed and read the *New
Yorker* or a novel. On weekends, if neither of us has to work, we
take walks in the neighborhood and have a few drinks with friends.
We are both in good health, we have no children, we rent, and we
have a cleaning person who comes every other week, so our shared
responsibilities consist entirely of doing the laundry and paying
the bills on time. There are, of course, the work stresses. Sometimes
one or the other of us gets too overwhelmed or too busy. But for the
most part, it is a good and easy life, without many surprises.

A few days ago, however, we came home to a strange smell. It was
like the smell of a zoo, that musty mix of straw and shit and the
bodies of unknown animals. But it was not exactly that smell—it
was one I knew better than that, but I couldn't quite place it. We
tried to ignore it, and figured that when Louis came to clean that
weekend, he would freshen the place up. The next evening, we sat
down to watch the news while we waited for *Project Runway* to
begin, and there was a report of a pig that had wings or the stumps
of wings found lodged in the suspension wires of the Williamsburg
Bridge. Tonight, we decided to make dinner instead of ordering in,
and I opened the oven to find it caked in ice, and this on a warm
September day. And then, when Alex opened the refrigerator to
take out the chicken he intended to bake, what he found was not a
pale-skinned body wrapped in plastic, but a live hen, feathered and
clucking, who jumped out of the refrigerator, shook herself, and
then ran around in circles on the kitchen floor, bobbing her head.

ISSUE 82

When I heard, from the coat closet, a distinct "baaa," I remembered what the smell was.

Alex froze against the kitchen wall and started shouting "What the fuck is going on?" and "Why is there a fucking—what did you do?"

I should have known, all these quiet years, that some day this might happen. I opened the closet door to let the goat out, and then I spoke to Alex in my most soothing voice.

"I didn't *do* anything, honey," I said, and "You're losing it. Please. Try and pull yourself together."

On the rare occasions when impossible events crash into an everyday day, I find I have one of two opposite reactions, usually whichever one the other person doesn't. I don't think I am alone in this. For example, when I was eight my mother and six year-old brother and I were on a train home to North Philly from downtown and there was a thunderstorm and a tree fell on an electric wire and then they both fell on the train, which derailed, and the lights went off. It was an hour before the conductor let us off the train and we walked between the rails a mile or so in a downpour to the station, where our car was parked, and got home very late to find my father calmly reading John LeCarré in the living room and smoking a pipe. My mother froze in the threshold between the dining room and the living room, so my brother and I froze too, in a rainy trauma tableau. Then my mother started shaking like a washing machine and saying in her highest most-pained-possible voice "We might have been dead, weren't you worried, how can you just sit there, don't you have feelings" and my father said "What could I do, I couldn't do anything about it, what good is worrying if I can't do anything about it, and you know, worse things could happen."

I am quite sure that worse things can always happen. You see, I know whose animals these are, and they're not Alex's. Alex grew up on the Upper West Side, wearing, or so I imagine, an adorable little sportscoat. Reportedly, when he was seven, his nanny let him collect as many frogs from Central Park as he could fit into a gallon jug and later his mother came home to find him naked in the bathtub covered in amphibians. For a while, he had a dalmatian named Dillon, but the rest of the animals were on television. When I realized, nine years ago, that we were falling in love, I thought I must have tricked him somehow, and so I said, "You don't understand.

The house I grew up in was dirty, and it smelled."

"Okay." he said.

"Okay." I told him that, but I didn't tell him about the animals.

A few months after the train wreck, my father got permanently sick, so my mother got calm, and moved us to Indiana to live on the family farm near our grandmothers. My brother and I were city children, and knew only the animals of the Philadelphia zoo, so on our first day on the farm, we saw thirteen snakes, not only garter snakes in the grass but black mambos in the bushes and anacondas winding through the stream and even pythons, thick as branches, wrapped high in the trees that lined our farm's dirt lane. We thought there were giant sloths and lemurs in the back woods, and brown bears napping in deep and hidden caves and that when we weren't looking, panthers chased gazelles and wildabeasts across the wild fields. We stayed in the yard.

Our parents decided to homeschool us, though, so gradually, since we had nowhere else to go, we became brave. With our first dog, Sasha, my brother and I followed the tracks of foxes, and searched for the latest litter of kittens hidden in the hayloft by their new mothers. I made friends with Tom, the patriarchal tabby, and he and I shared countless intense feelings as we ventured through the fields and hedgerows to the woods, where we would wait for deer to come to the salt lick, and try to understand what the birds were saying. And when the first crate of baby chicks came by UPS, I slept in the brooder house with them, enchanted, stroking their buttery down and wondering with them about their future lives as grown chickens.

But as my father became more and more sick, the animals changed. By the time I started leaving the farm to go to highschool, and my father started staying in bed much of the time, we were living with not only about twenty cats and a dog but a half-dozen roving demented geese and two ornery pebble-shit-spewing goats and a couple dozen hysterical hens and a tyrannical rooster named Sam, and they all needed some combination of feeding, tethering, egg-gathering, stall-mucking, herding, shit-scooping, and/or killing. The goats were always running away, the cats were always trying to sneak new friends into the barn, and the chickens were getting more and more stupid. And one day, Sam lost it completely.

ISSUE 82

I have loved, since I moved to New York, the feeling of living in an apartment; an enclosure inside another enclosure, walls within walls, our lives invisible and impersonal and yet surrounded by other human bodies, always nearby. From inside a New York apartment, the city can have the broad quiet feeling of a library. So this should not be happening, but it is happening: our apartment has become permeable in the strangest way. My bookshelves are alive with a soundless flutter of orange and yellow butterflies, and cardinals flash red from perch to perch, while a groundhog waddles secretively from under one couch to the other. I call 311, but when I try to explain our problem, the operator hangs up. There is a muffled knock at the door and when Alex opens it, a faun is shaking our welcome mat in his mouth. What else is there to do? He lets him in.

Our lives must stretch out not just in time but space; we can fall through any moment to another we thought was over forever. On the farm, Sam ruled us all with a frightening precision. Every morning he began crowing exactly an hour before the sun rose, after which the geese would attack the air with their wings and scream, and then the goats would begin to bleat in their stall in the barn, and then the hens would cluck their way out of the brooder house into the barnyard.

But one morning, the August before I left for college, Sam perched on a fencepost outside the brooder house at 4:00 a.m., began crowing, and did not stop. A couple hours later, he climbed into a lilac bush outside of my parents' bedroom and started doing a little dance inside it, a nonstop cockadiddledoo bush-shaking jig. After a while, my mother went outside in her nightgown and beat the bush for a while with a broom, but Sam wouldn't budge. When she went back inside, she saw that my father was in a coma.

Up too early because of Sam's mind-lacerating screams, I stumbled out to the barn to water the goats and pour dry catfood into tin pans. When I arrived in the kitchen cradling the morning eggs in my t-shirt, my mother was absent-mindedly scraping crumbling bacon around in a saucepan.

"There's something wrong with that rooster," she said. "And your father is in a coma."

"You're burning that bacon," I said.

ISSUE 82

I walked to the window to watch my brother shoot his fifty free-throws before breakfast. Despite the noise, he didn't miss a single one of his last eight shots. On his way back to the house, without looking, he hurled the ball at the lilac bush, but he picked it up again, brushed it off, and brought it inside.

There was no telling when in the night my father had slipped into the space between sleep and death. It was too dangerous to move him, said the doctor when my mother called, so we should just wait it out. Inside the lilac bush, Sam crowed and danced through every morning hour, and when my grandmother came at noon with frozen chicken patties, cole slaw, potato salad, and sweet pickles in plastic containers from Kroger's Market, the three of us ate lunch to the sound of a crazed screaming rooster flamenco. Sam crowed through the dishwashing and my furious early afternoon trip to move the goats to fresh pasture, and although my brother was in his room practicing his electric guitar all afternoon, I am sure he could hear the crowing after every chord.

My mother, grandmother and I were in the garden picking beans when, as the afternoon light turned suppertime golden, my brother went to the cellar stairway and took down our grandfather's old .22 caliber rifle from a rack on the wall. In the garden, my mother saw him first, walking out of the house carrying the gun.

"Would you look at that," she said.

"Where's he going with that thing?" asked my grandmother.

"I don't know," said my mother. "I don't think he's touched a gun in his life."

While we watched, my brother walked straight out the back door twenty feet, turned, took aim at some invisible point deep inside the dancing lilac bush, and shot Sam through the right eye.

Sam was an old rooster, too stringy to eat but good enough for broth. Giggling, my mother broke Sam's neck, and my grandmother plucked his feathers while he was till warm. I pulled out his insides, and then we set him to simmer in a big pot on the stove. When my brother stalked through the kitchen with his basketball to shoot his fifty free-throws before dinner, my mother asked, in the raised voice one uses with people who are always on their way out of the room,

"How did you manage to shoot that rooster right through the eye like that? Was it luck?"

"No," my brother said, and walked out to the barn.

"What happened?" asked my father, from the bedroom.

"Oh honey," said my mother. "You're awake, you're awake, you're awake."

Some part of me is waiting for Alex to fall ill. I've been getting ready to wait by his bedside, bring him grilled cheese sandwiches and pills and give him his shot. I have not been getting ready for what seems to be actually happening, our particular catastrophe. Yet most of these animals are familiar to me. I know the chickens, and the goat; I've seen the deer before.

But there are some I don't recognize, wilder and fuzzier around the edges. The frogs in the bathtub are not Indiana frogs. There's what sounds like a miniature animatronic great white shark thumping around in the kitchen sink. Alex and I are trying to watch Lost, volume cranked to drown out the noise. He seems less surprised than I am that there are meerkats tunneling through the stacks of magazines in his study, and a dalmation curled familiarly at his feet. Then Alex yelps and, a few seconds later, a tiny monkey, furry and chirping, is pogoing on the coffee table.

In minutes, there are dozens of them, some of them flying in stupid invented formations from kitchen to bedroom to study and back again through the living room, some of them banking and diving like crazed hornets. Alex is looking redfaced and ashamed. The other animals don't seem happy about his monkeys at all—they're ducking and chirping and bleating and clucking, and I've had it. I fill our largest pot with water and set it on the stove to boil. I'm not sure what I'm going to do, exactly, but I know I'm the one who should know how to deal with insane magical animals.

I take the elevator to the roof to clear my head, look along the long lit arc of the Williamsburg Bridge to Manhattan, Brooklyn's horizon, which curves to hold us. Everything that stands still is in its place, and everything moves at an appropriate pace. Coming toward me on the bridge, the J train passes a bicycle, a car passes the J train. I am tempted to hope that I still belong to these solid structures and these regular motions, that they will keep me moving in place, safe from the world to the west, from the Indiana where my mother lives, still, with the animals.

But they are here already. I should warn my brother, who has made his own home in Michigan, in the cleanest of suburbs, empty and safe, or so he thinks. I go downstairs to take care of business. But when I open the apartment door Alex is in overalls, chewing on a piece of straw, trying to cut chickenwire with my sewing scissors.

"There are six so far," he says. "I was thinking they could live in my dresser. I'm going to cut some holes in it."

"A brooder house," I say. "So you're a farmer now."

I can feel the gaze of dozens of animal eyes, not human but not empty, not threatening or friendly, just here. I turn off the stove and consider. I'll start with the monkeys, I guess; I'm thinking I can move the plants into my study to build a kind of jungle, get banana deliveries from Fresh and Direct so it's easy. It will not be as quiet a life any more. But worse things could happen.

David Lehman

Ode to Punctuation

A poem without punctuation is female.
                    – Pauline Ambrozy

The comma is female,
The exclamation point male,
The semi-colon is fem bi-curious sub 29 Virginia.

The apostrophe is prosperous, possessive (femme)
The colon looks both ways before crossing the street (m).
The fast-running dash can't make up his mind
about the curvaceous question mark lurking in the lobby. What to do?
The parenthesis (f, 30) needs attention and keeps interrupting.

Thus the sentence moves
from the solace of day
to the lunacy of night
in a dependent clause beginning "although."

Although it is past curfew,
the nouns in the woods
conjugate the verbs
unattended by adjectives and adverbs.

And the sentence drives to a climax
and ends in a unisex period.

ISSUE 82

Molly Peacock

The Diva

D was done with it
and it meant everything.
Done with demands, denial,
the drama of hope.
D hadn't lived all his decades for nothing.
Devotion? Spare me, D thought.
D was closing doors. Click-click—done.
When they were all shut behind him,
there opened a corridor of woods.

And another thing I'm done with,
D declared to himself, Sex.
I'm done with the dreck of it.
The minute he said that he felt both relief
and dismay.
Damn, I'm disoriented, he thought.
It was dusk in the dell.
Nothing to do but continue
through the dimming light.
Did he hear a divertimento?

Dreams. . . .
They were the forest corridor!
(He'd slammed all his doors like a demon
and now released his daimon.)
How dendroid he was, he noticed, shaped like a tree.
Why not close the last door? he asked himself in the dusk.
There weren't any doors anymore,
just the stuff doors were made of, the woods.

ISSUE 82

A dragonfly dove down
and flew up a damselfly.
D looked down then:
he was awfully old and disheveled and droopy.
He could be a man or a woman, it hardly mattered.
Oh why not, he thought?
have a bit of an adventure before the very end?
He made his choice.
D was Delta after all, the triangle.

A divan appeared in the dell.
D lay down, melting a little,
from dismissive to something like delighted,
but drier. He was a diva now, a dried diva.
His penis morphed just a little, to a more clitoral shape;
his old testicles were sort of shrunken anyway;
just a little bit more and they'd be labial wattles.
It was a soft landing when he jumped sexes.

D heard the sound of water.
Oh, was the divan near the beach?
D was glad she hadn't closed the door on dream.
She lay down, curling up,
with two hands under her chin
like a sleeping child or praying angel
as all dissolved, everything into everything else
air to water, water to air
disobedience into inclination
disappointment into a pleasant dampness
a humidity, a drink for her old dry skin
as the world dissolved from darkling to darling.

ISSUE 82

Interview with Molly Peacock and David Lehman

October 2009 – January 2010

An Interview with David Lehman, Editor of *Best American Poetry* and Molly Peacock, Editor of *Best Canadian Poetry in English.* Conducted by Jason Schneiderman.

Jason: Molly, David; I'm awed by how much you both do to promote poetry. David, you've been editing *Best American Poetry* for over two decades. Molly, you just oversaw the publication of the first issue of *Best Canadian Poetry.* I wanted to start by asking you both, what has been the biggest surprise of working on your respective projects?

DL: What continues to surprise me is just how many obstacles there are in the way of any effort at championing poetry, enlarging its readership, and honoring the poets. Even when you succeed – and *The Best American Poetry,* now in its twenty-second year, has succeeded beyond expectations – it sometimes seems like a losing battle. Perhaps that is one thing that draws some of us to poetry: on a bad day, it can seem that the worthiest causes face the longest odds. The newspapers ignore poetry except to proclaim the impending death of an art form, and when magazines or book reviews do allot some precious space to a poetry book, they employ notoriously malignant reviewers. Well, poetry will outlast newspapers, though it can give us no pleasure to see them fold. *The Best American Poetry* does its part to lift the morale of the poets chosen for our pages each year, and I'm glad of that, but it's sad that so many poets are prone to feelings of resentment, bitterness, and competitive envy.

On the other hand, it's very exciting that people in their 20s and 30s, knowing all they do about the problems we face, aspire with such sweet intensity and high ambition to join the bardic ranks. There is a lot of talent out there. Many more good poems are being written and published each year than the gloom-sayers will admit. And of course it delights me that there is a *Best Canadian Poetry* under Molly Peacock's general editorship. The impulse has spread abroad.

ISSUE 82

Christoph Buchwald's *Jahrbuch der Lyrik* has had a good long run in Germany. *The Best New Zealand Poems*, which the editors say they "shamelessly modeled" on "the successful US paperback anthology," made its debut in 2001, and *The Best Australian Poetry* (published by UQP) has been going since 2003; Anthony Lawrence chose the poems for the 2004 edition, John Tranter for 2007, and Alan Wearne in 2009. For a while there were even two competing "best" anthologies in Australia.

MP: Thanks back to you, David. I'm delighted to participate in this conversation. About that idea of surprise: part of the reason I undertook *Best Canadian Poetry in English* was to be surprised by the work of Canadian poets. I'm not nearly as familiar with Canadian poetry as I am with American poetry, so I never know what to expect. Since we're just beginning, I've only worked with two guest editors so far. I was flabbergasted that there were only six poets out of fifty in each volume who overlapped. It's a big landscape out there! I understand what you mean about the obstacles. Having helped to start *Poetry in Motion* with the Poetry Society of America about the same time as you started *Best American*, I was surprised that the poetry placards lasted as long as they did in New York — fifteen years — though they're gone temporarily. They'll be back on the buses, soon. The program still exists here in Canada, thriving on the Toronto subways. Because I am a citizen of both countries and go back and forth to New York all the time (though I live in Toronto) I run a continual compare and contrast essay in my head about poetry in my two countries. Poetry, even from small presses, is still reviewed in *The Globe and Mail* here, as well as in other newspapers across Canada. I fear that will decline as the newspapers decline. But in terms of poetry as news that stays news, it strikes me that in both countries the people who love poetry seem to find each other, whether that's in Moose Jaw or Miami.

JS: Molly — thank you for reminding me of the full title your anthology — *Best Canadian Poetry in English*. This brings me to the question of nationality. David, in looking through The Best American Poetry 2009, I noticed that Michael Johnson is unambiguously Canadian; Jade Nutter was born a British citizen (though she now works and lives in Minnesota); Derek Walcott is from St. Lucia; and Jim Harrison is coy about his birthplace. How capacious is *Best American* in its conception of "American"? Do you struggle not only with the idea of "best poem" but also the idea of "American poem?" And Molly, do you think that there would ever be a *Best Canadian Poetry in French*? You make a wonderful argument for a distinctly Canadian poem in your introduction. Would you consider, alongside the additional list of 50 poems, a list of Québécois Poems or First Nations Poems?

DL: We have always constructed "American" in the broadest sense to include Canada and the Caribbean. From the start the poets who served as guest editors of *The Best American Poetry* wanted to be ecumenical, and this predilection tallied with my own instincts. I favor the idea of being as comprehensive and inclusive as possible when surveying the landscape for an enterprise that confers, in the end, an exclusive distinction. The struggle I have is not with unsolvable questions of poetic value, the definition of "America," or the use of a superlative. The struggle I have is simply keeping up with the plethora of poems and poets out there begging for a hearing.

MP: We are always thinking of *La Meilleure Poésie Canadienne en Français,* though that would be quite a different enterprise. As far as First Nations poets are concerned, we will have poetry by at least one First Nations poet in our second volume. As the Series Editor, it's really important to me to find that broad sweep of voices and to include it in the anthology. That's why our longlist of 100 poems is so crucial. As for how we see the anthology in the North American context, that's a very different matter from the way David sees it. His is the point of view from what Canadians feel is the dominant culture to the south. Let's make an analogy from another part of the world. Think of Big China and little Thailand. Thai culture always feels the mammoth culture of China at its doors. Canada isn't little, area-wise, but it has had a unique challenge as it established its voice and cultural identity (perhaps I should say identities). Because of this challenge, the country got the rather amazing idea that its voice or voices, both for its own citizens and for the world, would be established by... its writers! As Canadian writers describe the Canadian experience, a nation is formed. *Best Canadian Poetry in English* is supported both by the national and the provincial arts councils. Because Tightrope Books receives its funding from the government, we actually have to report to the citizenship status of each of our poets. Coming from New York, this shocked me at first. It's not something I'll bet that Scribner gives a thought to. Yet the Canadian government's investment in its artists moves me. To be valued in such way is quite an incredible shift in the priorities of how a nation operates, and how it views its poets. I do feel that poets are more cherished in Canada.

JS: One of the things that I really like about both the *Best American Poetry* and *Poetry in Motion* is that they've never been coercive. I feel like a lot of the people looking to "promote" poetry either want to chastise poets and redirect their work, or chastise the public for not being good readers. I once saw Nadine Gordimer speak, and her defense of "the book" was couched in an attack on television and movies -- which seemed counterproductive to me. Poetry in Motion and your anthologies don't exactly take a laissez faire approach. They definitely put poetry in front of people who wouldn't otherwise be reading poetry, but without the guilt-trip. I was wondering if you guys get a lot of "conversion" letters from people who've discovered poetry because of your editorial efforts. Can you share any insights on what it is that makes a person a poetry lover or reader? And as poetry lovers yourselves, what is it like trying keep up with a full year's worth of poetry?

MP: As anyone who talks to teenagers knows, poetry that comes at a desperate moment in a life can feel as if it saves that life. Poetry lovers really, really adore poetry because they engage with it on so many levels, but particularly with the sense that the art responds in a crisis, an emotional one or an intellectual one. We do get fan letters for *Best Canadian,* but we haven't quite been around long enough to get "conversion" letters. However, I am on the Board of RPO, Representative Poetry On Line, a fabulous poetry website which has built on the work of scholars of poetry in English from the University of Toronto. RPO gets conversion letters from people who run across poems on line that sink immediately into their cores. It's very moving to me when this happens. There are people on dialysis machines, people on third rounds of chemotherapy, who discover poetry because it is so fearless in the face of disaster.

Yet, interestingly, the older I get, I don't expect sudden mass conversion to this intense art. Poetry takes time and focus and investment in language no matter what poet of which aesthetic conviction has written it. As an enthusiast, I personally am nourished by a huge variety of poems. Like David, I am not interested in representing a school of poetry, even though my own work has been identified with a school. I admire enterprises that go across aesthetic lines and beyond them. As David, whom I esteem, says about keeping up with poetry, yes, it's overwhelming (but a bit less so in Canada with about fifty literary magazines), but it feeds my restless intellect as well. My gamble, the gamble of Stephanie Bolster and A.F. Moritz, our first two guest editors, and that of Halli Villegas, the publisher of Tightrope Books, is that a wider audience for poetry is out there. The vectors that have converged for our marvelous sales are the excellence of the poems and the variety of the poets. That's what excites me, and that's what inspires this enterprise. Jason, I really appreciate the way you've moderated this conversation, and David, I really enjoy having had the chance to compare and contrast with you.

DL: Thank you, Molly – and let me add my thanks to hers, Jason, for arranging this dialogue. Like you, I don't want to chastise anyone except the chastisers. Coercion is the enemy of poetry. I can't do better than Frank O'Hara in "Personism." After noting that a strategy of "forced feeding" backfires, he writes, "Nobody should experience anything they don't need to, if they don't need poetry bully for them. I like the movies too." O'Hara is being deliberately pugnacious here, but his effort to separate poetry from obligation – whether the poet's obligation to society or society's obligations to the poet – is important. To perpetuate the audience for poetry is a worthy objective but guilt is a losing strategy. And the fortunes of our art form do not require us to refuse the charms of *Mad Men* on television or the Kurosawa retrospective at the Film Forum.

I don't know why some otherwise reasonable people become social Darwinists when it comes to assigning value to contemporary art and poetry. Sure, there is such a thing as bad poetry. There's always plenty on hand. But there's no reason to talk back to it. I like O'Hara's refusal to deal with a bad poem. He is convinced that it will "slip into oblivion" without his needing to give it a push.

Much of the mail I get is very gratifying. People write that a volume in the series, or a particular poem, had a decisive effect on them. Contributors say how happy they are to be included. They call it an honor. They've been reading the *Best American Poetry* from cover to cover for twenty years and now their own work is in there. I have heard from more than one contributor that their initial appearance in a volume of *Best American Poetry* was the best thing to happen to them in their professional lives. Even allowing for exaggeration, that's quite a statement. Some of the poems we have featured have become poetry "standards" (in the sense that "Body and Soul" is a jazz standard). It's nice to think that we played a hand in that or in the renewed popularity of a device like the abecedarius or a form like the sestina or pantoum. I also like the way the poems speak among themselves. Julie Sheehan had a poem in *BAP 2005*,

"Hate Poem," that inspired Martha Silano's "Love" in *BAP 2009*. There are other instances.

Poetry is unkillable. The very word is too useful. It remains the term of choice for a certain kind of grace (as when a journalist observes Oscar Peterson's fingers on the piano keys) or eloquence (as when political commentators repeat that "you campaign in poetry but you govern in prose"). When he found out that I write poetry, a software manufacturer congratulated me on practicing "a craft that will never become obsolete" – unlike last year's version of this year's operating system. Whether or not he meant to be ironic, the irony is he's right.

The desire to write poetry is a precious thing. It turns into a need on the one hand and a habit or practice on the other. If we were making a list of reasons to stay alive, and it seems we keep needing to do so, poetry would occupy a cherished place on the list. We have the testimony of too many people from any and every class, category, and income bracket, to doubt it. To the extent that these anthologies of ours bring to the publishing of poetry the same imaginative energy that goes into the writing of a poem, we will have succeeded in doing something important for the art itself, for our poets, and for readers prepared to embrace poetry if only it were presented to them in an appealing way.

ISSUE 82

83

Toby Barlow

A Diary of Food

the song of slicing
chickens' throats just north of Santa Fe
hanging them upside down from bare trees
their dark blood dripping down onto the dry soil
of the sangre de christo mountains.

and mornings spent humming in a winter barn
pushing around belligerent cows with stupid eyes
stepping, almost slipping, on black iced shit
then watching my breath steam out
over buckets of perfect white milk

and then the silence of that handsome shy boy
who sold street side horse meat
in the San Lorenzo district of Rome,
the boy my wife had a crush on
when she was on her way
to not being my wife.

ISSUE 83

Grace Bauer

Hand to Mouth

I've got a full report from the sandwich committee.
                    overheard in a hotel lobby

Of course, I think baloney.
Of course, I think ham and cheese,
peanut butter and jelly –
those familiar duos we grew up on.
The *ménage a trios* of BLTs.

But I know I must be missing
the context, some definition
homelier than bread, more filling
than what we commonly slip between
two slices and take in hand.

Perhaps the committee
could not commit – torn
between mustard and mayo,
between white, wheat and rye.
Oh, the awesome
responsibility of any choice.

Everything depends on depending –
that message in between
which words get said, the underside
of utterance full
of import and ellipsis,
which is what I've been
left out of in this instance
of eavesdrop. I sit, limp

as lettuce on a day-old sub,
dressed, wrapped and ready
for take-out, knowing that
whatever the committee decides
will be both right and wrong,
both not enough and too much.
That no report will ever be full
enough to satisfy hunger for long.

ISSUE 83

Abraham Burickson

At the Jobsite Friday is Barbecue Day

St. Agnes shouldn't let her girls go
but she does with shrieking bells

and could be they planned the wind
just for Sal: *why they make them skirts so short!*

his eyes grey and hot like the barbecue
burned too long, needs coal, Charlie

pours some and maybe he's embarrassed
until Sal unwraps the beef and says *See*

that's why it's a crime. Bloodwater splatters
the sidewalk. *The right hand giveth*

and the left hand. . ..The right hand giveth
*and the left hand. . ..*He's throwing meat

at the fire. Charlie's nervous; maybe
the man has slipped again, head full

of gristle – sometimes it gets hot –
They got mammies and they got pappies

a whole new kit, fresh out of the box ,
those little bodies all rubber and snap-dragon –

oooh it's just sunrise in those eyes! And lookit you
Mr. Noon! Sal's too close. Sal's too loud,

the girls are coming up the hill. Why think
of father and sister here, suddenly, your lost

teeth, suddenly, the blonde of your hair gone
brown, the torn-down house, the teenage drive

when you saw the white cow die, fascinating:
the viscera leaking out, fascinating: one might

know God by this design. But Sal's got Charlie
by the liver; burger's burning and Charlie's

leaping into hot metal: now everything falls
and the street's a fakir-dream of embers

Haha! shouts Sal. He's on the ground;
that's the smell of flesh burning

and smoke from his shirt – Charlie's
stretching a hand but Sal's got a coal

in the palm and a white smile:
that's what it is to buy it back youth,

charring skin to the fresh hand he was dealt.
Across the street the girls have stopped

and one grabs the fat of another one's arm
as their timid gaze falls on the mess of the men

while the others age in the sun
and cover their eyes and are gone.

Abraham Burickson

Sundays are for Market, Sundays are for Park

Lobsters agape in big glass tank. Bread and milk and eggs on shelf. Bread and milk and eggs in bag. And Charlie's getting Charlie's groceries. And hide your eyes, tuck your hands. And coat don't brush a banker; shoe don't touch a father; don't touch a husband father worker, don't touch a mother wife walker. And pig hung in window. Brain stuck like ham. Never notice; never wake; all the same; never wake. *How about tomorrow tomorrow tomorrow* thinks Charlie. But somebody *yesterday yesterday yesterday* says. And stand in the sun read the weather on the paper; stand in the bank read the future in your hand.

‡‡‡

Not to die like a dog.

ISSUE 83

Abraham Burickson

The View

He figures the air's there to carry words
for her. Charlie sees it. Her voice shivers it,
her voice: perfect, from a perfect body;

no, imperfect: what wreckage her young body
bore. You wouldn't think. Those chlorophyll eyes
that wash him, those hands, crushed once

under a world of rocks. That's the past:
a heart pumping poison, a brain aflame. *I
did it to myself,* she says, and Charlie

bends to put a hand in; she melts to him.
All that. He's only a feel and a touch now.
Too much: memory's a body

full of blood, they're wet with it.
I'm fine now, she says. She says!
The sound's a brass bell in a city street.

It's true! After so many days of night
of Charlie counting time in the door creak.
She says! Charlie would do anything for girl,

and she's kissing him now. Remember
when sky was brown at noon, Remember
rivers on fire? That apocalypse passed, too.

Now she's a ripple and a resting pebble, clear
at the bottom. He feels stones in her, that's
what happened: not a freeze but a foundation.

Charlie says he'll build a house there,
that ground come clean of chemicals, now she's
the black soil from which Earth grows. Earth!

ISSUE 83

Isn't that a mother born of cataclysm. No lovelies
without the fire, Charlie, she's a glimmering
and a forged metal. And you? Nevermind.

Girl's smile is a luminous unlocked door now.
Inside, a librarian is reading the future and Charlie
looks to see what he might hold and steps

into the veranda and the view and the armchair
on which Charlie might rest on which Charlie
might love to rest and to take a tea and to watch.

ISSUE 83

Lisabeth Burton

Sweet Fever

I eat like people who dog ear
the bottom corner of pages,
people in which
unrequited lust accrues.

Dear heavenly icebox,
I'm not brawling with my nature,
this is me appealing
for a conversation of the body.

Forgive us our engorged purple lamb chops,
the final fifty pieces
of pickled peach cobbler,
forgive us the sinless ability

to lose our lovely heads.
Absolve all the uncertainty
fondly clutching us like headwinds,
and deliver me

from the slick emotion
of stainless steel refrigerators,
for I am genuinely not
satisfied in this world.

ISSUE 83

Veronica Castrillon

Artichoke
(For E.)

Table set, fork in hand,
napkin on my lap:
sitting beside you, I
still look like someone civilized.

You're leaning forward, hands cupping your neck,
while I watch the slow
rise and fall
of your back.
Like you, I need to be broken into.

I imagine your head burrowed between my legs, fingers hooked
inside my mouth.

But I can't speak the way you speak.

Your blackberry hair is the dare of my body near.
Your mouth stained by the blood of beets is my mouth
meeting it.

The self-contained world of the snow pea is you inside me.

And the strange sound of artichoke, if said aloud,
would be my madness mouthed.

Meri Culp

Stalker

Keep your steely-eyed offerings,
your garden pretense, botanical bliss,

your reedy wisp of asparagus,
no longer green-speared, but gray-leaden.

Hold in check your artichoke words,
the petal pull of anger-dipped butter,

core-covering the heart of new spring,
my palmed heart, still tender, still looking

for unsullied celery, small boats of clean,
green sea washing to red sunset, rhubarb lined horizon.

Refine your sugar-shafted sight,
angled to hard cane truth.

Know that syrup can boil.
Spears can pierce,

and my heart can be shaded,
yet swayed, in one subtle trace.

Daniel Donaghy

Scrapple

Chances are, you've had it—
    maybe while you were high,
with creamed chipped beef and toast,

or out with relatives now long gone
    on a sandwich called
the Junk Yard Dog: fried pork roll,

fried bacon, fried scrapple and eggs
    on a soaked bun
you couldn't pick up. Maybe it's not

for everyone, but it's for you, isn't it?
    You love this stuff,
this bottom-of-the-barrel butcher

mush sliced thin and fried in fat.
    If you're old enough
to read this and you've made it

this far, you know exactly
    what I'm talking about.
Admit it: once or twice a year

you crave it the way you still
    crave the touch of a lover
who was just a bit rougher

than you were ready for,
    whose squints come back,
whose ass slaps come back

on long missionary nights
    because you're ready now,
it's clear. And you love how bad

it is for you, how you shouldn't
    let it near your mouth,
but because the choice is yours, you do.

Sage and pepper and cloves,
    onions and cornmeal,
ground pork brains and hearts —

you love every slimy piece
    of scrapple that drops
like a rock into your gut

to make sure you hurt
    the rare time you break
from the safe little script

of your life, each piece working its way
    into a jagged stone wall,
taking as long as it needs to settle in.

ISSUE 83

James Engelhardt

Pierogi (Polish)

Simple food, really, the sour shells
folded over filling—a kind of dumpling
to boil and fry with butter and onions

but imagine a boy
coming back to his house
of accented newspapers

after an afternoon watching Judy Garland
turn rosy after landing in Oz
and the smell of popcorn caught in his hair

crimped pierogi and country sausages
slip around on a plate
with blue and red designs

nothing in the house
as bright as Oz
as bright as the dark theater

he's supposed to pray in Polish
but he's thinking of yellow—
of light and film

Kate Ferencz

Pride in Your Work

Today when I was icing all the cupcakes—how many? Dozens or maybe hundreds, enough to keep me busy for six hours—I did not, not even for one single cupcake, make the effort to make sure I was putting a lot of love into it I usually do that. I think about how swirly the icing is, I think about the sensory experience of biting into the cupcake, and I imagine the person who buys it laughing a little because it's a kind of silly, indulgent, special-occasion thing to do. Maybe they were having an especially hard day today and they needed it, or maybe not, but I like to imagine that for some reason or other that cupcake changes their life for the better, because of the good wishes I put into it. I hope that the cupcake will make them remember that they deserve to be nice to themselves, and to give themselves little special treats or whatever it is they need to feel good. Or I hope they get that crazy manic feeling you get from too much sugar and end up spending the whole night dancing or doing something fun if wouldn't normally--- so that's basically the same thing. And sometimes the wishes are more ambiguous, open ended whispery ideas like, *break up with your boyfriend! Get out of New York!* Or even murkier, *I hope this cupcake is as fun to eat as it was to make,* and always, usually, love, love, love. Let this cupcake remind you what love is like. Let it remind you what pride in your work is like, but not today. Today I completely forgot.

ISSUE 83

Rachel Contreni Flynn

Ravenous

– for Noah

1.

The child holds on inside me:
pink bat, drowsy possum.

With quick teeth,
I eat handfuls of bread

and fruit the shape
of my own body,

pear juice like tears
coats the flesh of my arms.

2.

At night coyotes send up sparks of hunger and laughter from the
    frozen field.
I need to see shadows made into fire. At the window, my belly
    presses hard
on the cold glass as if the eyes inside also wake and blaze.

3.

I sleep a complicated circle
of desire and panic. Faces jut
from the underbrush claiming
we've found you and will keep you.

My hands are useless leaves,
my throat as dry. I clutch my breasts
and gut and come up with fists full
of bindweed and ragged feathers.

4.

If I have turned wild, long-haired, ravenous,
it is because there are so many ways grief

could come down, its paw impossibly
(but possible!) huge and sharp and sure.

5.

My husband gathers me up. Turning
the day to clouds and lilacs, he comes
with sacks of books, more fruit, then smoothes
our bed into a cool, pale square.

6.

There is nothing to do about the pulp and gore nestled in a sweet
     grass basket
except swing the bundle by a rope high above my head toward an
     icy fgully,

letting go again and again, and shrieking.

7.

Please live. I have dreams without reason.

8.

The boy I loved

seemed fierce
until the morning

I spied him alone
in the dorm kitchen

eating grapefruit,
lifting a wedge

ISSUE 83

of wet fruit gently

from its soft bowl,
bringing to his mouth

a bit of amber

with a spoon rimmed
in calm, blunt teeth.

9.

I have found you
and will keep you

from hunger
with my own body.
Please live. I know
the coyotes press in,

but I'll swing
my hair on fire

to ward them off
and bring you home.

10.

The morning I married the boy,
light caught the edge of his eye

and turned his face half-golden.
The cellos played. I gasped

as my dress streamed red.
With flowers, with flowers.

ISSUE 83

Sophia Galifianakis

Of What is Made

I.

Loose threads

reach down my rib and cross
the bone, the cage

of ink my body is; and then

II.

    travel through the needle's gaze:
to mend,

yes. Of strands and knots, let's say
a history

of stitches makes the garment whole.

For possibility:

III.

a hole.   What is cataracts,
after all,

but a waterfall before the passage:

IV.

like seeing, the philosophy of the divine.
Like culture

    waiting for its alphabet,
V.

banal, this body, inappropriate

Frankenstein
of formalities, decorated
as salt
                    thrust into oblivion
to bride
of all things,   clarity.   To be
that skin

VI.

effigial, looming in darkness
thick as flour
turning on a wheel.
Somewhere,

water rises water falls. We make our bread

VII.

of yeast and dialogue.

Jenny George

Notes on Pigs

A pig has eyelashes.
The pig's eyelashes function like our own eyelashes,
    but have a different meaning.
The pig is unadorned. A pig who cares about her looks
    is absurd.
A person who cares about a pig is a rare thing.
Many people live near animals.
A pig does not take a long evening bath, with a glass
    of sparkling grapefruit set on the porcelain ledge.
Neither a pig nor a person is invincible.
A pig is a tasty thing, when killed and cooked.
A person dressed in a pig costume is trying to be funny.
Pigs have superior eyesight.
A pig can see the silver belly of a plane moving across the sky.
Or a beetle crawling up a fence post.
Certain pink tulips, when the sun hits them, have the color
    of a clean pig.
A pig can only give birth to a person in a dream.
When a pig dies, it is either mourned by other pigs, or not.

Kristin Hatch

Sign of the Beefcarver Poem

we were at the break table swatting flies off the au jus. jerky kept
    laying his bald

head on my shoulder & i was like *i'm trying to eat my french dip,* but
    probably so timidgirl
it sounded like purr, purr.

(everything sticky, everything tan) the boys would smoke in the
    kitchen & probably
ash in your sauce.

i mean, don't we all want to be adored, but sometimes you just want
    a sandwich in some secret & no heads.
you don't have permission, pimples.

back on the floor & it was sunday afterchurch
so the place was buzz buzz whip/would you like some more coffee,
    sir & no tips
because of the lord's bigger.

& then suddenly smoke. not kitchen boy, i mean war.
i mean scream/boom (real bat man right here) poof/tinker/trick,
    trick (still).

when a lady drives into the Beef, it gets real quiet for a while after.

i wonder when you decide to keep eating.
like, when you assume no one is dead
or when the old woman climbs, churchclothed/alone, through the
    hole sorry or maybe
when manager jann (with two n's, mickey mouse tie) says to finish
    your fish.

& the cartoon-ties all talking in a circle & the lady shaking *oh boy* at
    the big
round table in the smoking room while they call her son.

ISSUE 83

you say *it'll be okay* like you know anything & like she asked
or like it will. purr, purr.

& then you just wait around it.

& their faces & the big hole by the fake fireplace looking out to the
parking lot.
& their faces & the big hole by the fake fireplace looking out to the
parking lot.

Elizabeth Hazen

Eve at the Stop N' Shop

There is a science
to my selection: I take two
of everything: artichokes

plastic bags of yellow corn
green beans asparagus
Peaches fist in my hands

My cart sinks:
nine gallons of milk six dozen
eggs butter sharp cheddar

burlap sacks of rice
boxes of pasta jars of sauce
frozen peas crinkling

like static I fill
three carts with tv dinners
two carts with cat food

and raw meat marbled
white with fat
In my hand I carry

a pack of doublemint gum
It takes four hours to ring
me up and six trips

to take everything home
The cabinets bulge
Goods ooze

through cracks
Pots and pans ring
disbelief

ISSUE 83

I soothe them with carrots
I add and add
The kitchen floods

with my mistakes   I have no one
to feed   I am starving
for cauliflower broccoli florets

The room deep with dismay,
thick with flour and meat
and all the recipes

I have failed to complete
The dishes rise to the ceiling
and fall Soapy water

fills the room   I have
forgotten what it was
I wanted

Jean C. Howard

Fruit Fly
—MOMA—NYC

Fat, little BB
of motion,
of minute flight,
weaving prayers
above sugar,
an open mouth
of wine and lemon
wedge.

Dreaming lazily
of summer,
its orchards
ripe and aching,
abstractions of fruit
at sun-cut angles.

Here you dip
toward watermelon,
haystacked with straws
of jicama,
then swerve
toward bleeding fig.

My thoughts go
out to you,
lured by the melody
of ruby flesh
and vinegar.
New York swirling
hot and restless
beyond my table,

I stab into a raspberry.
You'll drown,
I'm sure,
in blanc de noirs.

Mara Jebsen

Sundays in Lomé

By the jelly blue lights of an ocean
The day wakes, and breaks into sweat
Beach saunterers gossip of potions,
The power of juju, the wet

Face of a *madman*, whose wife, they said
put a spell in with the onions—
It was a Sunday of church, vodou, and knife
Her stewpots were seized by his cousins.

Jesus loomed in the market
Smiling benign and garish
Umbrellas and baskets of vegetable
Water in plastic bags, licorice.

Braid my hair, please, Madame, I said
Churchbells are singing, the sun has scored
It's way to noon, and here, my head
Rings with magic and blood, is shored

Against these fervent hallelujas
this ocean of hard palms clapping
I've that that the Lord is the color red,
Both lover and assassin.

ISSUE 83

Paul Lisicky

First Birthday

War in the news. Hunger in the news.
What of the following could stand up to that?

The waitress set down the plates. Car noise rolled in from the street. The rotisserie chicken so spicy and sweet, my eyes watered. After I'd finished my own plate, I started eating off of Mark's. The waitress came from the kitchen, laughed as if startled to see what she never thought she'd see. I cringed, blushed, though I went right on stabbing at his plate. Over and over, I lifted the fork to my mouth, shameless.

Around the corner to the nursery. Aisle after pleasantly messy aisle of sedum, spiral rush, mugo pine, more sedum. High sun on my forehead, seabreeze on my arms, legs, chest... The weather of my childhood, the weather of the shore house. (*She came back.*) Then it occurred to me: so this is what it's like to be alive again. It hadn't even occurred to me I hadn't been alive.

Yesterday just happened to be her birthday. My mother's first birthday since the day of her death.

ISSUE 83

Laura McCullough

Begin with a Bifid Tongue

Have you ever had turducken? That's turkey stuffed
with pork stuffed with chicken, a kind of gourmet diglossia,

or if you prefer, a glossolalia of protein. All boneless,
of course, which is best for the actual eating. Let's make

some, and while we eat it, let's share whatever words
we know in Tamil, Tagalog, Urdu. Let's draw pictographs

on our napkins in Chinese, Japanese, Korean, I don't care.
Can you stuff some spoken word in this poem or, better yet,

a double sonnet into a villanelle into a ghazal, no gravy,
to be sure, but what spills over, we can lick with our twin

tongues, salt and sweet dazzling our bifurcated muscles
into strips, no longer bifid but feathered, so we become

glossolalists, ecstatic, knowing only each other's language,
but unable to translate what we say, a kind of glossalgia

which means *pain in the tongue,* not unlike what happens
when you try to eat something right out of the oven, how

you can be that hungry, that desperate and that foolish.

ISSUE 83

Rose McLarney

We're Not Much for Words, But

Blackberries,
suspended in moonshine,

enlarged with alcohol,
skins stretched taut,
almost to bursting

and preserved, sit on the shelf.
They wait, purple and potent,

with the promise that, if we drink,
our skins will press together,
and our lips will split
in speech.

Wendy Noonan

Loom, Luminous

There's the platter of meats laid out for our guests;
wine, deviled-egg sandwiches; and the open field,
scrubby and littered, under the fire escape
where the kids go to smoke; there's the broken down
Toppys furniture truck in that field, and the old men
walking up Mississippi smelling like cigars and fifty years
of dumb hope. There's Bruce in his blue leisure suit, waving,
the horizon no longer far away: Mother toiling
with the family room— walker in a corner,
a rack of coats that go back sixty years.
For once, the mucked repetitions of home
don't loom like no-end streets, nor does the riff
of the beating heart, ahem, ahem.

Our guests sit at small plastic tables eating the food
we've laid out for them, their conversation,
the dog barking next door I've set my life against.
Grandma's in the bathroom rolling up her sleeves –
the rag in her hand, her husband in an urn
no longer yelling for her.

Look—there's me, there's me.

Rumit Pancholi

Appetite

Three-quarters moon, one-quarter barn: panoramic haze
of cattle bellows in a funk. Gray air trudges by
like wintered cornhusk, a dark bird pecks quietly its pile
of fodder on a straw hat the scarecrow refuses to wear
correctly like a rebellious child. From the cornfield
she emerges, the stolid, bonneted girl, a fat stray raccoon
cradled in her arms, a baby she's loath to surrender.
No sudden dash to his burrow. The prickling fur
at her forearm she ignores like a charm. It's past dusk—
her mother's nervous calls meander through sleeves
of moonlight, plumes of dark fog. The girl blinks away
her voice, the precariousness of night taking off
on the back of that dark bird at her will. Crouching over
the creature, fur chest she pillows, she tucks a kernel
of corn under the raccoon's tongue, waits for it to chew.

Janna Pate

Because You Were Older

You built your own table, the bare boards exposed.
By yourself, you kept the top clean, marble smooth. What's more,

you prepared for this dinner, you measured your sauces in stone
sake saucers, speckled with pinches of thyme and flicked sage.

You knew your spices. But, because you were a man,
you could fixate on broccoli, obsess over olives and limes.

Around you, steam blossomed and rose. Red wine swirled in a glass
the shape of a pear. Bulbous eggplants, recumbent inside a
      wire basket—

they spoke of your deep understanding, the way your dishes did
      not stack,
and there was no space for a layered dessert, no sense in a
      soft conversation.

As small, pensive sages, we sat instead, our legs crossed
on your vintage-style cushions; the smell was unnaturally new.

When the speed on the turntable surged, and then fell, you called
      that sound
"flutter," the fast form of *wow*. In the midnight moonlight,

I saw your spoon shake as I reached for more lamb.
Fork tines scraped my teeth. Could you hear me swallow?

ISSUE 83

Ricardo Pau-Llosa

Parable of the Chair

At the bar, the man's buddy's eyes
scavenge in arcs for women
ambulating as the man tried to explain
why he hadn't quite gotten over
his wife's betrayal and otherwise
moved on, ground these beans
of wisdom into flour, kneaded them into bread
and so forth, except the metaphor
of bread was like the seed thrown
to the barbarous thorns. So the man
said, Say you went to a banquet
and alone among the gorging sitting guests
your chair breaks and you fall
on your ass to the ground, where
you must ride out the banquet
for whatever reason on the damp grass
with your plate in your left hand
and spearing peas and potatoes with your right
while everyone else sits and gorges.
And maybe you should have shaken
the chair first when you took it,
as no doubt the others did theirs,
and noticed it was going to fail.
But no matter, there you are
on the grass, meal in hand,
table linen slapping your face
with each breeze. A redhead
passed behind the man, bringing
his buddy's eyes in line with his, briefly.
The man continued, So there you are.
Now, are you angry
because you lost your chair
or because you are sitting on the ground?
The friend can't figure the difference
as red curls and fake blonde strike up a conversation
nearby whose loudest key words
were Asshole and Real Estate. The man

plumbs the difference but no longer
caring if his interlocutor is following.
If you yearn for the chair,
you still love the woman who betrayed you.
But if what you lament is the fact
that you are on the ground,
then she is not the wound.
You have linked betrayal with life
on a conditional plane, the level that affirms
the inconsolable inextricability of the irremediable.
And with these last words he emerged loudly enough
from the sowing of his own thoughts
that his pal heard them
as he got up, mojito in hand,
to talk to red and yellow three stools away.
That's the problem, the buddy threw in
like change on the bar,
Too many *i's* in your words.

ISSUE 83

Sue Song

Lessons

I.

My father tears the body,
lines his fingers along
the fish's cracked back fin
and pulls against the head--
its eyes opaque from the fry.

He removes
the tender middle,
layered in tiers like feathers

holds the meat, still wet,
and asks Marie's mother
to open her mouth.

II.

At Sunday school,
a helper-mother
explains to me that birds
are creatures most without sin—
for they fly closest to god.

This same mother
often wielded a Beretta
to guard the convenience store
she and her husband ran
in West Philadelphia.

Once her husband
stabbed her for infidelity
with the store blade
used for slicing ham shanks.
At the hospital they told police
that a black man with a scar

splitting his left cheek
ransacked their place of business.

That night, at home
I page through a field guide
to North Atlantic birds,
studying lining, quill,
and large primaries
shaped like soft arrowheads.

I read of hollow bones,
those ancients
who studied entrails,
sporadic flight patterns

and consider the secrets
in those small hearts gorged,
white lungs blooming--
fists unraveling
in the open air.

III.

I remember
it was a day in December
I thought my mother
was beautiful
in a black wool coat
and houndstooth scarf.

That day she talked again
of how a starling
once snipped seed
right from her hand.

The bird cut her palm.
She bled a bit
and called it
pained blessing.

ISSUE 83

Rotate and Return

Beth watched the tip of the rod quiver, the motion sharp against the gentle sway of pine trees and white shells of aspen jutting from the boulders and cliffs surrounding them. She looked at her shaking hands and took a steadying breath, stepped ankle deep into the river. Her casts were neat, but they were falling short of the uprooted trees near the opposite bank by at least ten feet and the more she forced herself to aim for them, the more the exposed roots started to bend, blur into tentacles tangling in Micah's hair, holding him under until their father could pull him out.

She shook her head, turned the tentacles into roots again. This was the first time they'd been tentacles. Usually they were chains or barbed wire. Once, after a week of working at a craft store, they'd been colorful ropes of yarn, the strands lifting and weaving themselves into a doily-like restraint. Tentacles were a surprise even if the scene wasn't, probably the result of a Christmas with nothing but Star Trek DVDs to keep her company, one of the few things she managed to throw into her truck when she finally left Texas and the man who lived there. What she had to do was not think about it, catch herself before she sunk so deep into memory that she couldn't climb back out without help, chemical or otherwise. She reeled in her line and looked back at David, watched the warmth of his breath pool in the chill early morning air, air that caught the just breaking pink of the sun, sharpened it.

David's lips pulled to the side and his eyes crinkled at the corners when he caught her watching him, she blushed and looked away, still wasn't comfortable around him though he seemed relaxed around her. She tried to keep her eyes on her own cast, but caught herself watching him when she reeled in her line. He looked so much like their father, the same reddish hair and barrel chest, the same gray eyes and cleft chin, she wanted to see if he fished like him too, if his whole body hooked into the rhythm of it, the momentum traveling in a continued easy movement from his feet through the sharper bend in his wrist. It did, though she'd been a child when she watched her father, their father, and she hadn't paid as much attention as she should have, could still hear him telling her that she wouldn't learn

ISSUE 83

anything if she didn't stop fiddling with pebbles or the hackle or rock spiders. She wondered if David had ever heard that voice, if he had sat on the bank for more than a year watching before he was allowed to handle a rod. She doubted it, whatever mistakes their father had made with his first family he seemed to have gotten it right the second time. David studied architecture and played on a local soccer team, donated his spring breaks to building homes for the less fortunate. Depending on where he'd gone those past few years, she might have lived in one of them. But despite their different lives, despite the cold working its way across her neck and numbing her fingertips, despite knowing that he would ask questions she couldn't answer and that at some point she would have to repeat to herself that they were just tree roots, she was glad he'd called, was glad they were spending the day together.

She wrapped her pink fleece scarf tighter, blew on her hands. After a few minutes of hoping he would suggest a break she gave up and filled her chest with air, eased her feet deeper into the river. Her pulse kicked up but she took a few breaths, flexed her wrists, let out a little more line and threw the fly further upstream, let it float along the half-sunk tree. She remembered that, remembered her father pointing out the good spots, the still places in rivers. The current caught her fly, she reeled in, tried to judge the distance to the trees again, blew on her fingers.

"Hands cold?"

She jerked a little at his voice. They hadn't said more than a hello since she'd climbed into his truck early that morning and headed out. They hadn't spent too much time talking at all since he'd called just before Christmas to introduce himself, let her know he was interested in her life, that their father had died. Maybe that was why she'd turned her truck toward Colorado when she left Texas, she wasn't sure. But she was enjoying the quiet there, enjoying David, a man who could sit in quiet. A brother. She never thought she'd be able to say that again. She smiled at him and held up a reddened hand, "Got any gloves?"

A grin worked across his face, "might scare the fish." She rolled her eyes and turned back to her cast, listened to the light echo of his chuckle. Every man she'd been fishing with said something different scared the fish away. The one in Texas said stirring the river bottom, her father told her it was talking, told Micah it was deodorant. Apparently he'd told David gloves were to blame.

She let out a little line and took a few more steps, stopped when the water was knee deep. Now that she knew David was watching her she tried to make her arc perfect, make him proud of her. The reward from her father for a good cast had been Reese's Pieces or maybe a bologna sandwich. David had probably been given granola bars and bananas. But maybe they didn't have to eat. Maybe they could just sit and enjoy the quiet, that early morning quiet in the mountains even breathing seemed to violate. Something, anything other than stand in the river while tree roots morphed into tentacles.

She'd sworn after Texas that she wouldn't go anymore, that whatever fish were in those rivers, it wasn't worth it. But the first night they met, when David had peeked over her shoulder and seen her bait pole propped against the wall in her new apartment, he'd picked her up in a bear hug and told her that she was a disgrace to fish and humans alike and that he would teach her how to catch fish that were worth catching. It was the first time anyone had hugged her like that, like not hugging her would have been the awkward thing. She'd put her arms around his shoulders.

Later, over coffee, words tried to squeeze out of her throat, all of the words that would have told him she'd been fly-fishing, tell him about the men who had taken her, Texas, their father, tell him all the stories she was afraid would make him hop into his truck and drive toward a Habitat for the Homeless project, a place where he could do some good. But all of those words caught against one another in her throat. So she listened to him plan their trip and promised herself that she could handle it this time, that even if the river was nothing but tree roots and sucking mud she could tough it out.

What seemed like a decent sized trout nabbed her fly and ran behind the sunken tree before she could pull the line tight. She heard David call out but she was already heading toward the log, trying to get an angle around the tree so she wouldn't have to go too deep into the current. She eased her way along the bottom of the river, tested the water's power, she had to get closer but the rapids were strong and the roots were starting to blur again. She swallowed and tried for a larger step with her right foot. The current lifted her leg high and water rushed over her boot before she got her foot back down and into the river bed. The way it had filled her sneakers as she backed away from her father while he pumped her brother's chest, said "Micah," with each press on his rib cage, the tone strangely common, like he was calling him into the kitchen for dinner.

Beth gagged and the cold air hit her teeth, made them throb. She closed her eyes, tried to feel the fish out, block the sight of the beckoning tree roots. The toes of her left foot cramped but she kept them curled and choked back the bitter spit as it worked its way over her tongue. The pain in her thighs pushed a small humming moan out of her mouth. The moan she made when she tried to relax against pain, ride it. The moan she'd perfected while Texas pressed her face into bed springs while he fucked her from behind when she was strung out and didn't care. A moan she'd learned from a father that left her with a broken collar bone and two fractured ribs before he finally just left after he lost the son he'd always wanted.

Her eyes teared and she shook her head, blinked them clear. She wanted to yell for David, or drop the rod and let go, let the current take her somewhere else, maybe she'd wash up on a beach in California, learn to surf, leave men with fly rods and fish and never come back.

She exhaled, gripped the rod tighter, took two steps backwards, squatted deeper, pulled toward the shore. The fish was fighting less, his runs were shorter, and with every backwards step, every inch of line collected, the tentacles started looking more like roots, brown and innocuous.

The fish gave a few half-hearted flips out of the water but it was tired and small, a pretty little rainbow but nothing spectacular, nothing worth the work or the panic she'd gone through, not worth letting David see her like that. She turned to look for him when she had her thumb in its gill, jerked when she found him standing a few feet behind her. He'd never said anything, just stood there, and she knew by his expression that he'd noticed her weird display. He knew about Micah, she didn't know if he knew about the collar bone and the cracked ribs but she wondered if maybe he'd faced a few sprains and fractures too, if maybe he was standing so close because of that.

She held the fish up and tried to grin. He glanced at the fish then looked back at her, looked hard, asked if she was okay. She nodded, was hoping that if he did know that part of their father he wouldn't ask her about it, she wasn't sure she could talk about that yet. He reached out and put a hand on her shoulder, "You sure?" He squeezed a little bit, almost like another hug only gentle this time, and the words bubbled up again. But whatever it was, shame or fear or something she couldn't even name, it made her look down at the river instead. He kept his hand there for a while then nodded.

"Quite the little beauty," he said and walked back to the pack.

Beth took a few deep breaths. It was a clean catch through the lip, she could probably get it with her fingers, wouldn't need the pliers she assumed David was going for. She had the fly between her fingernails when she heard beer cans thudding against each other, looked up. David was standing above the contents of his pack, hands on his hips. He looked up, caught her watching him, smiled.

"Can't find the string line," he said, put his palms on top of his head and stared up at the sky. A gesture she recognized, the pose their father made when he had to think about something, needed to work out the details. He'd been a civil engineer, had needed to understand the chain of cause and effect.

She looked back at the trout and started walking toward David, maybe he hadn't really looked at it, maybe he'd just assumed from her spectacle that it was a fish worth keeping, big enough for a meal, a fish half-again the size of the one that was starting to bleed down her thumb. She hefted it into her hands to see if it was heavier than it looked, tried to picture the body split into fillets.

Rocks scattered, she looked up and saw him running back up the trail. He called over his shoulder that the line probably got caught on some brush when he went to pee, that it wasn't far, that she should just hold onto the fish, he'd be back in a flash.

She didn't think he'd really gone at first, stared at the trailhead waiting for him to reappear. When she didn't hear anything she looked back at the fish. If they were keeping it she needed to get it dead, rip its gills and let it bleed out, she remembered that, remembered that she needed a large flat rock to smash his head against.

She found one but sat on it instead and laid the fish in her lap, ran her hand over its head. She brushed the orange fur of the fly out of the fish's eye then worked the barb out of its lip. It mimicked an insect, she remembered that, and whatever insect it was supposed to

ISSUE 83

be it had done well, a disastrous breakfast for the trout. She looked at the rainbow's gills, gills that weren't moving against the flesh of her bloody thumb. The spotted black shimmer of its body scales were spotted with it, red that stood bright even against the pink stripe down its body. Maybe if they had let him live he would have learned not to bite the orange ones, that biting into one meant he would be yanked into the sky, taken to a place where he couldn't breathe the air, where floppy green things stood and watched as he gasped and crawled over the alien dirt. Then one of them would pull the gasping body onto its lap and a tentacle would melt shirt and pants, reveal pale stomach and nascent penis and rubber boot feet, leave a trail of river slime across Micah's blue lips.

She heard David's boots crushing through the brush. She took her thumb out of the fish's gill, wrapped her hands around it and took two steps, placed it in the water, let it go. It suspended near her left boot long enough before the current pulled it downstream to force a lunge and a sharp 'what are you doing?' when David got to her side and realized what she'd done.

He stood with his red hands tucked under his armpits, the string line dangling from under his crossed arms. He'd been so excited for her fish, for them to share something, she knew that. He stared at her then shook his head and started sloshing back upstream. She let out the breath she didn't know she'd been holding. The fish was dead, dead for at least a few minutes before she'd put him in the water. She knew David had seen its white belly as the current pulled it away from his hand.

David grabbed his rod from the bank and walked back toward her. Something about his walk made her back up until the flat rock caught her legs and she sat. He stopped beside her and looked down. "What do you think I'm going to do?" When she didn't answer he shook his head, marched past her. "Bad idea" he said. She didn't know if he meant releasing the fish or the trip or calling her to begin with, trying to make some sort of family from the wreckage their father had willed them. She heard him throwing things back into his pack, beer cans and sardine tins and extra clothes.

On the opposite bank the land flattened a little and there were early blue star columbines peaking out, their white faces softening the rocky soil. She wondered if there was a way over to that clearing, wanted to stretch her body out over the purple-blue leaves, drink beer, eat the sardines and oysters they'd brought in case they blanked. She wanted to talk to him about his girlfriend and his job, about his mother, she wanted him to describe the house he grew up in, tell her what sports he'd played in high school, what he thought of college, what life had been like with the man she'd known ten years before he was born. She didn't want to tell him why she'd just put a dead fish in the river. She didn't have any idea how to explain that.

The noise behind her stopped and she turned, afraid that he would be vanishing into the cut in the boulder as he took off up the trail, but he was standing with his hands on his hips, his head bowed. She tried to smile an apology.

"Don't" he said when he turned to her and saw her cheeks lifting. "I'm sorry I lost my temper. I do that sometimes." They locked eyes for a moment, long enough for both of them to grow uncomfortable and nod. Her eyes lowered and she turned back to the river, watched the water rush through the upturned roots. Alien hands kneading Micah's pale flesh, prodding his body while she and her father stood, hands at their sides, useless. She shook her head, it was *their* father, plural. She had a brother again. She lifted her eyes to the columbines, rubbed her hands together and blew on them.

"Cheeseburgers," she said. David turned to her but she couldn't look at him and do this so she kept her eyes on the flowers, tried to see every yellow center of every bloom. "Micah liked cheeseburgers so much and our father loved him so much that he let Micah eat them for breakfast."

ISSUE 83

Kim Church

Victuals

Picture a man walking into a grocery store — Harris-Teeter, say. An old man in a corduroy coat, tufts of acrylic pile spilling out the sleeves. He stops between the automatic doors, feels around in his pockets, checks his wallet.

No list.

He glances around, frowning, as if debating whether to soldier on without it or go back to his car. Other shoppers maneuver around him. There is no end of them; they come and go, come and go until he is dizzy. Finally he steps inside and plucks a small green shopping basket off the stack. His hand shakes — the slightest of tremors, hardly perceptible, but it embarrasses him.

His wife is waiting in the car. Is she crying?

They have just left my office. I am a lawyer.

"Our family lawyer doesn't handle these cases," the man told me. He and his wife, he said, wanted to sue their son's therapist.

Their son had always been awkward. Shy, clingy, didn't fit in with other children. "Maybe," the wife said, "because he was an only child. Maybe because we were older when he was born." A slumping, soft-spoken woman, with gray hair and skin and a beige skirt which she kept smoothing. Her husband sat fiercely upright, a book in his lap as if for ballast. He did most of the talking.

They had hoped sending their son away to college would teach him independence, but he didn't last a semester. He moved back home and signed up for computer classes at the local technical school. He completed a two-year program, found a job as a technician, eventually moved into his own apartment, eventually stopped coming home for dinner every night.

The "real trouble" started when he enrolled in his company's sales training program. "He should have known better," the man said, and looked at his wife. "Remember all those magazines, when he was supposed to be raising money for school?"

"He was *ten*."

He tried to cure his awkwardness by joining Toastmasters. He also, without telling his parents, started therapy.

His sales career ended after six months' probation, and he returned to his old job, again without telling his parents. He didn't tell them, either, when he bought a gun.

On Christmas Eve, he committed himself to Holly Hill. He was medicated, talked to, observed. His mother visited every day with small gifts: the crossword puzzle clipped from the morning paper; a handful of creme-filled caramels, his favorites. "She doted on him," the man said. "It was nothing," the wife said. "A few little treats he could look forward to. We didn't know how to help him."

After three weeks in the hospital, the son told his therapist he was feeling better and ready to get on with his life. He even asked one of the nurses out on a date, but she said no, she couldn't date patients. He was discharged. Two weeks later, he made another payment on the gun. Two weeks after that, he paid in full and took the gun home. The next night, he sat down and wrote his note: fourteen pages of college-ruled paper filled margin to margin with cramped, girlish handwriting. He wrote about his job, his embarrassment over the nurse, his fear that everyone must be secretly laughing at him. Mostly he wrote about his father, a painstaking list of grievances based on minor incidents from childhood. *He's never had faith in me,* he wrote. *He doesn't believe I have the nerve to do this.*

Then he picked up the gun and shot himself.

His body wasn't discovered for five days. For five days he lay on his kitchen floor, the gun beside him, the note — all fourteen pages — stacked neatly on the table.

His mother said, "We worried when he didn't come over or answer his phone for so long." His father was the one who found him — no doubt what the son intended.

"He was supposed to be in treatment," the man said. "We didn't know he'd gone off his medication. Cancelled all his appointments." In the month since his discharge from the hospital, the son had failed to report for therapy, and his therapist hadn't checked on him, not once. "That," the man said, his voice quavering, "is called abandonment." He lifted the book he'd been holding, a thick gray textbook, *The Treatment of Depressive Disorders,* and placed it on my desk as if he expected me to read it then and there. "Take a look at chapter seventeen. I think you'll agree."

I waited in polite silence for a moment. Then, as gently as I could, I explained the law: no matter how negligent their son's therapist had been, he couldn't be held liable for their son's death unless we could prove that he caused it. "In these cases," I said, "especially in an outpatient setting, causation is notoriously hard to prove." I use lawyerly language when I have to discuss difficult subjects, as a sort of verbal anaesthetic. "I'm sure you understand," I said, though I was sure they did not. Causation is a hard issue even for lawyers.

We would need to hire an expert, an independent therapist to review their son's records. This could be expensive, I said.

The man took a memo pad from his shirt pocket and made a note. "What about settlement?"

"I'll tell you what I tell everyone. Don't file the case if you aren't willing to take it to trial." Getting to trial, I said, could take years. And wouldn't be pleasant.

The man wrote something else, then tucked his pad back in his pocket.

"I'm not telling you not to pursue this," I said. "I'm just trying to prepare you."

During my speech, the wife's face had turned pink. Her cheeks looked scrubbed, her eyes pained. I could almost hear her thinking: *Go ahead, say it. Please, just say no.*

"You don't have to make up your minds now," I said. "You have some time. If you decide to take the next step, I'll start looking for an expert."

ISSUE 83

"What about the literature?" the man said. "This book..."

"I'll look at it," I promised. "I'm sure it will be helpful. Even so, we'll need a therapist who's willing to testify. That's the rule."

The man nodded. He nodded for several minutes. Then, tightening his grip on the arms of his chair, he pushed himself up. He stuck out a hand to shake mine; his was cool and hard, all bones. "We thank you for your time," he said. "We'll think things over." Then he turned and, with a tenderness that surprised me, helped his wife on with her coat. The two of them walked bravely out, the wife in front, the man behind her, his hand on her shoulder, for comfort or balance, I couldn't be sure.

Practicing law is painful. It was especially painful in my early years, when I had no experience or self-confidence and had to pretend. Pretending took its toll. I never seemed to know who I was: the new-lawyer me, with my suits and floppy bow-ties and pantyhose and pumps, my diplomas in tasteful frames, my office in a big marble building, or the me I had always been. My husband would call me at work and remind me of my other life, my life at home — we had bought a house, a brick ranch with a big yard, our own vegetable garden — and I would get irritated. One day he called to tell me our carrots were coming up. I wasn't exactly short with him, but I remember wondering why he thought I would have time to talk about carrots.

Later, after he moved out, I turned the garden back into lawn, which I hired someone else to mow.

After the man and his wife left, I opened the gray textbook to the chapter on suicide. Tucked into that chapter, marking a section titled "Special Considerations Surrounding Discharge and Follow-Up Care of Hospital Patients," I found a small sheet of paper torn from a memo pad, a list written in shaky blue ballpoint:

> tuna
> skim milk
> orange juice
> chicken broth
> seedless rye

The old man's shopping list.

His son was dead, his wife didn't want to do anything about it, but still the man had to buy food. I imagined him taking his groceries home, preparing a simple meal for his wife, sandwiches or soup. His wife sitting at the table, staring at her plate or bowl, not wanting to face him, not wanting him to see how she blamed him. "You have to eat," he would tell her. "I'm not hungry," she would say, and he would answer, "Eat anyway." Understanding, both of them, that everything they did, everything they would ever do from now on, they would do *anyway*.

The last place I saw my husband — my ex-husband, by then — was the grocery store. Wellspring, before it became Whole Foods. This was years after our divorce. He was finally leaving Raleigh, he told me. He was moving to New York or California to find a more creative job. There was something clear and hopeful in his eyes, and I wanted to encourage him. It was on the tip of my tongue, how I hoped he would find something worthy of his talents. But I didn't say it. I couldn't let my guard down that much, even then.

"I'll send you my new address and phone number," he said, and then, reading the *why?* on my face, added, "if you *want* to know."

"Sure," I said, "I'd like that."

But I wasn't convincing. He didn't send me his address. Later, when I found out he was sick, I asked my mother to get it from his mother.

Fourth Street, Berkeley.

If you had asked me beforehand how my husband would die, I would have guessed in a wreck or by violence or suicide. He was an alcoholic, dangerous when he drank. He drove fast, got into fights, got arrested. In our nice brick ranch house, he hurt me. I didn't tell anyone. I couldn't. I was a lawyer.

He always apologized afterwards. I would say to him, But how can you be sorry for things you can't remember? How can you make an *informed* apology?

Once he tried to kill himself. I wasn't at home — I had escaped during one of his rampages. He put an album on the stereo, *Rock of Ages* by The Band, and turned it up to full volume. Then he sliced his wrists, got into bed, lit a cigarette, and passed out. The bed caught fire and woke him up. He dragged the mattress into the yard and left it to smolder while he drove himself to the hospital and got his cuts stitched up. It was still smoldering when I came home.

He used to criticize me for being passive. "Your life just happens to you," he would say.

"What am I supposed to do?" I would say.

What *am* I supposed to do?

What to do about these clients, for instance? According to the old man's textbook, their son was in a high-risk category: young single male, living alone, just home from his first hospital admission. A competent therapist would have been more aggressive about follow-up care.

Would it have mattered?

No one can know, of course. But a fourteen-page suicide note, single-spaced, in longhand? I'd call that the work of a man who was hoping to be interrupted.

So why am I not pushing the parents to sue?

You know why. Five days. A jury may not forgive them for waiting five days to check on him.

My ex-husband would say, Then tell them no. Don't represent them.

But that isn't who I am. I'm a lawyer. I listen, I dispense information, I advise; but ultimately I allow my clients the dignity of their own choices.

I am not forceful like my ex-husband.

In the beginning I thought he was exotic: a Canadian, with that round-voweled, phonetically precise way of talking. Once I took him to a soul food drive-in and he ordered "the chit-ter-lings, please."

I wrote on my napkin, *victuals*. "Say this."

"Vict-you-wools," he said, and blinked his thick eyelashes.

How could I not love him?

His father was a veterinarian who'd given up a large animal practice in Ottawa to start a pig farm in North Carolina. He kept us in meat the whole time we were married — bacon, pork chops, ribs, sausage, all wrapped in white paper. Our freezer was always full of white packages. I wasn't fond of the pork — the bacon was sliced too thick, the sausage had too much sage. But my husband's father raised a few cows, too, and we occasionally got ground beef, a couple of steaks. My favorite was cubed steak, which I cooked country style, with gravy, the way my mother had taught me.

I did all the cooking in our marriage until my second year of law school, when I was injured in a wreck. During my recovery, my husband's father gave us extra beef, and my husband learned to make beef stew in the crockpot. He put in potatoes and carrots and turnips and garlic and red wine. We ate beef stew for two months while I healed.

One Friday in the fall of my third year, my husband surprised me with a picnic at the beach. We'd been given the use of a friend's house on the Intracoastal Waterway near Ocean Isle. He picked me up at school that afternoon and we got to the beach while it was still daylight. We unloaded the car and carried our things to the landing, our cooler and camp chairs and Hibachi. Then he took out the supper he'd packed: fresh bread, brie, a bottle of Merlot, and a thick steak, not from his father but from Fowler's in Chapel Hill, a gourmet shop we couldn't afford. He grilled the steak and we ate it slowly, in small bites. We drank the wine. We watched the sun set. We watched the

ISSUE 83

bridge turn to let boats pass. Birds skimmed the water. My husband smoked a cigar.

After I became a lawyer, we could afford all the store-bought meat we wanted. It stopped being special. Eventually he and I stopped having meals together. One night near the end of our marriage, my husband invited a friend over and grilled hamburgers for the two of them but wouldn't let me eat. He wouldn't let me leave, either; he disconnected wires in my car to keep it from starting. So I walked next door. The neighbor, an old woman we had sometimes mocked for her yard ornaments, fed me supper and made me a bed on her sofa.

In the end, my husband was the one who moved out. He rented an efficiency apartment so small he had to leave behind the kitchen table he'd built, one of the few things he treasured. He invited me to dinner one night to work out our separation agreement, and I sat at his counter. He cooked me pork chops, his father's. He sautéed them in a brown sauce. They were delicious. They broke my heart.

ISSUE 83

I wrote to him after he got sick. There wasn't much to say. "I'm sorry," I wrote. I had chosen a notecard with a picture of red shoes — a whimsical, light-hearted drawing, as if I believed a miracle were still possible.

He wrote back on stationery from the design firm he'd been working for. "Some luck with transplants," he wrote. "Otherwise, you pay your nickel and take your chances." He signed his note:

>Love
>Me

Like that, with no comma. His closing imperative.

Maybe my husband was right. Maybe I should be more of a take-charge lawyer. Spare this couple the burden of deciding whether to sue their son's therapist. I could call the old man right now and say, I'm sorry, sir, there's nothing I can do about your son. But the good news is, I found your grocery list.

My husband ran away from home when he was thirteen. He never told me why, only that he and his father didn't get along. He left his family in Ontario and moved to Vancouver. Three years later, he returned; by then he was bigger than his father, ready to forgive and be forgiven. But his father had moved the family to North Carolina, to my hometown. It took my husband another year to find them. His parents made a room for him in their garage, and he even worked for a while on his father's pig farm. When he and I were first dating, I sometimes visited on his lunch break. I didn't like the farm — the stink of the lagoon, the way the pigs squealed when they were kicked.

After he died, I went back to my hometown to pay my respects to his parents. It was the first time I'd seen them since the divorce. My husband's mother told me how happy he'd been after he moved to California. He grew lemons and broccoli, she said. He grew roses to give them away. "He should have lived there all along," she said.

ISSUE 83

His girlfriend, I guess you'd call her, the woman who took care of him while he was dying, Lisa Angel (her real name), phoned me with her condolences. Lisa had traveled from California to North Carolina for the funeral, hoping to meet me. She was sorry I hadn't come.

"He thought I would like you," she said.

She told me their history. They'd met the summer after he moved to Berkeley. The following summer, his symptoms started. Work exhausted him. He couldn't take a walk around his neighborhood without stopping to rest. " Then one night he was taking a shower," Lisa said, "and his hands and feet went numb and his prick turned blue." A quick stab of a word, *prick*: crude, too intimate.

Almost a year to the day after their first date, he was diagnosed with agnogenic myeloid metaplasia, a form of bone marrow cancer. He died six months later, on Valentine's Day.

" We never said we loved each other," Lisa said. "But every time I told him hello or goodbye, it meant *I love you*."

She needed to be with him, she said. "I got butterflies whenever I wasn't. The thing was, if he hadn't gotten sick, we wouldn't have stayed together. He drank. Not around me — I'm a recovering alcoholic myself, five years sober. There were a lot of nights we couldn't see each other because he was drinking. He was depressed. Even before he got sick, he wasn't interested in sex." She let the word hang in the air. "I stayed with him because it was my destiny," she said. "I believe that."

She tried to bulk him up with buttery mashed potatoes, rich cream sauces, a variety of eggy concoctions. But he had no appetite, and she ended up eating all the food herself. "I got fat trying to save him," she said. "I'm still trying to lose the weight."

I wondered how it was for him, being cared for by a woman he wasn't in love with or even attracted to, someone who kept getting fatter as he withered away. Someone loud and coarse, who disturbed all the other patients when she stood at the nurses' station and demanded to know why he wasn't getting better.

Is it easier to die if you're leaving someone you'd just as soon be away from?

That isn't what he told Lisa. After his splenectomy, after the chemo, after the bone marrow transplant, when he had wasted away to nothing, when he was bald and helpless and needed oxygen and couldn't eat more than a couple of spoonfuls of anything, when he was like an infant, she stayed with him in his hospital room. Once, near the end, as she was getting up to leave, he managed to say to her, "No, no."

When he died, my mother took his parents a ham (ham for a pig farmer! but it was what she had on hand), dinner rolls, potato salad, a Sara Lee cake. My mother is small and frail, and she struggled carrying the cooler to their front door. My husband's father came out and, without offering to help, told my mother no, no, they didn't need anything. She had to plead with him to take the food. "For when the other children come to visit," she said.

According to the medical examiner, my clients' son's last meal was pizza. A small cheese pizza from Domino's. The delivery boy, apparently the last person to see him alive, remembered little about him, just that he paid in cash — exact change, no tip. He ate the pizza, broke down the box and laid it flat in the recycle bin under his kitchen sink. He rinsed his drinking glass and upended it in the drain. Had he used something other than a gun, he might have left a clean kitchen.

I predict, and I hope I'm not wrong, that the old man and his wife will decide not to sue the therapist. A lawsuit won't bring our son back, they'll tell themselves. Maybe they'll blame it on money: they can't afford to pay for an expert without some guarantee of success, which of course I can't give them. The old man may tell me privately that his wife isn't strong enough to withstand the emotional upheaval of a lawsuit.

I understand, I will say. I will reiterate how sorry I am. I'll return the gray textbook and their son's records. But I will keep the grocery list.

ISSUE 83

Tonight as on most nights I stop in the gym on my way home from the office. A girl on a treadmill is talking to another girl on the treadmill beside her. Their faces glow in the light of the aquarium. "That's a triggerfish?" the first girl says. "I just ate one. I didn't know they were so pretty."

Before I was a lawyer, my husband and I used to go fishing. We fished from a makeshift platform on the girders of the trestle bridge over High Rock Lake, and the midnight train would rattle overhead and shake our tackle box.

At the Outer Banks he taught me to surf-cast for flounder.

On Saturdays when I didn't have to study, we would pack a lunch and find a spot along the bank of Abbott's Creek or the Eno. We would sit side by side, holding our poles, talking, not talking; waiting. We always caught something, and we always ate what we caught. Crappie, bream.

I remember the smell of fish roasting in the oven, six or eight small ones in a single pan, the kitchen full of the rivery smell of them. I remember their sweet white meat, their perfect, delicate, soft bones.

Mariko Nagai

Fugue

*(When I was a child, I was always hungry. We grew up not knowing
that some people were never hungry.* When I was a child, my parents
taught me that our bodies are not ours, but our masters', that we are
put on earth to bend as near to the ground as we can, bound in the
way seeds are bound to the earth. Our labors were our punishments;
our bodies our punishments. We were always hungry, my parents,
my brothers and sisters and I. After the harvest, when all we worked
for during summer was taken away by our landlord, we ate bark and
weeds and things even beasts would not eat. We ate less than three
lap dogs that the rich woman in fur always carried around in her
arms. The dogs all had jeweled collars, and the fingers of the rich
woman in fur glittered in colors we did not think possible, colors we
could not have ever imagined if we had not seen her. But now that we
had seen her, these colors were the colors we dreamed at night which
left our desires unfulfilled. When I was a child, I was always hungry,
we grew up not knowing that some people were never hungry.)

　　　　　　　*(When I was a child, I was always hungry. I
grew up knowing that there was a woman who never knew hunger,
who always carried three dogs in her arms.* She always wore the
softest fur, even in autumn when it was not yet cold, and she never
walked amongst us. Her small jewel-like shoes made in the city, clean
and unused on her, glistened as she sat in her carriage, looking at us. I
remember that even her dogs were forbidden to walk on the ground.
She was above us, always, she was the woman who never came down
to us, and we stayed near to the ground when we saw her, so our
worlds never collided. She never talked to us; she never moved. Even
our hunger did not touch her. When I was a child, there was a woman
who never knew hunger, who always carried three dogs in her arms.)

　　　　　　　　　　　　　　　　*(When
I was a child, there was a rich woman in fur who always carried three
dogs in her arms, and when we saw her, we knew that someone never
went hungry. She never went to bed knowing what hunger meant.* I
was only a child, and I only saw her from far away, like all of us only
allowed to gaze at her from a formal distance like beasts behind bars.
Then she stopped coming down to the village, and the rumor went

ISSUE 83

that she got sick of living in such a far away land from where she was from. Then some time after, rumor went that she died. Our Elder told us that the rich people were living in sin, thinking themselves above the land. God is merciful, he lowered his eyes, but God does not forgive sinners. That was the price they had to pay for forgetting about the land, about people's suffering. But she died and we forgot all about her, and we went about our days the same, hungry, toiling the ground, toiling our bodies to live for another day. But this is a story from when I was a child, when there was a rich woman in fur who always carried three dogs in her arms, and when we saw her, we knew that someone never went hungry, never went to bed knowing what hunger meant.)

(When I was a child, there was a rich woman in fur who had three dogs and she taught us that someone went to bed hungry, went to bed knowing what hunger meant, that there are many kinds of hunger and ours was not the worst. She was the child-bride of the man whose dead wife had three dogs. She had to take care of these dogs that she hated, and no one took care of her. She used to go to bed alone, in a big room, in a big bed that could sleep four, no seven of us; I was there, I saw her go to bed by herself, her sighs collecting like husks at the end of the harvest, wind carrying them far, but not far enough, and piling up in the heap by the edge of the field. She would gather her three dogs, but dogs are not faithful; they scampered away and found their own corner to nestle in, and she would cry into her pillow and call them names. She used to make me sleep with her, holding me tight against her like I was a pillow or perhaps her husband who was never home. You can be hungry, my mother used to say, but there are far greater hungers than the one of the body; when your heart is hungry, it can turn you into a ghost, already dead though your blood may run, though you may move like the living, breathe like the living. You are dead when the heart is hungry. She used to cry herself to sleep as she held me tight, and she died soon after in sleep, her arms still around me. When I was a child, there was a rich woman in fur who had three dogs and she taught us that someone went to bed hungry, went to bed knowing what hunger meant, that there are many kinds of hunger and ours was not the worst.)

(When I was a child, I was in love with a woman with three dogs but she never knew me. I loved her, and it was love so read, but I am an old man now, I know that my life is full for having loved her. I was not a child but not old enough to be called a man yet. I was in

ISSUE 83

love with her. She used to come down to our field with her three dogs, and would gaze at the land for a very long time. But I knew that she did not see anything; I knew that she was thinking of something far away. What was her name? I do not remember; it is such a long time ago, and I am a very old man, waiting out my last days in this feeble body. I loved her, though I was merely a boy, and I loved her for all the things people around me weren't: regal, sad, beautiful, and clean. You might ask, is this going to be one of those happy ending stories, in which she loved me back, and we lived happily ever after? When you are as old as I am, you can tell your children that happy endings are for the privileged few; these are lies we tell ourselves to keep ourselves going in this life, to make this life bearable. No, she was married, had no children, and she died. On the day she was to be buried, I went to her funeral, stood behind everyone, waited until everyone was done with their formal partings, and I touched her cheek, just once, her cheek cold as stone, as cold as the coldest feet, and that day, I became a man, no longer a child, a touch awoke me into a manhood that should've come so long time ago. I married another. A good woman. I had many children, many died and some survived. I tried to provide for her because she was a good woman, and in some moments, she became as radiant as the woman with three dogs. And I blamed myself; if I were a better man, my wife would have been as beautiful as the woman with three dogs; my wife's hands would have remained smooth and young. Now, she has died and I miss her more every day. When I was a child, I was in love with a woman with three dogs but she never knew me. I loved her, and it was love so real, but I am an old man now, I know that my life is full for having loved her.)

(When I was a child, I did not know that a happy life, a happy ending is a lifetime where a heart keeps breaking over and over, where we have too many partings. And out of partings come life itself. When I was a child, I was envious of the woman who came to watch us from her height with three lap dogs in her arms, I was envious of the dogs who never knew how to walk with their jeweled collars. I would close my eyes, lie under the tree and pretend that I was the woman lying on her bed with an arm over my eyes, her bed my carpet of leaves under the tree. I was envious for my parents whose lives were short, who could remain young in my memory, but memory fails me and my love for them, mythical in its heartache. But now that I am older than she ever was, I know that my mother would die of a broken heart if she could see me now. My mother was an old woman before her time. For each birth, she must've lost four teeth that by the time she was done giving birth to the youngest one, she had only one tooth left, but she said that having a tooth makes all the difference. I remember that she never laughed. I don't remember her smiling, only grimacing, her mouth collapsing to one side. My father was the same. He never laughed; he was old like other men in our village and I always thought that people were never meant to look young in our village until I saw the husband of the rich woman. When my father said that they used to play together when they were younger, I looked at him and I looked at the husband, and saw an old man against the middle aged man. My mother and father were old before their time; by the time I became old enough to remember their faces, they were done aging and they died from a simple cold. They did not grow old enough to see me like this. This is my story and I can make them become young, always young, always happy because I am not. *When I was a child, I did not know that happy life, happy ending is a lifetime where a heart keeps breaking over and over, where we have too many partings. But this is life.)*

Ann Lightcap Bruno

Notes on Hunger

1.   *The parent of all industries is Hunger.*
     - Henry Drummond, The Lowell Lectures
     on the Ascent of Man, 1894

Herr Doktor told me to arrive at nine, Sunday morning. Eat only lightly in the evening. Nothing after. That night Paul and I ate bowls of bean soup at the Formica table in our two-room pension, and after I packed a bag: flannel robe, American toothpaste, Austrian shampoo, Boccherini CD, small orange outfit donated by beautiful Iris, a secretary at the institute where Paul studied.

At eight-thirty, we walked along wet cobblestones, six blocks, to the Goldenes Kreuz hospital. At ten they put a suppository in me and by ten-fifteen I was doubled over in pain, the kind that makes you see your body from the outside. We have to slow them down, someone said, first in German then in English, although I could only half hear. The Boccherini was playing on a borrowed boom box, and even though the strains were familiar, Paul looked afraid and I didn't want to be touched. At some point it was no longer one long line of pain, just waves, and a little later they told me to push, and I did. Push. Do you want to feel the head? No, I said. Here, and the midwife grabbed my hand because I wouldn't do it and pressed the flat of my palm to the sticky surface pressing back. It was real then, that first moment of touching. So I held my hand there and bore down when she said, and the synapses fired and the colors in my head exploded orange, yellow, white, red, and there was no one's face, just light. Herr Doktor was behind me, supporting my back as I pressed hard into the place where my hand had touched (the head was now out so I could no longer reach). I broke apart then, as dying as I had ever been, but I wanted it actually, wanted to fall into the colors in my head and the open pain, so I pushed once more until I was empty and the pain slipped out of me and into the room. The midwife caught him and Paul cut him away. The baby was quiet but Paul was crying in that funny way he has that is nearly laughter. Herr Doktor put the baby on my belly and I ripped off the gown although it wasn't spoiled. Paul later told me that I called the baby by his name, although we hadn't decided for sure. We stayed like that for some time, belly to belly, eyes open. I asked for food, but all they brought was a tiny bowl of fruit from a can, which I licked clean like an animal might.

Later, at six, I was in a different room when a young nurse brought me a pot of good tea with cream and a sandwich of thick brown bread, bologna, and butter. I still remember that meal, how it made me alive again, and how I brushed the crumbs from where they fell on his soft, wrinkled head as I tickled his lips so he might open wider.

Hunger is the fundamental cry, and yet feeding must be learned, by both mother and child. It takes, perhaps, a young nurse, chomping improbably on Juicy Fruit, to cup the breast, pinch the nipple into something long and slender, and shove the whole thing in his mouth until he clamps on tight.

> 2.   *The hungry sheep look up, and are not fed.*
> *- John Milton, Lycidas, 1637*

As Presbyterians we did not gaze upon the emaciated form of Christ. That was strictly for the Catholics. Our icons were few. This made us feel better when, after the service, we allowed the ladies to ladle cups of sherbet punch and dole out slabs of pastry.

> 3.   *...La Motte and his family, encircling the fire,*
> *partook of a repast which hunger and fatigue*
> *made delicious.*
> *- Ann Radcliffe, The Romance of the Forest, 1791*

In high school the thing to do was not eat lunch, except maybe a waxy apple, maybe an ice cream sandwich, never breakfast. Then, 1984, it was about slipping into zipper-tapered stonewashed jeans that tucked into short suede boots. So we counted calories, aimed for 1000 a day or fewer. Apples were nearly 100.

The problem was that school was over before 2:00, and when I came home to an uninhabited house the freezer hummed like a siren. Inevitably I'd land in my father's recliner, TV tuned to "One Life to Live." When I finished one heaping mug of Light 'n Lively Mint Chip Ice Milk (the stuff my mother bought, the stuff I would buy myself for years until I went back to the real thing, thank God, when my children were small), I'd usually fill another.

ISSUE 83

So it was a constant give and take of hollow and solid, empty and bloated. When I think of this time, it is marked by that 2:00 hunger and how, as I crossed the threshold, it was like that moment just before you are allowed to drop your arms to your sides after holding them, shoulder height, for what seems like eternity.

4. *I started giving the three witches at the next table*
    the eye again. That is, the blonde one. The other
    two were strictly from hunger.
    - J.D. Salinger, The Catcher in the Rye, 1951

If you are hungry enough for love, you can believe anything, that he will leave his wife, that she is the incarnation of the redhead who lived next door when you were a child, that you could learn to love a car salesman, a former cheerleader, a picky eater. You can believe that he/she/you will never stop loving. My step-cousin Kevin is like this, a new "the one" every couple of months, averaging three a year until she beats him in a race or falls into shards from the pedestal. He has been through three fathers, my step-cousin, his sister two husbands, and when we gather at the holidays, they seem like they are starving despite the bounty.

5. *There was Mr. Cheeseman. . .admid a presence of*
    hungrifying goods.
    - Richard D. Blackmore, Springhaven, 1887

Most people see Thanksgiving in terms of ritual, celery casserole, green beans with fried onions, stuffing passed down from a dead aunt, cranberry with can ridges. But in my parents' house it is always a competition in outdoing the previous year, one my father has with himself, one we are not allowed to enter. And if I am lucky, he lets me make the shiitake-Madeira gravy, as long as I don't improvise.

My father plans at least a month in advance. On sheets of legal pad, he scrawls in indecipherable handwriting the choice for

ISSUE 83

each category: herb and porcini rubbed turkey, butternut squash gratin with rosemary breadcrumbs, cornbread, apricot and toasted pumpkin seed stuffing. He tags recipes in Gourmet with Post-its (targeting the ones with the best pictures). My aunt sometimes surprises him by bringing Jello salad or sweet potatoes baked with miniature marshmallows. This is what my children like.

We start drinking well in advance of the guests' arrival, our only real tradition.

6. *Hungry dogs will eat dirty puddings.*
    - John. Heywood, Proverbs, 1546

During my junior year of college, I grew nauseated and wan for no apparent reason. I only craved white food. After all the barium enemas and endoscopies and pregnancy tests (it would be another twenty years before I learned I was intolerant to gluten), my mother took me to Manhattan for recovery. At Bloomingdales, she bought each of us a slim suit and bright lipstick. As we walked to dinner, a bag lady with Medusa hair jumped into our path and screamed about the audacity of our clothes. My mother and I didn't speak of it. Later, we stopped to give our foil swan leftovers to a man sitting on a blanket and holding a sign that said, "AIDS – please help." He looked up at me with kind eyes, thanked me graciously, and took the ridiculous swans.

7. *She has hunger-struck in prison. She submitted*
    herself for more than five weeks to the horrible
    ordeal of feeding by force.
    - Emmeline Pankhurst, My Own Story, 1914

In magazines, they advise pulling a Scarlet O'Hara before a party if you are trying to lose weight. Eat before you leave home, fill up on carrot sticks. This way, you will forego scallops wrapped in bacon and chocolate fondue. Mammy did not force Scarlet to eat because of any diet, though. It just wasn't ladylike to be seen with fork in hand.

When I am cooking for a party, I eat as I go. I feast on the pieces, spears of asparagus, strips of pancetta, parmesan shavings, gingersnap crumbs. It is the privilege of the cook to rip freshly roasted skin from the chicken, to run the finger around the rim of the just frosted cake before anyone else has a taste. Once at the table I do not want to be Scarlet, a belle who does not eat, so I load up my plate. But I often consume so many parts that I cannot fully enjoy the whole.

8. *For seldom did she go to chapel-shrift;*
    And seldom felt she any hunger-pain.
    - John Keats, Isabella; or, The Pot of Basil, 1820

The anorexia mirabilis (miraculous lack of appetite) endured by women and girls in the middle ages is notably different from anorexia nervosa. This privation was in the name of God. It was desire for the delicious banquet of the afterlife. It was rebellion against convention, renunciation of the larger world. Angela of Foligno refused food but drank pus from the sores of the sick and called the taste as sweet as the Eucharist. Catherine of Siena only nibbled herbs, and Saint Veronica gnawed on five orange seeds during her three-day fasts, one for each of Christ's wounds. Sometimes these women lactated even though they were chaste. But there were no babies, so the milk dried up in due time.

9. *We have known swarms starved out of their hives.*
    Having made a few pieces of comb, and being without food,
    no eggs were set in them and the bees, through sheer want,
    cast themselves on the wide world. These are called
    hunger-swarms.
    - A. Pettigrew, The Handy Book of Bees, 1870

When she showed up we hugged by the hostess stand, and I told her she looked fantastic, and she took the compliment with equanimity.

But later, as she picked at her penne, she confessed the truth, that she hated everything that three pregnancies had done to her body. It didn't matter when I told her again that she was beautiful, complimented her new hair color, the antique silver pendant against her chest. It didn't matter that her husband thought she was beautiful too.

What I really want is time, she said. Is that too much to ask? And Max is just a baby still – seventeen years at least before I get any.

Time, she repeated, taking a bite at last. That or a boob job, and maybe a young guy to flirt with.

10. *The Word was made Flesh; which consequently is to be hungered after for the sake of Life.*
    - Daniel Waterland, Review of the Doctrine of the Eucharist, 1737

Presbyterians interpret body and blood as cubed Pepperidge Farm bread and vials of grape juice. My first communion was when I was two and able to hold the vial with minimal spilling. There was no ceremony, no bride dress, and no sense at all of mystery or meaning. For my son, baptized Catholic, there was ritual when the time came. In one of the classes, he pasted cut-out goblets and hosts to note cards and invited everyone he knew. Many showed up. It only occurred to us as we watched him at the altar that we had forgotten to teach him to put it in his mouth. Back in the pew, he still held it in his crossed hands.

11. *Being well hunger-pincht. . .[he] ran away from the rest of the Christians.*
    - Thomas Fuller, The History of the Holy War, 1639

The mountain fire leaped into angry tongues, splintering the logs and backlighting counselors strumming guitars. Over the hillcrest, behind the trees, was the log cabin my grandfather had built. When my father had been here in the fifties, the camp didn't have the born again slant it did now. I kept from my parents the knowledge that Jesus saved.

They lay down their guitars and passed out scraps of paper and tiny pencils like from miniature golf. Write down your sins, my counselor said. All I could think of was pale Dave who washed dishes and was heading for Bible college, how I wished there was something to confess. Instead I wrote that I called Sheila Schaeffer a bitch. Now put them in the fire, the counselor whispered, and we walked up to where the heat made our cheeks flush, sins folded tightly in our fists, and threw them in to turn to ash. Blessed are they who hunger and thirst for righteousness, the camp director called out, holding her worn bible aloft. She recited Matthew's version of the Sermon on the Mount rather than Luke who just said plain hunger and thirst, nothing at all about righteousness.

None of us here were hungry. Back in the cabins, we hid shoeboxes of Jolly Ranchers and Slim Jims under our beds. After taps, while our counselors snuck into the woods with the night watchmen, we gossiped about damnation and dug into our stashes.

> 12. *Young hawks should be plentifully fed, for if they are left one day without food, the hunger-traces will appear.*
> *- Sir John S. Sebright, Observations on Hawking, 1828*

Conversion takes over a child of mine who has gone too long without eating. As the blood sugar plummets, the face drains, and the child becomes a wrathful version of her regular self. When she is bad she is horrid. And then the revival: rice pudding from a plastic cup, wedges of apple, a dish of kalamata olives, whatever it takes. In minutes she is herself again, just like Sylvester as he wishes himself back into a donkey when his mother, there for a picnic, unwittingly lays the magic pebble upon the rock he had been.

> 13. *It is a wonderful subduer, this need of love,—this hunger of the heart,—as peremptory as that other hunger by which Nature forces us to submit to the yoke, and change the face of the world.*
> *- George Eliot, Mill on the Floss, 1860*

In my grandmother's hundredth year, her last, she lost interest in food. But my uncle was not ready and asked the nursing home doctor to prescribe appetite enhancers. After several days on the medication, she was ravenous although her body still couldn't handle the actual task of eating. She smuggled hard rolls out of the dining room even though her jaw was too weak to chew. She begged us to sneak a hot plate into her room so she could fry eggs. She hoarded vending machine crackers in her nightstand alongside her Bible. In her life she had abstained from all excess. Libation, fashion, language, flesh. Her only vice had been a small daily dose of chocolate. Now, she couldn't think about anything other than sating her desire. Eventually, my uncle recognized her misery and called off the drugs. Her death left him reeling.

On her last birthday, well before the appetite enhancer episode, we brought her to my parents' house for the party. But it was two days after Christmas, and she was too tired to do more than lie on the couch in her tidy suit. My three-year-old daughter tended to her like an undersized nurse. She covered my grandmother with a chenille throw and nestled a pillow behind her back. Here, she said, handing her a plate of cake. At first, my grandmother waved her away, but my daughter was insistent. It's your birthday. Like this, and my daughter showed her the way to break off a bite with the fork and bring it to her mouth. They took it one purposeful forkful at a time. And when the feeding was over, my daughter told her how well she had done.

Nina Furstenau

Biting Through the Skin

My first memories of trips to India while growing up are of my grandparents, a neighbor girl named Sweeti, and craggy faces of rickshaw drivers. Under these vivid mind pictures, though, is a feeling that loosens something under my sternum. It stems from the awe of seeing my father look taller, more vitally part of each meal, each conversation, like he returns to himself when we travel there, of watching my mother settle into an old routine that I had never seen. Laughter is relaxed, conversation fluid. I feel an easing of a tightly held tension I did not know we had.

I am six and sitting on a black bus seat alone. My legs swing, almost kicking the back of the seat in front of me. The windows have a horizontal bar to slide them open or shut and there is a small wedge open at the top of mine. Ahead of me about five rows are the backs of the heads of my family: wispy hair, surprisingly gray for a 40ish father, flies about through streaks of sun slanting through the windows revealing glimpses of a smooth bald brown pate. This, the very top of my *Baba*, is a head and shoulders above the tidy bun sitting quietly on my mother's neck and, stair-stepped down from her, is just the tip of my wavy-haired brother's head. I lift my chin to watch as others leave the bus to buy papaya juice, a mango, or stroll around the small highway pull-off until the driver is ready to continue on the switchback road up, up, and nauseatingly up through the blue Nilgiri hills near Chennai. My stomach feels queasy from sickness, but I have been told to eat, hence my bully separateness from the rest of my family.

I have a banana in my lap, the small brown Indian kind full of flavor, and have just finished a sandwich my mother packed this morning. A crowd has gathered around the bus and far below me I see a small child standing and looking straight into my eyes. He wears shorts and a buttoned shirt of some indeterminate khaki color and he seems to reach the elbows of the older children near him. No one else in the crowd looks at my window. His eyes stay steady though the crowd jostles him and the ragged hem of his shirt rucks up. I startle as I realize he has seen me eat the last bites of my bread. He has watched me swallow. I look at him more closely and see his hands are cupped.

ISSUE 83

I suddenly feel the bulkiness of the gummed bread still in my throat and stare at the banana in my lap. I want a drink but do not call out for one. My mother is talking earnestly, using her hands and tipping her head, making a point that causes my father to chuckle. *Do not waste your food, Nin,* she would admonish and I look back to the boy and lift my banana as if to peel it. But I cannot do it. I feel the black vinyl seat stick to the backs of my thighs as I lift my torso up. Not high enough. I stand and the vinyl pulls free of my skin. I reach the opened top of my window and toss the banana out and it drops and wobbles through the heated air. All else freezes as it makes its diver's arc end-over-end. The sounds of vendors, of the driver's radio, of talking tourists, mute. The milling people themselves, in their colorful saris, with their turbans and beards pulled tight under the chin, blur. Then, just before the boy's outstretched hand can close around the fruit, the smell of the idling bus engine suddenly reaches my nose and I sit back quickly. My grandparents said just last night not to "encourage them" so I glance up to make sure no one saw.

Now, the bread in my throat goes down and I make an audible swallow. I hope I will not be hungry later, and I look once more down to the boy. He deftly caught the banana, though sometimes I imagine it dropped in the dirt first before he snatched it up, and I watch as he takes quick bites through the bitter peel, as if someone might get to it still. I open my mouth to tell him to peel it first and it stays open until I look away. I imagine what banana peel tastes like and what the soft, fleshy fruit would feel like beneath it on my tongue. I rub my tongue behind my front teeth and grimace. Then, I am frantic. What if my mother sees that the peel is not in my trash? Will she ask what became of the fruit? She walks back and never looks into the wilted paper that had wrapped the sandwich. She pats my head, and goes back to her seat as the bus pulls away.

I realize now that I was seeing a child beg for food. I had seen beggars in India asking for money, but none had struck me as much as that boy. During our meals around a shellacked wood table in Kansas, I spent inordinate amounts of time hiding foods that I didn't like. Peas were pushed under crusts of bread, an Indian vegetable that my father and I called "blood purifier" to indicate its bitterness, I mashed with my fork to subdue. After the parts I didn't like were sorted to satisfaction, I ate the comfy foods, like potatoes with black pepper, like rice with minced meat, with such relish that I was done in five minutes the meal my mother wanted us to linger over. Every dinnertime, too, my father at exactly 5:30 p.m., ten minutes after beginning the meal, would turn on the national news with Huntley and Brinkley. All conversation stopped so he could hear. My back was to the television so I had nothing to do but look unfocused at the array of foods my mother prepared and rest my head on my hand.

The stories of starving children in India bandied about in Kansas to somehow force kids to finish their peas did not apply in my life until that moment on the bus. Now I see I formed an acute sense of privilege in being born who and what and where I was. My family, it seems lived with this dichotomy all their lives but that's when I saw it first. My grandfather had a sense that the economy ran by families hiring a cook, a driver, a gardener. They had a sense of keeping order by separating humanity into groups that serve and supervise. In many ways, I think that moment on the bus was the impetus behind my later development work in the Peace Corps, behind my teenage squabbles with my family over politics after I began turning around and watching the news unfold each night on TV. In the end, for me, there was that boy, eating a fruit with absolute concentration and no quibbling. Peel and all.

Jonah Lehrer

Food Memory

A few dozen pages into *Swann's Way*, after Proust has finished documenting his insomnia in clinical detail, the narrator dips a little cookie into a cup of lime-flower tea. Everybody knows what happens next: it's one of the most famous literary scenes of all time, in which Marcel recovers his lost memories of childhood in Combray.

"No sooner had the warm liquid mixed with the crumbs touched my palate than a shudder ran through me and I stopped, intent upon the extraordinary thing that was happening to me. An exquisite pleasure had invaded my senses, something isolated, detached, with no suggestion of its origin. And at once the vicissitudes of life had become indifferent to me, its disasters innocuous, its brevity illusory; it was me. I had ceased to feel mediocre, contingent, mortal. Whence could it have come to me, this all powerful joy? I sensed that it was connected with the taste of the tea and the cake, but that it infinitely transcended those savours, could not, indeed, be of the same nature. Whence did it come? What did it mean? How could I seize it and apprehend it? [i]

I drank a second mouthful, in which I find nothing more than in the first, then a third, which gives me rather less than the second. It is time to stop; the potion is losing its magic. It is plain that the truth I am seeking lies not in the cup but in myself."

These gorgeous paragraphs capture the essence of Proust's art, the truth wafting up, like steam, from a limpid cup of tea and some errant cookie crumbs. While the scene has turned the madeleine into a modern culinary fad - if it weren't for Proust, Starbucks wouldn't be selling chocolate dipped madeleines by the cash register – the passage really isn't about the cookie. Rather, the madeleine is merely a convenient excuse for Proust to explore his favorite subject: himself.

And so begins an epic and slightly self-indulgent search through Marcel's own memories, which lasts for several thousand pages and covers an astonishing range of topics, including the importance of jealousy, the epistemology of time and the funky smell of urine after eating asparagus. Of course, the sheer ambition of the novel makes the trigger for *The Search* even more peculiar. Why start with a cookie and a cup of tea? Wouldn't it have been more fitting to begin with something a bit more grandiose, such as the fleeting sight of a long lost love or a famous oil painting?

Proust, of course, had his reasons for starting with some crumbs of flour, sugar and butter. There is nothing accidental or haphazard about the madeleine. To understand why, let's take a closer look at Proust's description of how the madeleine elicited his memory:

> *"When from a long distant past nothing subsists, after the people are dead, after the things are broken and scattered,* **taste and smell alone,** *more fragile but enduring, more unsubstantial, more persistent, more faithful, remain poised a long time, like souls, remembering, waiting, hoping, amid the ruins of all the rest; and bear unflinchingly, in the tiny and almost impalpable drop of their essence, the vast structure of recollection."* [ii]

ISSUE 83

Embedded in these ornate subclauses are some prophetic insights into how our brain works. In 1911, the year Proust began writing his novel, anatomists had no idea how our senses connected inside the skull – the brain was three pounds of mysterious mush. One of Proust's deep insights, however, was that our senses of smell and taste bear a unique burden of memory. That's why he makes it clear that just looking at the seashell shaped cookie, which he'd glimpsed countless times in patisserie windows, brought back nothing; Combray remained lost. In fact, Proust even goes so far as to blame his sense of sight for obscuring his childhood memories in the first place. "Perhaps because I had so often seen such madelines without tasting them," Proust writes, "that their image had disassociated itself from those Combray days." [iii] Luckily for literature, Proust decided to put the cookie in his mouth. As he writes, it was "by taste and smell alone" that his childhood memories came flooding back. [1]

Modern neuroscience now knows that Proust was right. Rachel Herz, a psychologist at Brown, has shown—in a science paper wittily entitled " Testing the Proustian Hypothesis"—that our sense of smell and taste are uniquely sentimental. [iv] This is because smell and taste are the only senses that connect directly to the hippocampus, the center of the brain's long-term memory. All our other senses (sight, touch and hearing) are first processed somewhere else. As a result, these senses are much less efficient at summoning up our past.

But this anatomy doesn't simply explain how Proust was able to remember Combray in the first place. It also helps explain why his memories gushed forth in such an incomprehensible jumble. While some of Proust's ensuing mental associations are logical – it makes sense, for example, that taste of the madeline would lead to the memory of Combray - others feel oddly random. Why does the cookie also bring to his mind "the game wherein the Japanese amuse themselves by filling a porcelain bowl with water and steeping in it little pieces of paper"? [v] But this inchoate linkage is also a defining feature of memories triggered by smells and tastes. Because these memories tap *directly* into the hippocampus – they aren't filtered first – they give us a rare glimpse of our hard drive in its raw state, before we've had a chance to repress embarrassing details or polish the narrative. A sentimental smell or taste, then, is like a great pscyhoanalyst, effortlessly peeling back the layers of the past.

In contrast, memories that come from our other senses – such as looking at a childhood photograph - tend to inspire stories that are more coherent and causal, so that we understand *why* we are suddenly thinking about Combray. There is no surprise, no serendipity. We know where the memory has come from.

What's the problem with this? The reason Proust liked to be surprised by his remembrances, and thus the reason he was so often inspired by cookies and the smell of his post-asparagus pee, is that he believed such surprising epiphanies were more reliable. One of the paradoxes of *The Search for Lost Time* is that, for a book all about one man's memory, it's surprisingly skeptical of memory. Just before Marcel takes a sip of his lime-flower tea, he issues a bleak warning to his reader: "It is a labor in vain to attempt to recapture memory: all the efforts of our intellect must prove futile..." [vi] Why does Proust think our past is so elusive? Why is the act of remembering a "labor in vain"?

These questions cut to the core of Proust's theory of memory. Simply put, he believed that our recollections were phony. Although they felt real, they were actually elaborate fabrications. Take the madeline. Proust realized that the moment we finish eating the cookie, leaving behind a collection of crumbs on a porcelain plate, we begin warping our memory of the cookie to fit our personal narrative. We bend the facts to suit our story, as "our intelligence reworks the experience." Proust warns us to treat the reality of our memory carefully, and with a degree of skepticism.

ISSUE 83

Even within the text itself, the Proustian narrator is constantly altering his remembered descriptions of things and people, particularly his lover Albertine. Over the course of the novel, Albertine's beauty mark migrates from her chin to her lip to a bit of cheekbone just below her eye. In any other novel, such sloppiness would be considered a mistake. But in the *Search,* the instability and inaccuracy of our memory is the moral. Proust wants us to know that we will never know where Albertine's beauty mark really is. "I am obliged to depict errors," Proust wrote in a letter to Jacques Riviere, "without feeling compelled to say that I consider them to be errors." [vii] Because *every* memory is full of errors, there's no need to keep track.

What does this have to do with food? Proust's insight was that the act of remembering changes a memory, that to tell a nostalgic story was to alter the story you were trying to tell. (There's been some new scientific evidence suggesting that Proust, once again, was right. This is now known as "memory reconsolidation," or what Freud called retroactivity .) The corollary is that the most honest memories are those you think you've forgotten, since they haven't been corrupted by the remembering process. In other words, because Proust hadn't told the story of Combray countless times to his friends, because he hadn't rehearsed the sentimental scenes in his head, the memory still existed in a pure and honest state. This is why Proust was so obsessed with it.

But here's the catch: such surprising memories are most likely to come from a childhood dessert, or a whiff of your aunt's perfume, or the taste of an heirloom tomato. Every smell is like a mental worm hole, able to effortlessly transport us through time, back to another time.

[1] A.J. Liebling, the celebrated hedonist and New Yorker writer, once wrote: "In the light of what Proust wrote with so mild a stimulus (the quantity of brandy in a madeline would not furnish a gnat with an alcohol rub), it is the world's loss that he did not have a heartier appetite."

Liebling would be happy to know that Proust actually had an excellent appetite. Though he only ate one meal a day (doctor's orders), Proust's dinner was Lieblingesque. A sample menu included two eggs in cream sauce, three croissants, half a roast chicken, French fries, grapes, beer and a few sips of coffee.

i. "No sooner had": Marcel Proust, Swann's Way, vol. I (New York: Modern Library, 1998). P. 60

ii. "When from a long": Proust, Swann's Way, vol. I. P. 63

iii. "Perhaps because I had": Proust, Swann's Way, vol. I. P. 63

iv. "Rachel Herz": Rachel Herz and J. Schooler, "A naturalistic study of autobiographical memories evoked by olfactory and visual cues: testing the Proustian hypothesis," American Journal of Psychology 115: 21-32 (2002)

v. "the game wherein": Ibid. Marcel Proust, Swann's Way, vol. I (New York: Modern Library, 1998). P.64

vi. "It is a labor in vain": Proust, Swann's Way. p. 59

vii. "I am obliged to depict errors": As cited in: Landy, Philosophy as Fiction: Self, Deception and Knowledge in Proust. p.4

ISSUE 83

Molly Schultz

Cooking the National Dish of Uzbekistan

Here's a recipe that may seem novel, perhaps even formidable. But the pursuit, if you set yourself to the task, will not disappoint. *Osh-palov* (also *plov* or simply *osh*) is the national dish of Uzbekistan, a land-locked country in Central Asia not unlike Italy in shape, a right boot to match the left, with courtyards sheltered by canopies that drip with tight clusters of black grapes and sandy fields that glow with cotton bolls and sunflowers. I lived and worked as a teacher in Uzbekistan for two years: my first meal there and my last was *osh,* and countless meals in between were as well. It's a dish that fed travelers along the Great Silk Road in ancient cities like Samarkand and Bukhara and Khiva, where merchants today still stand in stalls sheltered by the same looming madrasahs as the ones their ancestors stood in the shadows of before them and they lure foreign travelers to their wares—spices, silk, ceramics. Alexander the Great of Macedonia partook of this dish. As did the fearsome, powerful Tamerlane. It transcends the rise and fall of empires, the creation and dissolution of nation-states, the upheaval that has characterized much of the region's history and does not elude it even to this day.

We'll have trouble replicating *osh* exactly, for there are various ingredients and cooking implements unavailable to us here that we must find substitutes for. There will be raisins, for instance, which are added to the dish during cooking. Boxed raisins could never be as fragrant and toothsome as those made from grapes grown in Uzbekistan. Of course you might endeavor to buy grapes and make your own raisins, and this would get you closer to the rich, dark pebbles of fruit in *osh* and how they grow soft from the cooking oil and the steam, but even then your grapes won't be Uzbek grapes culled from vines watered by the Amu Darya River, that ancient waterway, the *Oxus* in Latin, *Jayhoun* in Medieval Arabic, a word derived from *Gihon*, the biblical name for one of the four rivers whose waters originated from the Garden of Eden. It's no matter, a large handful worth of any raisins you have will do. Measure them out and set to the side for later.

For our purposes, we'll stick to the traditional ingredients: dark raisins, a generous scoop of chick peas, two to three whole bulbs of

ISSUE 83

garlic, and a string of withered, red chili peppers. Varieties of *osh* can also include chunks of honey-sweet fruit from the stubborn quince whose flesh must be cooked to a light amber or subtle pink to be eaten, perfect for the tenderizing effects of the long-cooking osh pot; or pieces of pumpkin, some dried apricots, pheasant, even boiled eggs. Then there's the matter of the fat source, the ingredient that excites every true gastronome's appetite. Fat from the rump of the fat-tailed Karakul sheep is considered the most delectable delight in all of the country. These sheep are a curious breed native to the Central Asian steppes. They have skinny legs and curly hair. Their rumps hang heavy from their hind legs like giant bifurcated tumors and bounce cumbersomely when the sheep are made to gallop. In the summer months and in the villages especially, Karakul sheep rumps are swollen with the plentitude of good grazing. While the meat on these sheep is considered palatable, certainly not something to waste, it is the sheep's rump fat (*dumba*) that is coveted.

At outdoor cafés and roadside restaurants, scallop-sized hunks of *dumba* are skewered to metal sticks one atop another and roasted over a flame much in the style of shish kabob, what Uzbeks call *shashlik*, an onomatopoeic term for the way the fire sizzles with dripping meat-fat. Of the varieties of *shashlik, oq sashlik* composed entirely of fat is the most coveted and thus the most expensive. Chunks of cooked fat glisten like pearl onions basted to golden translucence in a slow-cooking oven, and when eaten, they melt hot and tinny and coat the mouth's inner surface. Scalding tea might clear some of the residue, but hours after the meal, the fat will adhere to the roof of your mouth and to the recesses of your tonsils in a slick sheen.

There's a slim chance you might get your hands on some Karakul sheep of the fat-tailed variety in the US for your homemade *osh* since they're raised here today on a small scale. Char Luthy of Misty Acres Kennel in Bloomingdale, Michigan raises Turkish Karakul fat-tailed sheep. She offers honey, Nubian goats, rabbits and wool for sale on her website. Perhaps she could be persuaded to let go of a mid-size sheep with a good-sized rump from her Karakul herd for the right price. It's worth a try. Your *osh* will be made that much more delicious with the addition of *dumba*, for you'll need just over a pound of it. Chop a little more than half into bite-sized pieces and reserve the rest whole. Now, if Char holds her sheep close, as with the raisins, we'll make do with what we can. In this regard, we shouldn't feel much disappointment. A confession: tail fat is a delicacy in the preparation of *osh* even in Uzbekistan. Most people simply can't afford to purchase *dumba* and still have money enough for the requisite meat. They make do.

In addition to, and often in place of tail fat, Uzbeks use cottonseed oil culled from the seeds of the cotton plant. This works well for them, not least of all because it can be gotten by the bottleful and for cheap at any bazaar in any town or city across the country. Cotton is the country's charm and their pride, and yet it is also their bane. A Soviet scheme begun in the 1950s transformed this arid region of Central Asia into a fertile cotton belt, a seemingly nonsensical endeavor considering the adverse soil conditions in a country that's eighty percent desert. In order to slake the water-thirsty cotton plant, engineers built a vast maze of irrigation canals to divert feeder rivers away from the country's Aral Sea to the spreading fields of "white gold," effectively draining the sea to ten percent of its original size. The sea bed is a salt pan desert. It cradles the rust-down carcasses of fishing boats from under which the water dried up and shrunk away, marooning the fishermen who fished from them.

In the US, cottonseed oil is trickier to find in the quantities required for making *osh*. Considering, too, the conditions of the soil in Uzbekistan, the third largest cotton exporter in the world, the way dust storms pick up sand toxic with residual pesticides and fertilizers and scatter it wide, you might just stick to vegetable oil. Check your cabinets and make sure your bottle is more full than empty: oil will play a prominent role in this dish. Heat just under a quart of it in the thickest-bottomed pot you've got. Do this over high heat. In Uzbekistan, cooks use *kazanlar*, heavy half-moon pots made of blackened metal that vary in size depending on the occasion, some measuring six feet wide at their brims. A *kazan* of such magnitude costs nearly as much as a car and cooks who own one are in great demand, especially during the wedding season, and these cooks can make up the expense of purchasing an oversized *kazan* in three months time. The closest approximation in English to the word *kazan* is "cauldron." If you have a cauldron, here's your chance to break it out. A cast iron wok is also a viable alternative. I use my dutch oven with a roomy, tight-fitting lid to good effect.

You cannot cook *osh* without a flame to lick the sides of your pot and cradle it hot. For this reason an electric stove will not do. If you are without a gas stove, you might build a stokable fire outside and cook atop that, rigging a pot over the flame. It would be worth your effort. In this way you will most closely mimic the Uzbek-style of cooking with its tandoor ovens molded out of mud and hay that rural Uzbeks build in their courtyards and the gas pipes that they slide underneath to build a high flame that engulfs the sides of a cook pot. Wait nearby and watch the oil as it heats. When it's hot enough, the oil will smoke blue and grey. Let it, for Uzbeks believe bringing oil to its smoking point purifies it. If your quest for tail fat was a success, this is the time to add the chopped *dumba*—do this carefully—to the now steaming oil. Let the grainy fat shrivel, imparting the oil with an aromatic flavor that will scent your surroundings and bring your dog sniffing to your side. Scoop these glorified cracklings from the pot, and since it'll be another few hours before the *osh* is ready, top a runny egg on a slice of toast with them. Sprinkled with coarse salt and some ground pepper, they're better than bacon. The perfect chef's snack. Fortifying yourself afterwards with a swig of vodka of your own distillation poured quarter-ways up a tea cup and repeating this action every now and then during the remainder of the cooking process would be entirely copacetic with the making of *osh* as well.

ISSUE 83

Maintain the *dumba*-infused oil at a high temperature. In anticipation of your undertaking, you will at some earlier point have sought out a butcher and requested a combination of bone-in beef and lamb laden with equal parts meat *and* its parts: the cartilage, bone, gristle, tissue, and tendons—what we consider the extraneous and otherwise unsavory meat materials that butchers are accustomed to hacking from supermarket cuts before packaging. You'll need two pounds and change. Separate the meat into sizable chunks, but do not remove its extra material. The more unseemly the meat the more coveted by an Uzbek who does not, of course, consider it unseemly in the least. It should be clear by now that our palates are mere cultural constructions. This same Uzbek would lose his stomach at the prospect of eating a slab of meat in a shock of magenta at one of our American steak houses. The only "rare" meat in Uzbekistan is that which hangs from the eaves of a stall where flies swarm the flank and the sun beats it to purple. Likewise in Uzbekistan, esteemed guests— the town elder, say, and a visitor from faraway America beside him (that's me)—who find ourselves presented with a communal plate of *osh* topped by the most imposing of hunks of meat parts share different reactions. The elder rubs his beard in pleasure over it; and he pulls the meat apart with his fingers and places a portion of the choicest bits on the side of the mound of rice closest to me to eat and takes the others for himself; and he makes *kars-kars* noises with his back teeth as he masticates that meat between them with the pleasure full clear on his face. All the while, unconvinced that what he's shared with me is actual, digestable meat, I attempt to edge my portion closer to his side of the mound and further away from my own.

Over a high flame, fry the meat and the remaining tail fat in the oil until the edges are black-brown and crisp but the insides are still red. The meat will cook further and thoroughly to softness with later additions of water and rice. For now, remove it and set it aside. At some previous moment, you will have used a reliable knife to cut an equal portion worth of carrots to meat into thick-ish matchsticks, two to three inches in length. In Tashkent, the carrots used for *osh* are golden yellow. In the Samarkand region where I lived, orange carrots are customary. Regardless of their color, choose carrots that are thick and stump-like. Don't bother with the organic section and those darling finger-thin carrots, the statuesque ones that look as though they stand en pointe when held in an upright position. Think dirt-crusted and hearty. Think compact and knobby. Think of Matryoshka dolls rather than Kirov ballerinas.

Here's one way carrots are prepared for *osh* in Uzbekistan: my host-mother in Samarkand, Mavluda-opa, would drive her gunmetal knife into one plump carrot after another at quarter-pinky intervals until the whole of them had been rendered into long planks. Meanwhile she trained her eyes on a dubbed Mexican telenovella, a favorite around the country, that flickered from an ancient black and white television in the corner of the kitchen. She was preparing *osh* for the family's dinner. When the deeply-tanned heroine slapped a man across the face, Mavluda-opa gasped dramatically and said something unrecognizable under her breath to the villanous Carlos, then returned to chopping, piling the planks atop each other and cutting through them to the surface below to produce long twigs. Her thick fingers forced the blade through the flesh, a thwacking noise pounding along the floorboards with each chop.

In place of the meat you removed from the slurry of oil and tail fat, add a quarter of the cut carrots and twice as many in proportion of diced onions. Be sure to keep the heat high so any liquid that hits the oil immediately vaporizes. The vegetables meeting the oil will cause it to bubble. Stir. In a short time the carrots will grow limp and the onions soft. If you add water at this moment, which you have set to boiling a brief time earlier in preparation for this step, you will stop the cooking of the onions and your *osh* will come out light in color and unimpressive. The tyrant Tamerlane was known to have thrown men off the Tower of Death for lesser crimes. Show diligence and cook the onions further, but not so far as to burn them, and your finished dish will turn out a rich caramel color and will share that sweetness tinged with the bitter that onions fried to brown impart on a dish.

Others will argue it's the bone of the meat melting its marrow into the cooking liquids that gives *osh* its distinct, "noble" color and that this can only be achieved by the expert hands of a male cook. Even the honorary title for one who cooks *osh* is one only men hold: *oshpaz*. It's a source of pride for men awarded the title and is a position held in high regard by the rest of the community. In the public sphere, making *osh* is a task strictly guarded by men; but, and whatever the inferior results, making *osh* in the home most often falls upon women, the ones primarily responsible for feeding their families. *Osh* made by a woman's hand is generally acknowledged as a lesser version of the real thing and as such is suited only for lesser occasions. The gender divide is easily translatable: their *osh* is our BBQ; their *qazans*, our closely-guarded grills. Perhaps cooking *osh* is considered a male endeavor because it's an arduous task requiring brute and bulk for the sheer quantity that must be made by *oshpazlar* for special occasions and at restaurants and for the prep work for the ingredients that go into it. But ask a woman who culls the fields beside her husband, look at the hands of a woman who milks cows daily and bakes batches of bread once and even twice weekly, heaves water from far-away spigots and launders clothes by hand, and you'll realize this last bit, about brute and bulk, is nonsense. But it's a man's world, Uzbekistan, and such is the way the *osh*-making custom continues. My host-mother prepared all the meals for the family, including weekly *osh*. She was also the housekeeper. Bread baker. Animal tender. And a full-time teacher. The thing is, her *osh* was really nothing special, a mere mound of pale rice with bright carrots atop it. Her dishes might give credence to the claim that *osh* is best left to men were she not, simply, a miserable cook. So the woman can't do everything.

Return the meat to the pot. Let the bone do whatever it is the men say it will. Add enough boiling water to cover the contents of the pot then season generously with salt and pepper. Gather whole cumin seeds to fill the well of your hand but not overflow it. Flatten your palms together as if in prayer, careful to contain the cumin seeds therein. Rub your palms back and forth quickly and firmly across the seeds so that they break up and fall into the pot. Salt and stir. The concoction will have boiled sufficiently until the liquid evaporates, approximately one hours time, before you turn down the heat and add raisins, chick peas, and the remaining carrots. Remove the papery, outmost layers of skin from your bulbs of garlic, but leave the bulbs intact. Nestle them at even distances around the pot. Repeat with the chilies. Were your cauldron transparent, you would notice distinct layers, a veritable savory trifle: slick, orange oil at the bottom; meat; carrots; the black, white and red of the chick peas and garlic, raisins and chilies; and to top it all off, your next addition: rice.

The only proper rice used for *osh* in Uzbekistan is devzira rice cultivated by farmers for centuries on individual plots with small yields in the lush Fergana Valley, a land watered by the Zeravshan, the Amu Darya and the Syr Darya rivers. As early as the Samanid epoch of the 10th century, courtiers were eating *osh* made from devzira rice at their feasts. It has a pink-red hue with short grains. Run your fingers through the rice to catch stones and silt, and your hands will come away dusted pink with pollen. Devzira is well-suited for *osh* because it contains less starch than other varieties of rice and has a high tolerance for absorbing water without losing its structure. Because devzira is not available in North America, seek out Bhutanese red, or an Italian-style rice like Arborio. Do not make the mistake of using basmati. It will not produce the same resinous quality, the stickiness that characterizes the grains of rice in plates of *osh*. You will have rinsed two pounds of rice exactly seven times according to custom before scooping it into your *osh* pot. Flatten the grains evenly across the pot with a metal spatula or a flat-bottomed fat skimmer. Add water enough to cover the rice to the height of the first joint of your forefinger and then stand watch over the pot.

If they are not too great a distance from your station, your tea cup and your dwindling bottle of vodka might help you pass the time as you watch the water work its way into the rice. When the water has evaporated some and the rice has consumed it some and it has taken on a pearly shine but is yet opaque, skewer deep holes into the rice with a wooden dowel at staggered intervals. The water you have set to boiling on the stove should be poured therein. Use your skimmer to flip the rice a bit so that the top layer displaces the under layer and makes its way towards the heat at the center of the pot. Be absolutely sure not to disturb the meat and vegetables underneath. Imagine the local *oshpaz* and centuries worth of cooks before him standing over the *kazan*, faces reddened by steam, assessing the absorption of water to rice. You have joined their ranks. With the nobility suited to the task, take in hand your fat skimmer and gather the rice into a hill in the center of the pot. At this point, experienced cooks gauge the progress of the rice by tapping the hills with the flats of their skimmers. If the skimmer makes a plopping sound against the rice and releases from the impact with a slight pull, there is still water left to be absorbed. I have heard one cook describe the sound of a skimmer hitting near-done rice as closer to a dull "thunk." When you achieve this sound, cover your pot with a deep lid. Lower your flame to a minimum and allow the steam to gather under the lid and cook the rice finally. Uncover. Dig your fat skimmer to the bottom of the pot and turn the vegetables, meat, oil and fat together with the rice until the ingredients meld into proportion.

If the smell that you release when you lift the lid from the pot does not impress you the way it will the guests you have gathered around, do not feel defeated. It is a phenomenon widely acknowledged that a meal accomplished through strenuous labor results in exhaustion on the cook's part rather than hunger. But do as the men in villages do when they gather just before dawn during the wedding season to help the local *oshpaz* prepare wedding *osh* enough for three hundred or more villagers: reserve enough vodka to fill the tea cups of your arrived guests and yours as well or open a fresh bottle for the purpose of welcoming them to your feast. This tea-cupful distinct from the ones you took before it is meant to open your stomach, and it will.

In my village during the months of July and August there was a wedding to be celebrated nearly every weekend to which everyone was invited. Guests gathered in family courtyards to celebrate at midday and into the night. When I arrived at one such wedding and took a place with my host-family, the late August sun shone to candy-colors the plates at our table piled with watermelon slices here; sweet clusters of fried dough held together with honey there; the foil wrappers of candies; pomegranates scored from the top down into sections that bloomed with petals of red fruit; green-apple, cola, and pineapple-flavored sodas stacked in the center; and apricot seeds dusty with snow white ash. It was a long-awaited moment in the hot sun when plates of *osh* were placed in the center of each table and the elder with knotted fingers took the meat from atop the pile of rice and broke it into pieces, the meat falling away from the bone and the bone glistening soft and white, the edge of the platter ringed with a moat of oil the color of the hearkening autumn.

Make your own guests comfortable at the table upon which you have arranged dishes of nuts and candies, round disks of bread your guests should pull apart with their hands and distribute along the table; a salad of chopped tomatoes, cucumbers, and furry stalks of dill; bowls of sour-milk yogurt, grated turnips, grapes and shelled walnuts; bottles of vodka and neon-colored sodas—all, accompaniments for the meal. Present the *osh* to your guests on large, round platters onto which you will have scooped a generous portion enough to satisfy four people and atop which you will have placed a piece of meat scavenged from the pot and a bulb of garlic from which the cloves should cleave away effortlessly and squeeze soft from their skins into your guests' hands. Place each dish in the center at either end of the table in position for your guests to reach comfortably.

Uzbeks traditionally eat *osh* only with the right hand and without the aid of utensils. To bring the rice from plate to mouth requires a practiced technique. Give it a try in the privacy of your kitchen before you attempt it in front of your guests. Forgo a fork and instead cup the fingers of your right hand together like a hook with your thumb held firmly at the crook of your bent index finger. This is the "*plov* claw." Use your fingers to grab a mouthful of *osh* to the edge of your plate. Gather it into a compact ball and scoop it into the crook of your fingers and bring it to your mouth. Pull your hand down your open mouth and catch the *osh* with your lower lip as your fingers draw together finally into a fist. With your hand in this position over your mouth, you have the vantage of swiping any stray rice or dripping oil that may have caught on your lips and chin before you remove your hand from your mouth. With this practiced technique, partake from the section of the mound of *osh* closest to you and allow your neighbors range enough to do the same.

As the plates of *osh* grow nearly empty, guests in Uzbekistan lean back on pillows and enjoy half-cups of hot tea. But if you were my ancient host-grandmother in this moment whose thin braid slipped out of your headscarf and trailed long down your hobbled back and who had no age and no birth date, who had lived through the siege of empire like ancestors before you, like generations to come after you, never having left the village of your birth and upbringing, who knew the vastness of hunger and the riches of the harvest—tomatoes that beat red, figs split pink, syrup-sweet melons—you would give thanks at the end of the meal, soaking your fingers into the oil left at the edge of the plate, cupping your hands like gold-dipped wings open towards the sky. And you would whisper an invocation to your

God, Allah, and draw your fingers from the top of your forehead
down your face, your eyes closing as your fingers passed over them,
anointing yourself, lifting your head to the heavens, in the last breath
sighing: *omen*, and those who surround you will join in chorus,
grateful for the meal.

Rachel Abramowitz is a PhD candidate at the University of Oxford.

Meena Alexander has published six volumes of poetry including *Illiterate Heart*, which won the PEN Open Book Award, *Raw Silk* and *Quickly Changing River*. She is the editor of *Indian Love Poems* and author of the memoir *Fault Lines*. Her new book of essays, *Poetics of Dislocation* is published by the University of Michigan Press, Poets on Poetry Series. Her fellowships include those from the Guggenheim Foundation, Fulbright Foundation, Rockefeller Foundation and Arts Council of England. She is Distinguished Professor of English at Hunter College and the Graduate Center CUNY.

Eric D. Anderson is the director of "Way of the Puck," a feature-length documentary film about professional air hockey.

Nathalie Anderson's first book, *Following Fred Astaire*, won the 1998 Washington Prize from The Word Works, and her second, *Crawlers*, received the 2005 McGovern Prize from Ashland Poetry Press. Anderson's poems have appeared in such journals as APR's *Philly Edition, Atlanta Review, Denver Quarterly, DoubleTake, Inkwell Magazine, Journal of Mythic Arts, Louisville Review, Natural Bridge, The New Yorker, Nimrod, North American Review, Paris Review, Prairie Schooner, The Recorder, Southern Poetry Review,* and *Spazio Humano*. Her work has been commissioned for the Ulster Museum's collection of visual art and poetry titled *A Conversation Piece*; for the catalogue of the retrospective exhibition *Sarah McEneany* at the Institute of Contemporary Art of the University of Pennsylvania; and for the artist's press book titled *Ars Botanica* published by Enid Mark of ELM Press. Her work appears in *The Book of Irish American Poetry From the Eighteenth Century to the Present* (Notre Dame), and her poems have twice been solicited for inclusion in *The Year's Best Fantasy and Horror* (St. Martin's). She has authored libretti for three operas – The Black Swan; Sukey in the Dark; and an operatic version of Arthur Conan Doyle's *A Scandal in Bohemia* – all in collaboration with the composer Thomas Whitman and Philadelphia's Orchestra 2001. A 1993 Pew Fellow, she serves currently as Poet in Residence at the Rosenbach Museum and Library, and she teaches at Swarthmore College, where she is a Professor in the Department of English Literature and directs the Program in Creative Writing.

Arlene Ang is the author of four poetry collections, the most recent being a collaborative work with Valerie Fox, *Bundles of Letters Including A, V and Epsilon* (Texture Press, 2008). She lives in Spinea, Italy where she serves as staff editor for *The Pedestal Magazine* and *Press* 1. More of her work may be viewed at www.leafscape.org.

Amanda Bales hails from rural Oklahoma. After leaving the prairie she fell in love with mountains and bummed around a few before landing on a (large) hill in Ireland. Her work has been nominated for the *Best New American Voices* series and has appeared in such journals as *Bateau* and *The Southern Humanities Review.*

Toby Barlow lives in Detroit. His writings have appeared in *The New York Times, N+1,* and *Artangel.* He is the author of *Sharp Teeth* and winner of the 2009 Alex Award.

Grace Bauer's most recent book of poems include *Retreats & Recognition* (Lost Horse Press) and *Beholding Eye* (CustomWords). She is also co-editor, with Julie Kane, of *Umpteen Ways of Looking at a Possum: Critical and Creative Responses to Everette Maddox* (Xavier Review Press). Her poems, stories, and essays have appeared in numerous journals and anthologies. She teaches in the Creative Writing program at the University of Nebraska-Lincoln, and is currently guest editing a special of *Prairie Schooner.*

Erin Bealmear's poetry has been published in *The New York Quarterly, Margie, The Santa Clara Reivew, In Posse Review, Opium, The Cortland Review, CrossConnect, Main Street Rag,* and *Identity Theory,* among others.

Jene Beardsley was born and raised in Mount Vernon, New York. He received his MA in English literature at the University of Illinois. He now lives in the suburbs of Philadelphia. His poems have appeared in *The Amherst Review, The Haight-Ashbury Literary Journal, The Journal of the American Medical Association, Soujourners, Fulcrum, New Letters,* and *The Lullwater Review* among other magazines.

J. Matthew Boyleston is an Assistant Professor of Writing and English at Houston Baptist University. He received a PhD in Literature and Creative Writing from the University of Houston and an MFA in Creative Writing from the University of South Carolina. His poems and essays have appeared widely in journals such as *Puerto del Sol, The Spoon River Poetry Review,* and *The New Orleans Review.* He has also taught at Bloomsburg University in Pennsylvania and at the Malahide Language School in Dublin, Ireland.

Ann Lightcap Bruno, a native of Latrobe, Pennsylvania, graduated from Brown University and Boston College. Her writing has appeared in such publications as *Elimae, Memoir (and), The Rambler,* and *Mississippi Review Online.* A teacher of English at the Wheeler School in Providence, Bruno lives in Cranston, Rhode Island with her husband and children.

Abraham Burickson is a poet, essayist, and conceptual artist. His work has appeared widely, in such publications as *Blackbird, The Painted Bride Quarterly, Time Out Chicago, Southwestern American Literature,* and the *Best New Poets 2008 Anthology.* A chapbook of his poems, *Charlie,* will be published by Codhill Press in Spring 2010. Mr. Burickson currently teaches writing at the Academy of Art University in San Francisco, CA.

Lisabeth Burton lives in Brooklyn, New York and works for W. W. Norton & Company. She is a recipient of *Poets & Writers Magazine's* Amy Award and the Stephen Dunn Prize in Poetry. Her poems have appeared in the *Denver Quarterly, the North American Review,* and *Tin House.*

Madelyn Camrud, born in Grand Forks, North Dakota, and raised in rural Thompson, has degrees in visual arts and creative writing from the University of North Dakota. She is the author of *This House is Filled with Cracks* (1994) and a chapbook, *The Light We Go After* (2006). She retired from Audience Development Director at the North Dakota Museum of Art in 2001, and in retirement paints and writes poems.

Veronica Castrillon grew up in Asbury Park, where the view from her bedroom window was a carousel, The Pink Flamingo hotel, the Palace Amusements, and a porno theatre.

Rachel Chalmers is an Australian writer living in San Francisco. She keeps a blog at http://www.yatima.org.

Kim Church's last story in *Painted Bride Quarterly*, "Bullet," was included in *Flash Fiction Forward: 80 Very Short Stories* (W.W. Norton), *The Great Books Foundation Short Story Omnibus*, and translated into Farsi as the title story in the 2009 Iranian anthology *Golouleh*. Her stories have also appeared in *Shenandoah*, *Mississippi Review*, *North Carolina Literary Review*, *Northern Lights*, and other journals. A Pushcart Prize nominee, Kim has been awarded writing fellowships in fiction from the North Carolina Arts Council, the Virginia Center for the Creative Arts, and Vermont Studio Center. She recently completed her first novel, *Byrd*, a fragmented family history of a child given up for adoption.

James Cihlar is the author of *Undoing* (http://www.littlepearpress.com), and his poems have appeared in *Painted Bride Quarterly*, *Quercus*, *Bloom*, *Minnesota Monthly*, *Northeast*, *The James White Review*, *Briar Cliff Review*, *Verse Daily*, and in the anthologies *Aunties* (Ballantine), *Regrets Only* (Little Pear Press), and *Nebraska Presence* (Backwaters Press). His reviews have appeared in the *Minneapolis Star Tribune* and on the poetry site *Coldfront*. The recipient of a Minnesota State Arts Board Fellowship for Poetry and a Glenna Luschei Award from *Prairie Schooner*, Cihlar lives in St. Paul.

Jona Colson's poems have appeared in *Crab Orchard Review*, *Subtropics* and *Harpur Palate*. He received his MFA from American University and currently teaches at Goucher College and American University.

Julie Conover is an attorney and part time law professor living in Philadelphia. "The Voucher" is her first published short story.

Rachel Contreni Flynn was born in Paris in 1969 and raised in a small farming town in Indiana. Her second full-length collection of poetry, *Tongue*, won the Benjamin Saltman Award and was published in 2010 by Red Hen Press. Her chapbook, *Haywire*, was published by Bright Hill Press in 2009, and her first book, *Ice, Mouth, Song*, was published in 2005 by Tupelo Press, after winning the Dorset Prize. She was awarded a Fellowship from the National Endowment for the Arts in 2007. Her work has often been nominated for Pushcart Prizes, and she received two literature grants from the Illinois Arts Council. She is an instructor in poetry at Northwestern University and a graduate of Indiana University and the Warren Wilson College MFA Program. Rachel lives north of Chicago with her husband and their two children.

Meri Culp has been published in various literary journals, including the *Southeast Review, Apalachee Quarterly, BOMB, Nomads, Sweet: A Literary Confection, Snug, The Northeast Chronicle, Cider House Review* and online in *True/Slant* and *USA Today.* Her poems have also appeared in two anthologies: *North of Wakulla and Think: Poems for Aretha Franklin's Inauguration Day Hat.* She is currently working on a collection of stalk vegetable poems and Gulf oil spill poems.

Blythe Davenport first job was dressing up as the Easter Bunny at the local mall; she has come a long way since then. Or has she? Her poetry has appeared in the *Noneuclidean Cafe, Chronogram, Mad Poets Review* and *Grasslimb Journal.* She lives and works in Philadelphia.

T. M. De Vos received an MFA in 2004 from New York University and a Hopwood Award in 1999 from the University of Michigan. Her work has appeared most recently in *HOBART, Dossier Journal, Bosphorus Art Project Quarterly, Tidal Basin Review, Dossier Journal, Sakura Review, The Whistling Fire, Shady Side Review, Umbrella Factory Magazine,* and the *Los Angeles Review.* She is a staff member of *Many Mountains Moving,* a performer with the Poetry Brothel, and a contributor to *Fiction Writers Review.*

Alex Dimitrov is the founder of *Wilde Boys,* a queer poetry salon in New York City. His poems have appeared or are forthcoming in the *Boston Review, Yale Review, New York Quarterly,* and *Best New Poets 2009.* He works at the Academy of American Poets and frequently writes for *Poets & Writers* magazine.

Kristin Dombek lives in Brooklyn and teaches in the Princeton Writing Program. This is her first fantastical essay.

Daniel Donaghy has published two books of poetry: *Streetfighting* (BkMk 2005; Paterson Prize Finalist) and *Start with the Trouble* (U. of Arkansas Press, 2009). Both books feature the city of Philadelphia prominently.

K.E. Duffin's book of poems, *King Vulture*, was published by the University of Arkansas Press. Her work has appeared in *Agni, Bellingham Review, Cadillac Cicatrix, The Cincinnati Review, CutThroat, Denver Quarterly, Harvard Review, Hunger Mountain, Jabberwock Review, Kestrel, MARGIE, Minnetonka Review, Pleiades, Ploughshares, Poetry, Poetry East, Prairie Schooner, Quiddity, Raritan, The Sewanee Review, Shenandoah, The South Carolina Review, Southwest Review, The Spoon River Poetry Review, The Sun, Verse*, and many other journals. Her poems have also been featured on *Poetry Daily* and *Verse Daily*.

C.S. Ellis is an archivist for the Marine Corps. His work has appeared in *Metal Scratches* and *Modern Drunkard*. He lives in Fredericksburg, Virginia.

James Engelhardt's poems have appeared in *Lilies and Cannonballs Review, Elsewhere, Hawk and Handsaw and Paddlefish*. His ecopoetry manifesto can be found at octopusmagazine.com. Originally from Western North Carolina, he is now in Lincoln, NE pursing a PhD in poetry. He is the Managing Editor of *Prairie Schooner*.

Kate Ferencz lives in Brooklyn and writes songs and sometimes plays them in front of people. She's working on a fourth album and recently put out a little book of mostly lyrics and drawings called *You Can Be Whatever Character You Want*.

Christine Flanagan teaches writing and literature at University of the Sciences in Philadelphia.

Joe Fletcher's chapbook, *Sleigh Ride*, is published by Factory Hollow Press. His work has appeared in *Jubilat, Octopus, Poetry International, Slope*, and elsewhere. He lives in Raleigh, North Carolina.

Wendy Fox has been published in *ZYZZYVA, The Pinch, The Expatriate Harem: Foreign Women In Modern Turkey* (Seal Press 2006), *The Madison Review*, and others. She lives in Denver, Colorado.

Emily Fridlund grew up in the Twin Cities and earned her M.F.A in fiction from Washington University in St. Louis. She has published fiction in *Boston Review, New Orleans Review, The Portland Review,* and *Philadelphia Stories*, among others.

Nina Furstenau teaches food and wine writing at the University of Missouri, writes a food column for *Missouri Life* magazine, and received the International Regional Magazine Association's Award for Food Writing in 2009. She has recently completed a food memoir, *Biting Through The Skin: Tales from an Indian Kitchen*. She was a month-long resident at the Vermont Studio Center in Johnson, Vermont, in 2008. She received an M.A. in English/Fiction in 2006, a B.J. Degree in journalism in 1984, both from the University of Missouri. She was raised in a small town in Kansas in the 1960s-70s, cooks Indian food constantly, and visits India as often as possible with her family.

Sophia Galifianakis received a dual B.A degree with honors in English and Philosophy from the University of Maryland. She went on to get her MFA in Creative Writing from the University of Michigan in 2001, and subsequently taught English Composition and Creative Writing courses until 2002, when she had her first child. Currently, she is an adjunct lecturer at the University of Michigan, Ross School of Business, where she teaches in the BBA and MBA programs.

Jenny George lives in New Mexico where she was recently poet-in-residence at the Harwood Museum in Taos. She has an MFA from the Iowa Writer's Workshop.

Elizabeth Green holds a BFA in acting from the University of the Arts. In 2007, *The Secret Prince* was published by the online literary magazine, *Flask and Pen*. Some of her plays have been produced at the University of the Arts as part of the Equinox Play festival as well as in the 2008 Philadelphia Fringe festival. Recently, her play *Fiction* received a staged reading at the Painted Bride Art Center. She was also nominated for the Christopher Brian Wolk award with the Abingdon Theatre Company for her play, "Anchorhold."

Eryn Green is a graduate student in the creative writing program at the University of Utah, where he also serves as an editorial assistant for *Quarterly West*. He was a nominee for the 2007 Ruth Lilly Fellowship, awarded by the Poetry Foundation. His work has appeared or is forthcoming in the *tiny, Bat City Review, H_NGM_N, Word for/Word, Rhino* and *Denver Quarterly*.

Kristin Hatch's work has recently appeared or if forthcoming in *Bat City Review, Black Warrior Review, Court Green, Fence, Forklift, Ohio* and *Quarterly West*. She has an MFA from the Iowa Writers' Workshop and lives in San Francisco.

Elizabeth Hazen's poems have appeared or are forthcoming in *Bellevue Literary Review, Fourteen Hills, Nimrod, Smartish Pace, The Threepenny Review* and elsewhere. She lives in Baltimore.

Brian Patrick Heston grew up in Philadelphia, Pennsylvania. He has a Master's in English and Poetry from the University of New Hampshire and an MFA in Fiction from George Mason University. His poetry has appeared in *Pennsylvania English, Confrontation, Slipstream, Cake Train, Poetry Southeast, West Branch, The Bitter Oleander, Many Mountains Moving, Philadelphia Stories, Portland Review,* and *Gargoyle*. He currently is an MFA candidate in Poetry at Rutgers University in Camden New Jersey and is an Assistant Editor with *Many Mountains Moving Press*.

Sean Patrick Hill is the author of *The Imagined Field* (Paper Kite Press, 2010). He earned his MA in Writing from Portland State University and was awarded residencies from Montana Artists Refuge, Fishtrap, and the Oregon State University Trillium Project. His poems appear or are forthcoming in *Unsaid Magazine, Exquisite Corpse, diode, In Posse Review, RealPoetik, New York Quarterly, Copper Nickel,* and *Juked*. He lives in Kentucky and reviews poetry for *Bookslut* and *Rain Taxi*. His blog site is theimaginedfield.blogspot.com.

Jean Howard is an award-winning video and performance poet, organizer, producer, and participant in the original development of the internationally-acclaimed, "Poetry Slam," has poetry published in over one hundred publications, including *Harper's Magazine, The Chicago Tribune*, and her own book, *Dancing In Your Mother's Skin* (Tia Chucha Press).

Kathryn Hunt lives in the village of Port Townsend, on the northwest coast of Washington. Her poems have appeared in *Rattle, The Sun,* and *Open Spaces*, among other magazines. She earns her living as a freelance writer. When she is not at her desk, she can be found in her garden, trying to stay ahead of the weeds and deer.

Todd Jackson is a writer from Ontario, Canada.

Mara Jebsen is a poet, performer, and New York University language teacher. She hails from Philadelphia and Lome, West Africa, and is a 2009 New York Foundation for the Arts fellow.

Siel Ju writes 17 blocks from the beach in Santa Monica, Calif. Her poems and stories have been published in *Gargoyle, ZYZZYVA, Hobart, How2, So to Speak, The Mad Hatters' Review, Shampoo,* and other journals. She just received her PhD in Literature and Creative Writing from the University of Southern California. While trying to figure out what to do with said degree, Siel blogs at greenlagirl.com.

Caledonia Kearns is the editor of two anthologies of Irish-American women's writing, *Cabbage and Bones* and *Motherland.* She lives in Brooklyn, NY with her daughter.

Nancy Krygowski's first book of poems, "Velocity," won The Agnes Lynch Starrett Prize from the University of Pittsburgh Press.

Keetje Kuipers was the 2007 Margery Davis Boyden Wilderness Writing Resident. Her poems have appeared most recently in *Agni* and *Southeast Review,* among others. You can hear her read her work at the online audio archive From the Fishouse. She lives in Missoula, Montana with her labradoodle, Bishop.

Christina LaPrease was raised in the backwaters of Louisiana. Her work has appeared, or is forthcoming, in *Beloit Poetry Journal* and *Black Warrior Review,* among others. She lives and works in New York.

David Lehman David Lehman was born in New York City. He initiated The Best American Poetry series in 1988 and remains series editor of the annual anthology. He is the author of seven books of poems, most recently Yeshiva Boys (Scribner, 2009). Among his nonfiction books are *A Fine Romance: Jewish Songwriters, American Songs* (Nextbook, 2009), *The Last Avant-Garde: The Making of the New York School of Poets* (Anchor, 1999) and *The Perfect Murder* (Michigan, 2000). He edited *Great American Prose Poems: From Poe to the Present* (Scribner, 2003) and *The Best American Erotic Poems.* He edited The Oxford Book of American Poetry, a one-volume comprehensive anthology of poems from Anne Bradstreet to the present. He teaches writing and literature in the graduate writing program of the New School in New York City. He lives in New York City and spends summers in Ithaca, New York.

Jonah Lehrer is a contributing editor at *Wired* and the author of *How We Decide and Proust Was a Neuroscientist*. He graduated from Columbia University and studied at Oxford University as a Rhodes Scholar. He has written for *The New Yorker, Nature, Seed, The Washington Post* and *The Boston Globe*. He's also a contributing editor at *Scientific American Mind* and National Public Radio's Radio Lab.

Teresa Leo is the author of a book of poems, *The Halo Rule* (Elixir Press, 2008), winner of the Elixir Press Editor's Prize. Her work has appeared in *The American Poetry Review, Poetry, Ploughshares, Women's Review of Books, New Orleans Review, Barrow Street, Poetry Daily, Verse Daily, Italian Americana, Xconnect,* and elsewhere. She has received fellowships from the Pew Fellowships in the Arts, the Leeway Foundation, and the Pennsylvania Council on the Arts. She works at the University of Pennsylvania.

Ada Limón's first book, *lucky wreck*, was the winner of the Autumn House Poetry Prize and her second book, *This Big Fake World*, was the winner of the Pearl Poetry Prize. She's won the Chicago Literacy Award and fellowships from the Provincetown Fine Arts Work Center and the New York Foundation for the Arts. She is the Creative Director for *Travel + Leisure Magazine* and teaches a Master Class for Columbia University. Her third book of poems, *Sharks in the Rivers*, will be published by Milkweed Editions in 2010.

Paul Lisicky is the author of *Lawnboy, Famous Builder,* and two forthcoming books: *The Burning House* (2011) and *Unbuilt Projects* (2012). His work appears in recent issues of *The Iowa Review, Story Quarterly, Black Warrior Review, The Seattle Review, Sweet, Lo-Ball,* and other magazines and anthologies. He teaches at NYU and lives in New York City.

Jeff G. Lytle, an Idaho native, earned an MFA in Poetry from the University of California, Irvine and currently lives in Greenpoint, Brooklyn. He has won two Academy of American Poets awards, and has been nominated for a Pushcart Prize. His poems have appeared in *Redlands Review, Faultline, Swerve, Croonberg's Fly, Factorial* and *Dust-Up,* and has serialized epic poem on thepeterprincipal.org.

Tony Mancus lives in Rosslyn, VA with his fiance and a chinchilla. He teaches literature and writing at Emerson Prep and runs workshops with Writopia Lab DC. He is co-founder of Flying Guillotine Press and his poems have appeared or will be appearing in *Verse, H_ngm_n, Handsome, CUE, Forklift, Ohio,* and elsewhere.

Desirae Matherly is a Harper Fellow at the University of Chicago where she teaches in the Humanities. Her most recent essays appear in *Pleiades, River Teeth,* and *Lake Effect.* She is a contributing editor for *Quotidiana,* an online anthology of classical essays, and in 2004 she finished her Ph.D. in creative nonfiction at Ohio University.

Suzanne del Mazo is a poet, teacher and activist from Oakland, California. When she is not at the page, you may find her identifying plants, teaching writing workshops, digging in her vegetable garden or attempting a poetic installation. She has self published a chapbook entitled *Voluming Blue* and has appeared in *Breadcrumb Scabs* while completing her MFA at Mills College.

Marilyn McCabe's poetry and essays have been published in such magazines as *Nimrod, Beloit Poetry Journal, Natural Bridge,* and *Hunger Mountain.* Two chapbooks produced in collaboration with poets Mary Sanders Shartle and Elaine Handley were awarded best poetry book prizes in 2006 and 2007 by the Adirondack Center for Writing. In 2004, she was awarded a New York State Council of the Arts Individual Artist grant. She is currently pursuing her MFA in poetry with New England College.

Kerrin McCadden is a poet and teacher who lives in Central Vermont. No matter what she does, she ends up living and working at the edge of the Winooski River. Her poetry has appeared recently or is forthcoming in *Rattle, Poet Lore, New Delta Review* and *The Fiddlehead.*

Kyle McCord is a graduate of MFA program at the University of Massachusetts-Amherst. His book, *Galley of the Beloved in Torment,* was the winner of the 2008 Orphic Prize. He's received awards or grants from the Academy of American Poets, the Vermont Studio Center, and the Iowa Poetry Society. He has work forthcoming or published from *Cimarron Review, Columbia: a Journal of Art and Literature, Cream City Review, Gulf Coast,* and elsewhere. He currently lives and teaches in Des Moines, Iowa.

Laura McCullough has four full length collections and two chapbooks of poems, *Panic,* winner of the 2009 Kinereth Gensler Award (forthcoming, Alice James Press, Jan. 011), *Speech Acts,* (forthcoming, Black Lawrence Press, fall 010, *Women and Other Hostages,* Flip Kelly Chapbook Contest (forthcoming, spring 011, Gobhill Chapbook Series, Amsterdam Press), *What Men Want, The Dancing Bear,* and *Elephant Anger,* online, Mudlark Chapbook Series. Her work has appeared recently or is forthcoming in *The American Poetry Review, The Writer's Chronicle, The Painted Bride Quarterly, Prairie Schooner, Spoon River, Guernica, Crab Orchard Review,* and others. She is in the Critical and Creative Writing Doctoral Program at Bangor University in Wales, and her scholarship focuses on the poetry and essays of Stephen Dunn.

Rose McLarney's book, *The Always Broken Plates of Mountains,* will be published by *Four Way Books* in 2012. McLarney earned her MFA from Warren Wilson's MFA Program for Writers and is the Joan Beebe Teaching Fellow at the college. She grew up in rural western North Carolina, where she continues to live and raise a variety of livestock.

Ashley McWaters is an instructor at the University of Alabama, where she is the Coordinator of Undergraduate Creative Writing. Her manuscript, *Whitework,* was a 2006 finalist in the National Poetry Series, the Four Way Books Intro Prize, the Elixir Press Prize, and the Nightboat Books Prize. She was a 2007 finalist for the Stadler Fellowship. Her work has appeared or is forthcoming in *Northwest Review, Caketrain, Spinning Jenny, Fairy Tale Review,* and *Pindeldyboz,* among others. She lives in Tuscaloosa with husband Scott, daughter Posey, and dogs Tallulah and Olive.

Erika Meitner is the author of *Inventory at the All-night Drugstore* (Anhinga Press, 2003), and *Ideal Cities* (Harper Perennial 2010), which was a 2009 National Poetry Series winner. She is an assistant professor of English at Virginia Tech, where she teaches in the MFA program, and is also simultaneously completing her doctorate in Religious Studies at the University of Virginia.

Dante Micheaux has published poems in various journals and anthologies, in the United States and abroad. His honors include the Oscar Wilde Award and fellowships from Cave Canem Foundation and The New York Times Foundation. *Amorous Shepherd,* his debut collection of poems, is published by The Sheep Meadow Press. Micheaux resides in London and New York City.

Yvonne C. Murphy lives in Queens, NY. She is an Associate Professor of Cultural Studies at Empire State College.

Mariko Nagai's writing has appeared in *New Letters, The Gettysburg Review*, The Southern Review, and other journals, and has received fellowships from the Rockefeller Foundation Bellagio Center, Yaddo, UNESCO, to name a few. Her book of poems, *Histories of Bodies*, was the winner of the 2005 Benjamin Saltman Award and was published by the Red Hen press. Her forthcoming collection of short stories, *Georgic*, won the 2009 Chandra Prize and is forthcoming from BkMk Press in 2010.

Peter E. S. Nichols holds an MFA in fiction from the Bennington Writing Seminars. His work as a visual artist often informs his writing, as in his "Orlando Slocum – The Story of a Young Artist" (Truax Press). He is currently at work on a memoir.

Wendy Noonan lives in Portland, Oregon with her son, boyfriend, and Frankenstein, the cat. She teaches freshman composition at Portland State University. Her poems have appeared in *Permafrost, Diner,* and *Bolts of Silk,* but her only permanent gig is with the Noonan family *Christmas letter.*

Charles O'Hay is the recipient of a 1995 Pennsylvania Council on the Arts fellowship in poetry. His poems have apperared in over 100 literary publications including *Gargoyle, South Carolina Review, Brooklyn Review, Slipstream, Rattle,* and *New York Quarterly.* As a member of the Deadpool Poets, his work appeared on the audiocassette Taedium Viate (1994). His chapbook, *Curio,* was published by Kali Momma Press (1996). Broadcast appearances including a reading on WXPN's Live from Kelly Writers House (1997) and an interview on WWDB's The Comfort Zone (1999).

R.G. O'Reilly lived half of his life in Brooklyn and currently lives in exile in another borough. He is a practicing attorney and writer.

Zachary Pace is an MFA student at Sarah Lawrence College. He curates Projection: A Reading Series at the Center for Performance Research (http://www.cprnyc.org) and lives in Brooklyn.

Andrew Palmer is a recent graduate of the MFA program in fiction at Johns Hopkins University. He lives in Brooklyn.

Rumit Pancholi has an MFA from the University of Notre Dame and a BA from the University of Maryland at College Park. He currently resides in Maryland and works for a nonprofit publishing firm in Washington, D.C.

Catherine Parnell teaches writing and literature the University of Massachusetts, Boston, where also she works as the Cultural and Program Liaison for the William Joiner Center for the Study of War and Social Consequences. She recently co-curated a book art show titled *Somewhere Far from Habit: The Poet & The Artist's Book,* which premiered in Cambridge, MA in November of 2009. She's on the masthead at *Salamander* and *Arrowsmith Press.* Recent and forthcoming publications include her memoir *The Kingdom of His Will* (2007), as well as stories and reviews in *Dos Passos Review, Stone's Throw Magazine, Salamander, Consequence, Another Book, roger* and *Diverse Voices Quarterly.*

Janna Pate received her MA in English from TCU, where she studied poetry with B.H. Fairchild and fiction with Cynthia Shearer. Her fiction has appeared in *descant.* Janna currently resides in New York City.

Ricardo Pau-Llosa's sixth book of poems, *Parable Hunter* (2008) is from Carnegie Mellon University Press, as were his previous three titles. He has new work in *Margie, Stand, The Fiddlehead, Salmagundi, Virginia Quarterly Review, Kenyon Review & Agni* (both online). He was recently featured in *The Writer's Chronicle* and *Saw Palm.*

Christopher Payne, a photographer based in New York City, specializes in the documentation of America's vanishing architecture and industrial landscape. His first book, *New York's Forgotten Substations: The Power Behind the Subway* (Princeton Architectural Press, 2002), offered dramatic, rare views of the behemoth machines that are hidden behind modest facades in New York City. His new book, *Asylum: Inside the Closed World of State Mental Hospitals* (MIT Press, 2009), which includes an essay by the renowned neurologist Oliver Sacks, is the result of a six-year exploration of America's vast and largely abandoned state mental institutions. Trained as an architect, Payne is a graduate of Columbia University and the University of Pennsylvania. His interest in historic buildings and industrial architecture began shortly after college, when he documented cast iron bridges, grain elevators, and power plants for the Historic American Engineering Record of the National Park

Service, and, later, produced measured drawings for New York University's excavations at Aphrodisias, a Greco-Roman city in Turkey. He has been awarded grants by the Graham Foundation, the New York State Council on the Arts, and the New York Foundation for the Arts.

Molly Peacock is the author of six volumes of poetry, including *The Second Blush*. Her poems have appeared in leading literary journals as well as in numerous anthologies, including *The Best of the Best American Poetry* and *The Oxford Book of American Poetry*. She is the Series Editor for *The Best Canadian Poetry in English* and serves on the Graduate Faculty of the Spalding University Brief Residency MFA Program in Creative Writing. Her latest work of nonfiction is *The Paper Garden: An Artist Begins Her Life's Work at 72.*

Lisa Heiserman Perkins has a PhD from the University of Chicago. She taught at Tufts, Harvard, and Emerson College, and then left academia to write and to produce documentary films. Her work has appeared in *Dislocate, Quiddity, Under the Sun,* and *Front Range Review* and she has work forthcoming in *The Fourth River*. Her film, *Secret Intelligence: Decoding Hedy Lamarr*, is in post-production. Lisa lives in Somerville, MA.

Allison Power is an editor for Rizzoli International Publications and edits the poetry journal *MAGGY*. Her chapbook, You Americans, was published by Green Zone Editions in 2008. Her poems have appeared or are forthcoming in *Pax Americana, The Best American Poetry Blog,* and *Post Road,* among others. She is an MFA candidate in Poetry at the New School.

Josh Rathkamp's first book of poems *Some Nights No Cars At All* was published by Ausable press in September. His work has appeared in numerous literary journals, including *Indiana Review, Meridian, Passages North, Puerto Del Sol, Gulf Coast, Sycamore Review, Verse Daily,* and *The Drunken Boat.* He is currently the Coordinator of Creative Writing at Mesa Community College.

Susanna Rich, author of *Television Daddy* (Finishing Line Press, 2008), Fulbright recipient, and Collegium Budapest Fellow, tours a series of one-woman, audience- interactive, poetry experiences. Professor of English and Distinguished Teacher at Kean University, Susanna has been published in dozens of venues, internationally, including the Emmy-nominated baseball documentary *Cobb Field.*

Joseph Rogers' fiction of Joseph Rogers has appeared recently in *Bridge, Opium, Pindeldyboz* and *Verb*.

Tomaž Šalamun has had books translated into most of the European languages. He lives in Ljubljana and occasionally teaches in the USA. His recent books in English are *The Book For My Brother* and *Row. Woods and Chalices* was published by Harcourt in Spring 2008.

Robin Beth Schaer is the recipient of fellowships from the Saltonstall Foundation and the Virginia Center for the Creative Arts. Her poetry has appeared in *Denver Quarterly, Barrow Street,* and *Washington Square*, among others, and recordings of her work are featured on "From the Fishouse." She has taught at Columbia University, Cooper Union, and Marymount, and worked as a deckhand aboard the HMS Bounty.

Jason Schneiderman is the author of *Sublimation Point*, a Stahlecker Selection from Four Way Books, and *Striking Surface,* winner of the 2009 Richard Snyder Prize from Ashland Poetry Press. His poetry and essays have appeared in numerous journals and anthologies, including *American Poetry Review, The Best American Poetry, Poetry London, Grand Street, The Penguin Book of the Sonnet, Story Quarterly,* and *Tin House.* He has received fellowships from Yaddo, The Fine Arts Work Center, and The Bread Loaf Writers' Conference. He was the recipient of the Emily Dickinson Award from the Poetry Society of America in 2004. A graduate of the MFA program at NYU, he is currently completing his doctorate at the Graduate Center of the City University of New York.

Molly Schultz is studying to receive her MFA from the University of Idaho. She spent two years in Uzbekistan as a Peace Corps volunteer, and now resides in Moscow, ID. "Cooking the National Dish of Uzbekistan" is her first published essay.

Matt Schumacher, educated at the University of Maine and the Iowa Writer's Workshop, is a vagabond transplant who considers himself an Oregonian. His first collection of poetry, *Spilling the Moon*, was published by Wordcraft of Oregon in March 2008, and his second, *The Fire Diaries*, is forthcoming from the same press in 2010. His poems have recently appeared in *Clare, Anti- and The Shepherd*. He is currently pursuing doctoral studies at the University of Wisconsin-Milwaukee.

Rochelle Jewel Shapiro's novel, *Miriam the Medium* (Simon & Schuster), is being sold internationally. She teaches writing at UCLA Extension.

Britton Shurley holds an MFA in Creative Writing from Indiana University and is currently an Instructor of English at West Kentucky Community & Technical College. His chapbook, *Johnny Depp Saved from Drowning*, was published by *Permafrost*, and his poems have appeared, or are forthcoming, in the journals *Bateau, Epicenter, Passages North, Salt Hill,* and *Whiskey Island*. He is married to the poet Amelia Martens and has a dog named Hoosier.

Sean Singer's first book *Discography* won the 2001 Yale Series of Younger Poets Prize, selected by W.S. Merwin, and the Norma Farber First Book Award from the Poetry Society of America. He is also the recipient of a Fellowship from the National Endowment for the Arts. He is a Ph.D. student in American Studies at Rutgers-Newark. He lives in Harlem, New York City.

Ed Skoog's first collection of poems, *Mister Skylight*, was published by Copper Canyon Press in 2009. Other poems have appeared in *Paris Review, The New Republic, American Poetry Review, Poetry,* and *Ploughshares*. These poems are part of "Words in the Wild," a collaboration with photographer/novelist J. Robert Lennon, responding to his photographs of words in their natural environment, and exhibited in Ithaca, NY.

Sue Song lives and works in New York City. She received her MFA from New York University. Everyday she is grateful to be in love.

Hillery Stone's poems have appeared in *Sojourner, Paterson Literary Review, Gulf Coast Magazine* and *Painted Bride Quarterly*. She teaches in the Expository Writing Program at New York University.

Joannie Kervran Strangeland is the author of two poetry chapbooks. Her poems have also appeared recently in *Raven Chronicles, Iota Magazine,* and *Valparaiso Poetry Review.*

Mathias Svalina is the author of numerous chapbooks and the book *Destruction Myth*, from The CSU Poetry Center Press. He lives in Denver, CO and has a new puppy named D'Count.

Rob Talbert is a former Corrections Officer from San Antonio, TX. His poetry has appeared in *American Poetry Review, Ninth Letter, the Portland Review,* and others.

Elizabeth Thorpe's short stories and excerpts from her novel-in-progress have appeared in *Puckerbrush Review, The Maine Review, Stolen Island Review,* and *Pitkin in Progress.* She teaches at Drexel and in the pre-college program at the University of the Arts.

Lauren Watel's work has appeared in *Ploughshares, Poetry International, Triquarterly,* and *Five Points* and is forthcoming in a poetry anthology entitled *One for the Road.* She lives in Decatur, Georgia.

Francine Witte is a poet, playwright and fiction writer living in NYC. Her poetry chapbook, *The Magic in the Streets,* was published by Owl Creek Press. Her flash fiction chapbook, *The Wind Twirls Everything,* was published by MuscleHead Press. She is a high school English teacher.

Jason Zuzga is currently a PhD student in English Literature at the University of Pennsylvania focusing on natural histories and poetics. He received an MFA in Poetry and Nonfiction from the University of Arizona. He is the nonfiction editor of *FENCE* magazine, and his poetry and nonfiction have appeared in such journals as the *Yale Review, jubilat, Tin House, Seneca Review* and *VOLT.* He was the recipient of a 2001-2002 residential fellowship from the Fine Arts Work Center in Provincetown, MA, and was the 2005-2006 James Merrill Writer-in-Residence in Stonington, CT.